"In more than 35 books, [Scott Young] has hardly ever inflicted wretched prose on his readers . . . [**The Boys of Saturday Night**] covers the era comprehensively and smoothly. This one's an evening by the hot stove." – Alison Gordon, *The Toronto Star*

"Skillfully revives memories . . . [Young] shoots and scores another winning goal." – *Halifax Mail-Star*

"Young covers the entire ice surface here . . . This book . . . has been a long time coming, and it turns out to be worth the wait." – *Regina Leader-Post*

"A welcome addition to the history of hockey." – *Hamilton Spectator*

SELECTED TITLES BY SCOTT YOUNG

Scrubs on Skates (1952)
Boy on Defence (1953)
A Boy at the Leafs' Camp (1963)
The Leafs I Knew (1966)
Hockey Is a Battle [with Punch Imlach] (1969)
Face-Off [with George Robertson] (1970)
War on Ice (1976)
Conn Smythe: If You Can't Beat 'Em in the Alley
[with Conn Smythe] (1981)
Heaven and Hell in the NHL [with Punch Imlach] (1982)
Hello Canada! (1985)
Face-Off in Moscow (1989)
100 Years of Dropping the Puck (1989)
Power Play [with Alan Eagleson] (1991)

SCOTT YOUNG

The Boys of Saturday Night

Inside Hockey Night in Canada

An M&S Paperback from
McClelland & Stewart Inc.
The Canadian Publishers

An M&S Paperback from McClelland & Stewart Inc.

First printing October 1991

Copyright © 1990 by Scott Young

All rights reserved. The use of any part of this publication reproduced, transmitted in any form or by any means, electronic, mechanical, photocopying, recording, or otherwise, or stored in a retrieval system, without the prior written consent of the publisher – or, in case of photocopying or other reprographic copying, a licence from Canadian Reprography Collective – is an infringement of the copyright law.

All enquiries regarding the motion picture or other dramatic rights for this book should be addressed to the author's representative, MGA Agency Inc., 10 St. Mary Street, Suite 510, Toronto, Ontario M4Y 1R1. Representations as to the disposition of these rights are strictly prohibited without express written consent and will be vigorously pursued to the full extent of the law.

Canadian Cataloguing in Publication Data

Young, Scott, 1918 –
The boys of Saturday night

"An M&S paperback."
Includes index.
ISBN 0-7710-9097-8

1. Hockey night in Canada (Television program) - History. 2. Hockey night in Canada (Radio program) - History. 3. Sportscasters - Canada - History. 4. Television broadcasting of sports - Canada - History. 5. Radio broadcasting of sports - Canada - History. I. Title.

GV742.3.Y6 1991   070.4'49796962'0971   C91-094368-0

Cover design by Andrew Smith
Cover photographs: of Ron MacLean and Don Cherry courtesy CBC Television Sports; of rink surface by Greg Holman

Printed and bound in Canada

Published by arrangement with Macmillan of Canada

McClelland & Stewart Inc.
The Canadian Publishers
481 University Avenue
Toronto, Ontario
M5G 2E9

ACKNOWLEDGEMENTS

Research for this book required many dozens of interviews by telephone, fax and in person. To all those mentioned in the book who helped with anecdotes, observations, bitchy opinions and cheerful recounting of personal experiences alike — Ted Hough, Frank Selke, George Retzlaff, Gerald Renaud, Harry Neale, Bud Turner, Roger Mallyon, Ward Cornell, and Ralph Mellanby among them — my thanks. Special thanks also to Dick Irvin for permission to use a passage from his own book, *Now Back to You, Dick*. But the biggest stroke of luck for me was that Bob Gordon, having bade farewell to Hockey Night in Canada after 33 years of faithful service, agreed to head up the overall research. He did a magnificent job. If there are errors or omissions, I'm the culprit.

SCOTT YOUNG
Summer, 1990

CONTENTS

Prologue **1**

Chapter 1 "The Truck" **5**
Chapter 2 Hockey or Show Biz? **16**
Chapter 3 Who Gets on the Air? **27**
Chapter 4 Big Deal on a Little Golf Course **38**
Chapter 5 Goodbye General Motors, Hello Imperial **53**
Chapter 6 The Landing of Hugh Horler **64**
Chapter 7 The First Masters: Retzlaff and Renaud **80**
Chapter 8 The Golden Era of Ward Cornell **103**
Chapter 9 The Sayings of Chairman Ralph **118**
Chapter 10 Bad Day in Pittsburgh **140**
Chapter 11 Goodbye Esso, Hello CBC **157**
Chapter 12 The Good Guys and the Bad Guys **169**
Chapter 13 Memories, Memories **188**
Chapter 14 The Molson-ization and CBC-ization of Hockey Night in Canada **208**

Index **219**

The BOYS OF SATURDAY NIGHT

Prologue

In a nation where one of the principal preoccupations is hockey talk, with gossip, prejudices, truth and untruth inextricably mixed, hockey broadcasters — The Boys of Saturday Night — know more about the pro game, past, present and future, than most. It's not only what they see and hear covering games in 22 cities for more than nine months of the year. In the average week during the season a professional broadcaster with a home satellite has a choice of watching something close to three dozen NHL games. When Don Cherry gets off a zinger about this player or that, this team or that, you can be sure it is not hearsay. He's seen it. He'll stay up until two in the morning or later to get the end of a game on the Pacific coast, and if that means he misses some other game he wants to see, he often can get it on a repeat that night or the next morning. Besides Hockey Night games on the CBC, on the Global network, or The Sports Network on cable, anyone with a satellite dish and the appropriate de-scrambler, if necessary, can get anything on several U.S. all-sports networks and even some that are televised in only one local market.

To take one representative period, from March 24 to March 31, 1990, there were 41 NHL games, almost all available somewhere on satellite. When the playoffs started April 4, there was hockey on television almost every night for six weeks.

In covering all that hockey, a special relationship develops between at least some of the broadcasters and the hockey players, coaches, managers, trainers and other personnel. They're all in the same game, one way or another. When Harry Neale was fired as coach of Detroit Red Wings in 1986, two of the Sutter brothers skated up the next time they saw him and, calling him Mr. Neale, said they were sorry. Most players know what it is to be fired, or traded, or sent down, and can relate to someone else it has happened to.

And when broadcast crews come into a rink several hours before game time, it's to a sort of private hockey world, with a limited number of initiates. To follow one specific pair, Bob Cole and Harry Neale: One February night when Pittsburgh was in Toronto they went straight from the production meeting ending at around six and headed out through the all-but-empty rink toward the broadcast booth to go over their notes on the people they'd be watching; but also they picked up a few impressions along the way, seeing things the fans didn't see. That night, for instance, all-star Pittsburgh defenseman Paul Coffey was taking his ease dressed in undershirt, shorts and not much else in a gold seat at Maple Leaf Gardens, chatting with Leaf assistant coach Garry Lariviere; they'd been teammates with Edmonton a few years earlier. Neale stopped and got into the conversation. Back near the players' benches Ron MacLean was talking to Wendel Clark. In the open area outside the visiting team's dressing room under the stands, Randy Hillier and Mario Lemieux — still healthy then — and others, half-dressed, were customizing their sticks, while a few feet away facing the necessary hot lights, visiting broadcaster Jiggs MacDonald was taping his own opening. Players, broadcasters and all the rest exchanged opinions, gossip and real news. Trainers who have been around forever were doing their pregame tasks.

Coaches have been fired, players traded, promoted, sent down. A chance conversation might make an item on the broadcast that night or another night; the participants are in a little world of their own, before a game, after a game, between games, while riding the same aircraft, staying sometimes in the same hotels. They know, and have critical or kindly opinions about, this official or that. It all hangs out.

Prologue

Even for broadcasters who travel across the continent it's a tight little ship, much more so than the relationship, say, between active coaches in the league. Harry Neale and Scotty Bowman live not far from one another in East Amherst, a suburb of Buffalo. They do the same job for Hockey Night, providing commentary and analysis, Neale a regular in Toronto and Bowman in Montreal, working the same game only sometimes when Montreal plays Toronto and the crews are mixed. When they were rival coaches in the NHL, they would, of course, seldom have occasion to speak to each other. Now, they are colleagues, able to share a familiarity not possible before.

"We're good friends now," Neale says, "but when you coach against Scotty, you're the enemy. There's no friends. He was always one of those guys who was looking for an edge somehow, and he didn't care whether it offended you — that was the game he had to win tonight."

Now that both are rated among the best color men in the game, they rarely work in the same place at the same time, but talk in person or by phone two or three times a week. Maybe Bowman is coming up to a game involving a team whose game Neale had done a few days earlier. Or vice versa. In such cases they'll compare notes on everything useful to broadcasters — how certain individuals are playing, how the team is playing, balance, weaknesses, strengths. It's all part of the preparation by two men, former coaches, each with pride in doing well whatever they do — Bowman with his Stanley Cups in Montreal, Neale, rarely having had the same quality of gunners, once coming close with Vancouver. Long in hockey, new in friendship, from time to time they see sides of one another that they didn't know existed.

"I'll never forget one time last year [spring 1989]," Neale relates. "Scotty had been out west, including Calgary and Edmonton, about four games in six nights, and you usually get good games when you go out west, and we're chatting and he says, 'You know, Harry, Calgary's not going to win — they're not going to win the cup.'

"I say, 'Well, what about Edmonton?'

" 'No. Not this year.'

" 'Well, what about Philly?'

" 'No.'

"Finally we'd gone through about five teams that he's saying haven't got a chance and I say, 'Scotty, at the end of May they're going to give that cup to somebody, whether you like it or not.' "

That year, Calgary proved Scotty wrong. Neale did not rub it in.

So, witty or serious, salty or tame, the mix is there, bringing us night after night for two-thirds of the year what we want to see and hear: who won, who scored, the ever changing state of the game.

Star players, coaches, managers, owners, referees and just about everyone else in the game have had books written about them. This one is about the broadcasters, and the men and women who work out of microphone and camera range, to deliver hockey to air, on time, excitingly, rousingly, sometimes even grammatically. The Boys of Saturday Night.

Chapter 1
"The Truck"

> *Does this mean my mother has to stay up until two o'clock in the morning to see my name in the credits?*
> — voice in The Truck during pregame run-through

At three o'clock one Saturday afternoon in the 1989–90 hockey season a big vehicle that looks like a semi-trailer but that hockey-television people know as The Truck, or more formally as The Mobile, is parked on the south side of Wood Street near Church in downtown Toronto — as close as it can get to the north wall of Maple Leaf Gardens, where a hockey game will begin at eight that evening. The downtown street is heavy with traffic and the south sidewalk is crowded but not blocked by The Truck; around it cold concrete, junk-food wrappers blowing in the cold wind, the gawking of curious passersby, the distant sound of ticket scalpers crying, "Extras! Who's got extras?"

About halfway along the narrow passage between The Truck and the old hockey temple's yellowish brick wall, people who look as if they work for a living move up and down a set of portable steps to get in or out of the vehicle. On this particular night The Truck has the Global Television Network logo on its side. The Global equipment is rented by CBC from time to time when the CBC's own truck is working elsewhere. The internal configuration differs slightly between the two — a row of six intent people facing the monitor rack in the CBC truck, two rows of three people in the Global — but functions and staffing are the same. Starting roughly five hours before game time and revving up from there, hockey television's intense pregame activity rises to an excitement not easy to convey fully without the sound effects and music and kibitzing and a few f-words.

Up a few steps, through a door into The Truck. To the left a few feet is the crowded tape room where isolation director Paul McKeigan holds sway over technicians tending four tape machines. To the right of the door and between a row of hanging parkas, leaning people and stray bits of apparatus, a small crowded room is filled with what looks like two tightly packed rows of occupied triple seats in a bargain aircraft. All are facing the monitor rack. Six youngish people are in the seats. They intently face a wall of ever changing monitors displaying pictures and emitting sounds.

Their starting lineup in row one, left to right, is producer Mark Askin, director Terry Maskell and the duty switcher (who punches the buttons). In row two are Chyron operator (the person in charge of electronic titles) Jerry Preston; statistician Ron Harrison, Jr., whose father is executive producer of hockey games in Toronto and Los Angeles this night and working a football playoff in Calgary the next day; and production assistant Karen Lapointe, new to this job but a veteran of other shows.

Behind a glass wall to their rear is audio man Julien Bergeron, wearing earphones connecting him to Mark Askin, who is calling the shots.

As he does so, the urgent chorus of sounds in the room is of voices overlapping not only one another but also words and music from the monitors. The crew is running through all those segments that can be shot, honed and refined in advance for tonight's unusual two-city doubleheader (Toronto and Los Angeles). These segments include scripted intros and voice-overs to pretaped features, throws to standby games, throws to commentators, throws to commercials, throws to intermission interviews or out-of-town score updates, and to a form of the advertising art designed especially for regions where plugging beer on TV is forbidden and therefore the beer-and-girls-and-guys dreamland of your normal beer commercial is extinct, giving way to something no doubt much, much nicer. Producer Askin at the extreme left of The Truck's front row calls, "Okay, cue up the no-beer opening!" And a good deal later, "Cue up the no-beer closing."

But this day we're not at the no-beer part yet. One monitor shows a few scalpers working the wet pavement in front of the Gardens, one a lanky man with the cuffs on his drooping jeans wet from the slush. He is loudly crying, "Leaf tickets! Leaf tickets! Who needs tickets?" (He might have been given a few bucks to persuade him to use those lines exclusively, due to the fact that the more standard cry of "Who needs a pair?" would not be specific enough to be in keeping with the intricacies of this item's script.)

Think of six pairs of eyes plus Julien Bergeron's ears all concentrating on the screens. Each of those present is watching or hearing or speaking his or her own specialty, so while voices individually make sense to *someone,* the overall sound comes off like a contrapuntal chorus, impractical to explain succinctly:

"Perfect!"

"Okay, thanks!"

"I'm thinkin' this does need . . ."

"So I'll just use five there. . . ."

They're all watching the ticket-scalping scene. Producer Askin is thinking aloud along with each few seconds of film and sound: "As soon as he says, 'Who needs tickets?' we go to the VTR. Sneak the music in there. So let the natural sound tell itself, Julie. Actually, *now* go in! The package! Right. So we just gotta get it out. Take my count and take it out. Okay?"

Production assistant Lapointe: "Just there, five seconds to green, to blue." (Each color denotes a different tape machine.)

Askin on his microphone to Bergeron: "Okay. Now Julie, the music you're using, does it have a hard in? So we could try it.

Have it come in hard at the transition 'cause it'll make more sense...."

Jumble of voices. Instructions to re-cue. An occasional loud cackle of laughter.

Isolation director Paul McKeigan has recently become a father, and once when he makes a mild fluff a voice calls, "That's all the kids you can have, Paul. Being a father is getting your head all screwed up." His work both in The Truck run-through and in a production meeting to come later emphasizes his importance to the on-air product. Being intuitive is an advantage for an isolation director. One of his jobs is to anticipate, sometimes on his own and sometimes following the script, when the play-by-play commentary can be complemented by a few feet isolating this player or that involved in a goal, a fight, a scoring streak, or something else in the game. Whenever the commentator or play-by-play man speaks of, say, Gary Leeman, Jimmy Carson, John Kordic, Steve Yzerman or anyone else involved, McKeigan will have a few seconds of action ready, featuring that player. The switcher in The Truck will cut it in on cue.

Askin: "Stand by, everybody! Wait for my cue, Chris, please." This to Chris Cuthbert, tonight's broadcast host, who is doing the voice-overs. "Okay, stand by to roll green."

Voices, Askin and Lapointe, in unison: "Three, two to green, one. Roll green. Two, one. Up on green..."

Lapointe: "Five to blue. Four, three..."

Askin: "Roll blue..."

Lapointe: "Two, one..."

Askin: "Music cue. Cue!"

From the monitor, as the picture leaves the scalper crying "Leaf tickets!", Chris Cuthbert's voice-over is vibrant, urgent, picking up instantly on the ticket-scalping scene just shown. What he's doing is selling excitement.

"*Tonight* the hottest ticket in town is one scalpers *can't sell* because we have *your* seats reserved! First at front row in Maple Leaf Gardens in Toronto as American star Jimmy Carson makes his first Canadian appearance as a Red Wing!" The screen shows Carson donning a Detroit Red Wing sweater.

"Later you have a *box seat* —" we see Larry Robinson pulling on a Los Angeles Kings' sweater "— waiting at the Great Western Forum in Los Angeles, California. Larry Robinson dons his new sweater against his old team for the first time as the Kings entertain the Canadiens. It's a *double feature! Tonight! From Toronto and Los Angeles! On Molson Hockey Night in Canada on CBC!*"

Blare of music, a few seconds of reflective silence, then Askin: "Okay, now let's mix the openings, which will be, ah . . . item one will obviously play back off the red, I guess?"

"You got it."

"Paul, this is the one that's coming off, this is the one that's gonna go over to Co-Ord, correct?" Co-Ord is the CBC studio a block away that handles cutting in commercials, promos, other set pieces.

Brief comments back and forth, then Askin: "Let's play back what we just did and we'll go right into the opening . . . Now [to Cuthbert] do you want a count to the music or do you like not having a count in your ear? Do you want to just read the music yourself?"

"No, no, it doesn't matter, whatever. Maybe we should just . . . Could I just see it once, make sure?"

"Yeah, sure. . . . Paul, can you give us a playback of the Molson Canadian opening, please?" Burst of music. "Here it comes. . . ." Portentous voice (that's the best kind): "The following is a live presentation of CBC Sports. . . ."

And so it goes, nearly two hours of run-throughs of what could be checked and double-checked and refined to the ultimate in bang-bang crispness toward the time when the real unscripted and unscriptable action on the ice begins. One of the final jobs is to record the credits which, tonight, will appear only at the end of the Montreal–Los Angeles game, which immediately follows the Toronto game.

Mournful unidentified voice: "Does this mean my mother has to stay up until two o'clock in the morning to see my name in the credits?"

This was only a slightly out-of-routine night for Hockey Night in Canada. The difference was strictly the doubleheader, not the total volume of games. With 21 teams in the National Hockey League, it is possible to play 10 games in one night across the United States and Canada, but that happens rarely — only twice in the 1989-90 season. It is also theoretically possible in one night to televise seven games, one for each Canadian franchise whether the teams play at home or in the United States.

No more than three of those on any one Saturday night would be on the CBC network; the others on Global Television, TSN (The Sports Network) or on individual local stations — such as when, for instance, Edmonton at New York, produced and with on-air staff by Molstar Communications, is seen only in Alberta and by those elsewhere who can pick it up from Madison Square Garden on satellite dishes.

This night five of the league's eight games involved Canadian teams, the doubleheader on CBC national, the others regional. What made the doubleheader possible was the three time zones between the most easterly (Toronto) and most westerly (Los Angeles) games.

At about 5:00 p.m. Askin and some of those in The Truck, plus others concerned with the on-air, as well as the technical side of the broadcast, gathered for a production meeting in the Gardens intermission studio. This takes place at ice level and across a wide corridor from the Toronto team's dressing room. Everyone present at the production meeting was armed with a copy of the 11-page script. On the cover page's distribution list appeared, if you were looking for it, an indication of a fact of life in the NHL: in accordance with the contract outlining conditions of the sale of broadcast rights, copies of each show's script go routinely to owners and senior executives of the teams concerned.

Among those on this night's list were Leafs' owner Harold Ballard, general manager Floyd Smith, coach Doug Carpenter, rink public-address announcer Paul Morris, publicist Bob Stellick, and timer's bench boss Joe Lamantia.

Don't think these worthies don't read the script with care. If someone in authority isn't happy with one or more of the on-air people listed, feeling that this or that individual in the talent list has been too negative or overly critical lately, or is just a plain mealy-mouthed little snitch, they instruct Molstar Communications, which produces the shows, to give the guy the bum's rush.

That right of the club owner has been there forever. Still, when it makes headlines, as happens from time to time, it is greeted with reactions ranging from ho-hum (those in the know) to outrage (some writers and editorialists previously unaware that free speech does not extend to hockey broadcasts). Over the years there have been many instances, some never reported, of clubs controlling the broadcasts or segments thereof, and banning use of gents they considered to be unfriendly. Frequently the exercising of this right has caused some potentially lively television to be lost to the hockey world. In the late 1970s when Leaf coach Punch Imlach didn't want team captain Darryl Sittler interviewed on a show originating from Toronto, Sittler was bumped. The same happened with an intermission show called "Showdown", on which Imlach had refused to allow Sittler and goalie Mike Palmateer to appear. The club's contractual right to censor gave Imlach the power to ban it from Toronto television, which he did — so "Showdown" had to originate from Montreal that season and was not seen in Toronto.

In later years when Harold Ballard didn't appreciate the outspoken work of broadcast pros Brian McFarlane, Dave Hodge or Pat Marsden, these offenders were ruled off. Those who cry out against such interference with the right of free speech historically cry out in vain; they have never won yet.

The most notorious example of this kind of censorship happened in 1959. In the season semifinal between Chicago and Montreal there was a riotous ending to one game in Chicago. Bobby Hull had been tripped in the dying moments and referee Red Storey didn't call it. The fans were still screaming bloody murder and some on the Chicago bench were giving the choke sign when, with 82 seconds left to play, Claude Provost scored the winning goal for Montreal. Beer cans, money and at least one chair were thrown at Storey. Two fans jumped over the boards to go after him and were fended off, bleeding, when Montreal's Doug Harvey swung his stick in Storey's defense. The demonstration lasted 20 minutes. It was one of the most referee-threatening contests ever played in the NHL.

At the height of the uproar Storey considered calling the game and appealed for help, advice, support, *anything*, from NHL president Clarence Campbell, who was watching from rinkside. Campbell had nothing to offer. Storey finished the game. That night he didn't sleep much. The next day when he read the newspapers he found that Campbell not only failed to recommend Storey for a bravery medal, but strongly criticized him — one of the league's best and most senior referees — for losing control and even adding to the danger of the situation by the way he had acted. Storey then loudly vowed that he would never referee another game for Campbell, and he blasted Campbell for throwing him to the wolves.

However, both showed up a day or two later in Boston where Leafs and Boston were involved in the NHL's other semifinal. In the lobby of the hotel where the hockey press and most other hockey people were staying, Storey had a large audience as he colorfully described the Chicago scene and the outcome of his appeal late in the game for Campbell's support.

"When you went to him, what did he say?"

"He was too scared to say anything. His face looked like what you see when you lift the lid of a coffin. Then the next day in the papers he blasts *me* — the guy on the firing line."

Question from a writer then with Hockey Night in Canada: "Would you come on the TV intermission tonight and describe what happened?"

"I sure would!" Storey said.

At the Hockey Night in Canada production meeting later that afternoon in a suite in the same hotel, the proposal was made to interview Storey as part of the game coverage. The wild finish in Chicago was front-page news wherever hockey was played. Now, Campbell and Storey were in the same Boston hotel, Storey willing to talk on television, and Campbell not answering the phone in his room, and even — for a while — ignoring knocks on his hotel-room door. How about Storey as an intermission guest?

There was a discussion. The television people were gung-ho all the way. But sitting in at that production meeting was Ken Reardon, a former star player and by then an executive with Montreal Canadiens. He was at the production meeting to represent the league and its owners. Some of those present believe that when the proposal was made to use Storey on television that night, Reardon phoned, not Campbell, but Conn Smythe of the Leafs in Toronto, Frank Selke of the Canadiens in Montreal, or both.

Whoever gave the thumbs-down, the answer was no. The good name of hockey was felt to be at stake. Storey had a rough tongue. Hockey couldn't prevent him from talking to reporters, but they could prevent him from laying out the facts and his opinions to a national audience on hockey television. Which they did.

On this night in the 1989–90 season, 30 years after Red Storey was forbidden his big chance to be hockey's good-guy sheriff in a television intermission shootout, there was nothing in the lineup to object to. Several of this evening's broadcasters — Chris Cuthbert, Bob Cole, Scotty Bowman, Don Cherry, Harry Neale and Ron MacLean — have been known to have sharp tongues, but when criticism is called for, they, except Cherry, are inclined to use needles rather than sledgehammers to get the job done. They don't see it as a badge of honor to get fired for knocking the product that, in truth, they love.

At this afternoon's meeting in the studio set, the sounds were mainly of pages turning as Askin quickly read through the entire 11-page script, which described every off-ice element of that night's Toronto broadcast. His reading was in detail not only for technical reasons, so that everyone would either understand or ask for clarification, but also to let the on-air people know everything they might have to handle. Chris Cuthbert, who as the show's host had the function of keeping it all knitted together, was there along with Bob Cole, who would do the Toronto play-by-play, and Scotty Bowman, the color man.

Askin began by detailing the opening segments, as seen and checked earlier in The Truck.

Then: "Chris, we'll come down to you on camera, welcoming us. You'll have about 50 seconds for your live on-camera between the benches. The only add-in there will have the current Norris [division] standings and other games played, as well as the points, okay? Off [that] you'll throw upstairs to Bob and Scotty." Again, live upstairs: "Thanks, Chris." Several players had been listed tentatively in the script as possible subjects for live comments from upstairs. "On the Leafs, scratch Ed Olczyk and Gary Leeman, you'll talk about Allan Bester. On the Wings it'll be Steve Yzerman, so scratch Jimmy Carson. Off the end of the live piece upstairs, which we will rehearse, we go one through four [numbered items in the script], and Coley [Bob Cole] will throw off to commercial one with the cue stated."

Out of commercial one the script then called for a throw to Chris Cuthbert in the studio, whom Askin instructed, "Look down to F [this item in the script read 'Possible Leaf–Wing memories from the past']. You'll have about a minute before you throw upstairs to Bob and Scotty for the drop of the puck...."

Askin went painstakingly through every promo, commercial, live on-camera segment and interlude for the entire 11 pages. The only thing that couldn't be scripted, of course, was the live action on the ice and the player interviews. Thus the foreseeable was covered, the unforeseeable left to Cole's play-by-play, Bowman's color comments and the players themselves.

When the production meeting ended, those present moved off separately or in small groups for an hour or so, some for dinner. Cole and Bowman walked through the empty Gardens to the escalators that would take them up two levels, then the stairs the rest of the way to the gondola, where they would go through the lineups player by player, study their notes, get ready.

Not present at that meeting, because they were working the Los Angeles game, were Don Cherry, the presiding iconoclast of "Coach's Corner", and Ron MacLean, whose gadfly role in the Cherry segment keeps the great man moving from one controversial pronouncement to another. Part of Cherry's arsenal of the unexpected is that while most weeks they discuss possible subjects — and sometimes get to none of them — they do not actually rehearse. This leaves them open to tackle, if they wish, something that happened 10 minutes earlier. Cherry gets ready by thinking of what might come up, and what kind of a shot from the hip he'll take if it does. His ammunition is frequently not quite what the head of CBC Sports or other erudite citizens would like him to use, but that fact alone gets wide public approval, and not only from the yahoo constituency.

Still, there are dissenters.

Chapter 2
Hockey or Show Biz?

The way they're doing hockey right now, it's almost like show biz, which to me is wrong. It's not show biz — hockey is hockey.
— George Retzlaff, CBC's first hockey czar

This would make a good text for a half-day seminar at the CBC's annual Lake Couchiching festival of bigdome viewing with alarm — if only for the excitement that would be engendered as Don Cherry dealt with the rush of behavioral scientists who'd promised their kids they'd get his autograph and also let them know firsthand what Cherry was really like.

Cherry and his straight man, Ron MacLean, are precisely what Retzlaff is talking about. When Cherry gets going on what he'd do to foreigners stealing our fish from under the noses of those grand people in Newfoundland, or puts on his amazing act of being simultaneously lugubrious and fiercely nationalistic about how Canadian junior hockey players are being robbed of their birthright by foreigners — who are possibly on sabbatical from stealing our fish — it is show biz all right, and anyone who really wants to hear about the hockey game in progress is often plumb out of luck.

There are counterarguments, of course: that some people — I keep hearing that these are mainly women — who won't budge from their steam irons to listen to anybody else talking hockey, will drop everything for the intermission's three and a half minutes with Cherry and MacLean. In some rare instances, in fact, Cherry is not the main attraction.

Hockey Night's executive producer Ron Harrison says his wife *hears* Cherry, all right, it's hard not to, but she really watches MacLean.

"Look at his face!" she'll say, as MacLean struggles vainly to remain expressionless at Cherry's verbal barrage while at the same time trying to figure out what he'll say to both leaven the more outrageous opinions and stir up others.

"It used to be that in 'Coach's Corner' we'd come in close on Cherry as a one-shot," Ron Harrison says. "But when Cherry couldn't see someone else on his monitor he had the feeling that he was just talking to himself, and he didn't like that. That's why we pull back and make it a two-shot."

And thus, in addition to Cherry, let people see how MacLean reacts to it all.

In his criticism of the show-biz trend, old pro Retzlaff does not dispute the appeal. But he would rather see and hear the interplay of three or four knowledgeable hockey men, maybe including Cherry, discussing the big plays, good and bad, of the on-ice action that preceded the intermission. That format actually was tried from 1952 to 1957, converting the old radio "Hot Stove League" to television. But it didn't work, because while the participants could be themselves on radio, once they were on a set with an actual hot stove and cameras and floor directors and all the paraphernalia of television, they could not be themselves, or even fake it. They weren't actors; they were hockey men. The idea was stubbornly given a good run before it was dropped.

In the 1980s on American television a program called "Sportswriters" was introduced, featuring *sportswriters* — mainly old guys in shirt sleeves, some smoking cigars, who argued and yelled at each other over sports issues of the moment in boxing, hockey, racing, football, baseball, golf, any target of opportunity; Retzlaff, if he still ran hockey, would want that approach — to give viewers a lively discussion of the game, not necessarily without laughs, but featuring lively critics in the old style that once prevailed — which might also turn out to be show biz.

That being said, Cherry is a genuine wonder of hockey TV. His persona, understood by all and nurtured by his references to his minor-league past, is that of a blue-collar guy who made so little money as a player in the minors that he had to work in construction every summer to keep bread on the table. He sometimes refers to himself as a beer-hall guy, and talks as if he is addressing the folks in a noisy beer hall where, unlike those responsible for his conduct at the CBC, nobody gets a sick headache if he says "nothin' " or "nothink."

Indeed, before Cherry's name disappeared from the *NHL Guide's* active-player list in 1970 when he was 36, the beer-hall sites in question could be guessed at by the number of clubs he played for. One was Boston Bruins; he played one game for the Bruins against Montreal Canadiens in the playoffs of 1955 when he was 21, chalking up no goals, no assists, no penalty minutes. He tends to make jokes about this; meets a fan, laughs and says, "Here's a guy says he saw me play in the NHL!"

The fact is he had earned his tryout at the top honestly, with a good record as a defenseman with Hershey in the American Hockey League: 63 games, seven goals, 13 assists and 125 penalty minutes. Many NHLers have made the big time on less. If NHL expansion had come a few years earlier than it did, Cherry no doubt would have played those years in the enlarged NHL, when an experienced tough defenseman standing five-foot-eleven and weighing 180 pounds would have made a place for sure. But in 1955 when he had gone to Boston's camp in the fall with his hopes high, he was up against Doug Mohns, Leo Boivin, Fern Flaman, Bob Armstrong and Bill Quackenbush. Didn't make it. One game in the bigs was it. He went back to the minors, and it was in long-ago Hershey, Pennsylvania, in the season of 1955–56 that he met a tiny and beautiful Italian Catholic girl named Rosemarie "Tootsie" Martini. He asked her if she'd come some night and watch him play and when she said yes, he pressed a couple of tickets into her hand.

Hockey or Show Biz? 19

"It was the first game I'd ever seen," she told Tom Slater of the *Toronto Star* after Cherry had become famous. "About two minutes into it, Don was in a brawl. I said, 'These Canadians are barbarians.'"

Some weeks later when Cherry was dragged up the front walk of Rose's home for the mandatory meeting with her parents, "I was beautiful," Cherry said. "I had stitches on my forehead, my eyes were a mess. What an impression."

They were married on March 21, 1956, although Rose said her mother still thought that there was nothing but wild Indians in Canada "and Don hadn't helped to change that much."

Leaving Hershey two seasons later, his next stop was with Eddie Shore in what was called the Siberia of hockey, Springfield, Massachusetts, also in the AHL. Then Three Rivers in the old Eastern Professional Hockey League, Kitchener-Waterloo in the same league, Springfield again, Sudbury in the EPHL and Spokane in the Western Hockey League. In all this traveling he'd moved around NHL farm systems a bit, from Boston to Detroit and then to Montreal. Sam Pollock, Montreal's resident genius, decided in the spring of 1962 that he needed some muscle to protect his smallish forwards. According to Cherry's own self-deprecatory memoir, *Grapes,* Montreal got Cherry for two rolls of tape and a jockstrap.

One night he went out for a few beers with a goalie named Claude Dufour. The next day Pollock called him in and said he had plans for Cherry in the Montreal organization, but that a club rule banned drinking. Would Cherry promise to observe that rule? Cherry politely declined on the grounds that he liked beer and didn't want to promise to give it up. Pollock thanked him and asked him to come the next morning for his ticket. When Cherry reported in, Pollock asked, "How would you like to go to Washington?"

Cherry thought that would be great — not far from Hershey, Rose's hometown. He phoned and told her that there they'd be, right in the nation's capital, and if he couldn't play for Montreal, Washington would certainly be okay. It was not until he inspected his ticket that he found it was for Spokane, Washington.

After Spokane it was into the Leaf farm system: Rochester, Tulsa in the Central Professional Hockey League, then Rochester again, where he also coached, successfully. It was as a coach that he finally got back to the big league: Boston Bruins from 1974 to 1979, and Colorado Rockies in 1979-80. After Colorado fired him, he began to turn up regularly on CHCH-TV Hamilton's mid-week games, especially when Boston played Toronto.

H. E. "Ted" Hough, head of Hockey Night from the early 1960s to the late 1980s, through various MacLaren Advertising Company Ltd. subsidiaries — Videotape Productions, Maple Leaf Sports Productions and finally Canadian Sports Network — recalled his first sighting of Cherry on hockey TV. At the time, 1980 or 1981, CSN had been helping the NHL with an ad-hoc network of televised afternoon games in the United States, supplying the production people or recommending the on-air talent. In command of CSN's participation was producer Don Wallace. Wallace's budget for the U.S. games was fairly small, and he had also been asked to use commentators who were known to American fans. Cherry's long career in the minors, backed by coaching in Boston and Colorado, fitted those requirements. He'd often been interviewed by the press and on television, and had a reputation for saying what he thought, which hadn't always been popular with his superiors or officials of other clubs. Wallace figured he had a good slot for Cherry: Boston at Buffalo, where Cherry's former Boston and Rochester connections might strike some sparks.

"I didn't think Cherry was very good that first time I saw him," Hough confessed. "I winced at a number of his comments because I was a good friend of the Buffalo people, especially Dave Forman, who was Buffalo's vice president in charge of everything, a man I dealt with a lot.

"Lo and behold, the next day Dave called me. The first thing he said was, 'I thought you were a friend!'

"I said, 'I thought I was, too. What's wrong?'

Hockey or Show Biz?

" 'How did you let that bleep-bleep Cherry on the air for that game yesterday? I thought you were producing it *for* the NHL, not against it.' "

The beef, of course, was that Cherry was being Cherry, even that early on. He knocked the product. According to Hough, Forman stormed, "I don't want him ever coming out of Buffalo again!"

Forman was not the only person Cherry offended in those days. That didn't matter much — executive producer Ralph Mellanby was bringing him along slowly. Ron Harrison was a Hockey Night director then, working under both Mellanby and Wallace. "In those real early days we'd use Cherry as a color analyst and he was *brutal*," said Harrison. "He would say exactly what he thought, and as color man he was on the entire show. That was too much. Partly it was inexperience, but it was also Cherry — and now that he's only on the one segment of the show, 'Coach's Corner', of course that very individual approach is what makes him so good."

Ted Hough, another Cherry booster: "He added a breath of fresh air to what was becoming a pretty dull and predictable telecast. He's hockey's Dizzy Dean."

CBC functionaries used to protest angrily the way Cherry mistreated the English language on the grounds that his grammar and syntax might cause irreparable harm to impressionable young minds. Such protests have diminished somewhat in the face of Cherry's present eminence: the most recognizable person on Hockey Night and one of the most recognizable in the whole country. And so it came to pass that within a few years, assessing an upcoming hockey TV season, it was fairly common to read headlines such as this one in the October 11, 1989, *Peterborough Examiner*: DON CHERRY HIGH PRIEST OF HOCKEY BROADCASTING.

"I spend a lot of time with Cherry, especially in playoffs, and he is without question the most recognizable guy I've ever been around," said Harry Neale, color man on many midweek non-CBC games, as well as in the regular Toronto crew with Cole, Cherry and MacLean. "He's got this great thing going — act, schtick, charade, whatever you want to call it. I've told this to a hundred people, and they do ask, 'What's Cherry really like?' If he's sitting there having a beer and there's just two or three of us, you'd think this guy is a little out in left field, just a good guy, but if he saw a mike over there somewhere, into his act he goes.

"You can't go anywhere with him and have a beer without somebody coming over — it's almost like a rock star. If you like him, you can't wait to hear his next tirade. If you don't like him, you still want to hear it so you won't like him *more*."

Cherry acknowledges that often he still talks first and thinks afterward. "I feel that someday they're going to come to me and say, 'Well, you've just gone too far.' "

There has long been tension between the CBC and Hockey Night in Canada over when, and why, the CBC should interrupt a hockey game for a newsbreak. Once, in the late 1980s, Cherry was scheduled to interview Boston's Cam Neely between periods. Neely's face had been cut quite noticeably during play a few minutes earlier. He showed up to keep his appointment with Cherry anyway, dabbing at his wounds with a towel, tired and in pain. Then came the prelude to explosion. Cherry was told that he'd have to hold the interview until *after* CBC News had cut in with a couple of items — one a report on a development in Poland's Solidarity movement, and the other a filmed parade of antique Mustang automobiles. Philosophically, there must be some level at which interrupting a program in progress for major news is justified. But . . . in this case?

Cherry blew his stack, fuming against whoever back in the newsroom that night, without a thought for what else was involved, cued that newsbreak — really more of an assertion of the CBC's God-given right to interrupt than anything to do with real news. Cherry watched and listened with growing disbelief. When he did get on the air with Neely he came right to the point. If he was the Boston coach, he said, he'd never let another Boston player appear on CBC television in such circumstances. Period.

Hockey or Show Biz?

CBC News didn't like that, but possibly someone decided that it didn't really want to take on Cherry's fans along with Cherry. This raises another point, which Cherry didn't happen to mention during his tirade but probably would have if he'd thought of it. CBC runs as many as nine commercials, as well as promos for its own shows, during the average 15-minute, sometimes stretched, intermission. Does anyone ever break in on that perhaps financially necessary but surely not sacrosanct sales period for a newsbreak? Promo-weary viewers sometimes wish to hell they would. In such an eventuality there'd be a fighting chance that there would be cries of welcome for Knowlton Nash right across the land. In fact, the so-called newsbreak itself is really only a thinly disguised CBC promo for the *National*, which follows the hockey game. The CBC talks loftily and a lot about journalistic principles, but if the news items it uses on Hockey Night were really news, they would go on TV when they *happened*, not wait for an intermission.

Cherry got into more big trouble in 1989 because he blasted Winnipeg Jets' general manager Mike Smith for hiring a Finn, Alpo Suhonen, to coach the Jets' farm team in Moncton. Bringing in a Finn sent a message to North American coaches that they weren't very good, Cherry fumed. And then came the *coup de grâce*, which was widely and justifiably deplored. "Alpo," he added. "That's a dog food, isn't it?"

The Winnipeg club's NHL governor, Barry Shenkerow, demanded that Cherry apologize, and said that if one was not forthcoming, the club would take the matter to the courts. An apology was seriously discussed. On the night it was supposed to happen, the matter was on Cherry's mind — as well as on Ron MacLean's. At the end of "Coach's Corner", MacLean gave Cherry his chance to be humble.

"He turned to me and said, 'Anything else?' "

"I said no."

Cherry appears not likely to change, but he doesn't risk legal action for most of his more inflammatory comments. He habitually hammers away at the number of European players taking jobs, as he puts it, that might otherwise be available to Canadian juniors. One night in the 1989-90 season he brandished for the cameras a multi-signed letter from players of the Ontario Hockey League's Niagara Falls Thunder applauding this stand.

That season also, he opened a new antiforeigner front. This was at a time when Canadian fishermen in the Maritime provinces were much in the news. Fish-processing plants were being closed and many fishermen thrown out of work because of the depletion of fish stocks by foreign fishing fleets. The Canadian government was trying ineffectually to get the foreign fleet to go home, or at least cut down on its take.

And then, in the world junior-hockey championships in Stockholm, a player named Norris from one of the places where the fish war was hottest, Newfoundland, scored the winning goal against the Soviet Union, giving Canada the gold medal.

Cherry, on January 6, 1990, during a game between Los Angeles and Toronto:

> And how about that Norris kid from Newfoundland, is he something else? Way to go from The Rock! I know they don't like to call it The Rock but I call it The Rock anyhow. He said, you know, here's what he said, "You steal our money on the tours, you steal our fish, you steal our fishing, you foreigners, but you can't steal the gold!" Way to go!
>
> Ron MacLean: This is a new area of expertise, I guess.
>
> Cherry: Yeah, and I'll tell you one thing down there — I would like to be the commissioner of fisheries. I'll tell you, no foreign boat would take *one* of our fish! That's what I'd like to do. You guys, eh? Norris, you've got the hockey straightened out! Straighten out those guys in the fish!

Sometimes viewers are sure Cherry is loaded for bear, about to open another battlefront, when suddenly he stops. MacLean always has the last word, throwing to a commercial. The way this is achieved on time is by MacLean's moving his left knee sideways a few inches to nudge Cherry's. That's when Cherry

Hockey or Show Biz?   25

stops talking, sometimes abruptly. The two-shot vanishes, and "Coach's Corner" is over for another night.

The only instance anyone can remember Cherry being totally flummoxed he was not on camera. At the time, Bob Gordon was a Hockey Night in Canada producer. He had worked his way up to that high estate from being a 20-year-old rookie in the late 1950s, one of his early jobs being to shoot an intermission film on how hockey was played in the American South by the Charlotte Checkers of Charlotte, North Carolina, in what was considered strictly a hackers' league.

From there he'd become a jock of all trades, traveling tens of thousands of miles with Foster Hewitt on radio-broadcast trips, and later working on television as producer in mobiles parked outside rinks across Canada and the U.S., one of Hockey Night's most dedicated all-rounders. He also had a son named Todd who was a high scorer in kids' hockey.

In one game, Todd, who had already scored a few goals that day, had a breakaway, accompanied by a little kid who wasn't any Brett Hull in the scoring department. As the two of them zoomed in on the opposition net, Todd Gordon faked the goalie out of position and slid the puck over to the other boy, who scored his first goal ever.

This unselfish act so profoundly impressed his father that, encountering Cherry a few hours later, Bob Gordon told the story in all its moving details.

A day or two later he took Todd with him to Maple Leaf Gardens for the usual morning skate that teams go through on game days. The media crowd usually attends, as well, doing interviews and catching up on the gossip. It's free-and-easy time. Cherry was there. Noticing young Todd, he went over and said in his most official on-air carrying voice, "Hey, Bob! Is this the kid who passed to the other kid so he could get the goal?"

"That's him, all right," Bob said.

Cherry turned to Todd. "Now listen, kid! I'm gonna tell you something! The guys that score goals in hockey are the ones that everybody hears about! Everybody! Those guys that score goals, lots of goals, they're the ones that drive Cadillacs!

"The guys that pass them the puck to *let* them score the goals, kid, they're the guys that drive Volkswagens! Now, think about it, kid! What do you want to drive when you grow up?"

Todd didn't even have to think about it. "I'd like a motorcycle."

Chapter 3
Who Gets on the Air?

In the assignment of talent, Hockey Night takes into account the idiosyncrasies of the various clubs and the necessity of cross-pollinating various programs, the basic crews being local but with always the presence of at least one person of national Hockey Night stature.

— Ted Hough, Hockey Night's longtime chief botanist

Cross-pollinating might be considered an unnecessarily professorial way to describe the process of deploying the talents of some of the best-known men in Canadian sports broadcasting, but Hough didn't reach his eminence in hockey broadcasting by being imprecise. Although the CBC by 1990 was converting to its own people as rapidly as it could manage, leaving a few bodies along the way, a good proportion of the on-air talent going into the new decade was from the era in which Hough as president, Frank Selke as vice president and Ralph Mellanby as executive producer ruled pretty well supreme.

All three had earned their stripes in the trenches. Hough in 1936 was a lanky kid just out of high school with a job at Imperial Oil that allowed him to insinuate himself into Foster Hewitt's gondola on game nights and move up steadily through top jobs for 52 years thereafter. Selke was raised from

childhood in the hockey family headed by the older Frank
Selke in both Maple Leaf Gardens and the Montreal Forum,
easing his own way in as Montreal Forum public relations
director and hockey television host before leaving Montreal in
1967 to become president of the expansion California Seals.
Mellanby on occasion could outdance them both, a sort of
riverboat gambler show-biz type who learned fast and added a
few dance steps of his own. What they ran was the biggest
long-running sports-network-cum-soap-opera in the world.

In their later years with Hockey Night, Hough's "cross-
pollinating" referred to the sometimes delicate business of
assigning on-air men to games in 21 NHL cities across North
America, wherever Canadian teams played. At least as delicate
were broadcasting relations with the 21 owners and general
managers, plus the league in all its control functions, as well as
networks and sponsors. But all depended finally on the product,
the broadcasts to millions of fans, keeping the standards high
enough to dominate the field. This in turn depended on the
play-by-play men and color analysts who fronted the entire
operation, a staff constantly in a process of change through
expansion: six teams to 12 in 1967, two more in 1970 and others
later to the total of 21 that have survived into the 1990s. Over
the years CBC, while keeping a firm grip on Saturday nights,
eventually was joined in the broadcasting roster first by CTV
for a few years of midweek games, then by Hamilton's CHCH,
Global, and The Sports Network. This required a vastly expanded on-air staff. While all clubs were usually served partly
by local talent in on-air crews, there were times when the crews
were mixed, dropping some individuals, promoting others.

By 1990 the production company in charge of all this was
Molstar Communications. Molstar, holding exclusive contracts with many of the high-profile on-air people, joined CBC
to supply the on-air crews for all games, while CBC and the
other broadcasters provided the technicians, including cameramen. All assignments, from national shows to the regionals,
take some juggling and much attention to logistics. Every
regular, and those who do not work as often, has his entire

Who Gets on the Air?

season's schedule by early October, with hotel rooms booked far in advance to take advantage of special group rates, expenses paid on a per-diem basis, and the hockey travelers with individual flight preferences booking their own flights, paid for by Molstar.

Hockey Night doesn't really think in terms of a farm team; more like a talent pool doing regional or midweek broadcasts before, in some cases, eventually reaching the stature of the national guys. It's a tough league when you're trying to get into that top few. Once you make it, the good news is that you're probably there for as long as you can hack it, or believe you can hack it, which is not always the same thing. The bad news is that in the constant search for new faces, voices and styles, the cast does change fairly frequently — and it's rarely because of resignations.

The turnover is especially high among color men, sometimes called analysts. Among the most prominent and warmly received color men since they were first invented have been Howie Meeker, Eddie Fitkin, Bob Goldham, Gary Dornhoefer, Brian McFarlane, John Davidson, Gordie Howe, Bobby Orr and Andy Bathgate. They all had a shot — some long, some short — and then fell back.

Of those who didn't stay long, Orr might have been the best if he'd been on the job when radio was king; he's an excellent analyst but did not feel comfortable on camera.

Meeker, in his era, was as big across the country — in the hearts, minds and heartfelt convictions that he was wonderful, as well as in heartfelt wishes that he'd go away and never come back — as Cherry is today. Their approaches, however, were — and in Cherry's case, are — radically different.

Meeker's quirky, doctrinaire and sometimes devastating analysis focused strictly on plays, with no untouchables. He once dared to criticize Jean Beliveau during a game broadcast from Montreal. This was followed by a fast telephone call from the Club du Hockey Canadien to Hockey Night in Canada offices in Toronto, the details only to be guessed at but invoking the club owner's right to ban whom they don't like, in this case Meeker.

In contrast to Meeker's basic mixture of professorial pronouncements well peppered with golly-gees, Cherry's comments are based on hockey, but he shoots at anything that moves. During the season he shows up mostly on the Toronto games — 11 times from Toronto against three from Montreal in one 1990 two-month period. Montreal does not have a Cherry equivalent, perhaps because the attitude toward him in Montreal is not overly favorable if one takes a temperature reading from influential Montreal *La Presse* columnist Réjean Tremblay. In the wake of Phil Esposito's being fired as general manager and coach by New York Rangers in the spring of 1989, Tremblay wrote: "Mouthy people like the big Italian always find a job somewhere in hockey. It's Don Cherry who should be looking over his shoulder. Hockey Night in Canada could easily find a big mouth capable of shouting louder and making more outrageous statements per minute than him."

Goldham, in contrast, was just plain warmly likable, his easygoing style based on his years as a great junior with Toronto Marlboros, a World War II spell in the Royal Canadian Naval Volunteer Reserve on active duty as a leading seaman, and as a fine NHL defenseman with Toronto Maple Leafs, Chicago Black Hawks and finally Detroit. After a long stint, he eventually was replaced by a new face and voice.

Dornhoefer was by no means easygoing, but had powerful credentials. In his NHL years, mostly with Philadelphia Flyers, he'd been in there fighting for a piece of the ice in front of a thousand nets. Because he never backed up, and so did little to brighten the lives of those who tried to move him out from the edge of the crease, fans around the league often wished they could provide him with a one-way ticket to the moon.

At the same time, good hockey coaches liked his style. After 16 years as a pro and two Stanley Cups, he was one of a courageous breed much prized in hockey. Later, as a Hockey Night in Canada color man, he knew one when he saw one,

Who Gets on the Air?

which was a great asset, but eventually he, too, gave way to a newer analyst.

Among hosts, the longevity record is better. The shortest term in history as a Hockey Night in Canada host was served by the writer of this book, at the time a daily newspaper columnist, removed from regular TV duty after a year and a bit, but staying a few years longer on radio. The next two Toronto hosts were Ward Cornell and Dave Hodge, both extremely competent and experienced broadcasters, neither really ready to leave when, for vastly different reasons, the word came down that the ax had fallen.

For 20 years Brian McFarlane was color man, host, writer, producer of intermission film features, a dependable all-rounder kept on by Hockey Night in Canada to work from Montreal and other cities even after Harold Ballard banned him from Toronto broadcasts.

Like most Hockey Night regulars, for much of his career he was paid by the game. Before the 1988-89 season this system changed somewhat to a guarantee of being paid for a certain number of games, whether worked or not. In McFarlane's case this was a low $30,000, compared to others who made two or three times that. He didn't like the contract and didn't sign until the season was over. In the 1989-90 season, he did mainly intermission film features, which he is good at; but he was being eased out, another victim of the fact that in Hockey Night in Canada, nothing is forever.

Play-by-play men apparently have the most security, perhaps because they have to be more than just another pretty face. Danny Gallivan worked 32 years at play-by-play before retiring of his own volition. He now is in both the Hockey Hall of Fame and Canada's Sports Hall of Fame — as was Foster Hewitt, of course, the first great one. Foster's son Bill had a good run of 25 years or so before he packed it in, his decision hastened by temporarily poor health.

Dick Irvin in Montreal is a cross-over person in this respect: his intelligence and personality, long experience in his own and other shows for private television — CFCF, Montreal — and the fact that he grew up practically behind the bench in a hockey family (his father, Dick Irvin, a famous coach with Montreal, Toronto and Chicago) helped make him supremely capable as a host, color man, rinkside commentator and interviewer, as well as on play-by-play.

One way or another, he has been a Hockey Night in Canada regular out of Montreal since the mid-1960s and during that time has been close, despite the occasional media-versus-coach arguments, with Scotty Bowman, one of the game's most successful coaches (five Stanley Cups in Montreal before moving to St. Louis and then Buffalo). Bowman now works as color man alongside Irvin on most Montreal games. Don Wittman is another veteran on play-by-play, one of the best, working mainly on western games.

Irvin's play-by-play counterpart on the Toronto broadcasts, Bob Cole, is a Newfoundlander who lives in St. John's and flies back there to his home and family after each of his broadcast stints. As a long-standing sideline, Coley, the name his broadcast familiars call him, owns his own fish-processing plant. He read the CBC news for years, was host of a popular non-hockey show called "Reach for the Top", and called Hockey Night in Canada games on radio beginning in 1969 and on television since 1973, eventually replacing Bill Hewitt as Toronto play-by-play man after Hewitt decided he'd had enough. Cole has few equals, if any, on play-by-play. When big-play excitement is building, his voice seems to go up, plateau by plateau, until the play's climax, when it drops as the teams regroup for another push. Cole drives himself. His conviction is that every broadcast he does should be perfect. The witty former coach Harry Neale is usually his color man.

Like Bowman, Neale is a world-class expert on the quirks and quarks of dressing rooms and players and what players may do right or wrong in game action. After coaching various teams in the World Hockey Association, including Hartford, he reached the Stanley Cup final with his Vancouver Canucks in 1982 and finally coached in Detroit, where he was fired. The frontline hockey experience of Bowman and Neale, added to

Who Gets on the Air?

the broadcast professionalism of Cole and Irvin, supply these two preeminent broadcast teams, or any cross-pollination among them, with an informative and entertaining mix. A look at the talent assignments in one two-month period from December 30, 1989, to March 31, 1990, does something to illustrate the basic pecking order.

The Toronto on-air lineups through that period were usually Cole and Neale in the gondola, with Ron MacLean working as the show's host, doubling as Don Cherry's ringmaster in "Coach's Corner" and interviewing newsworthy hockey executives or players, such as 70-goal scorer Bernie Nicholls on his feelings about being traded from Los Angeles to New York Rangers in January 1990.

For Montreal games, Dick Irvin — who could fill any job on any broadcast — usually called the play-by-play with his old sparring partner Scotty Bowman as color man and Chris Cuthbert of the CBC as host. When Montreal and Toronto played one another the crews were, well, in Hough's term, crosspollinated. On January 27, 1990, in Toronto (Montreal 5, Toronto 3), Irvin and Bowman joined MacLean and Cherry while Cole and Neale were assigned to a Vancouver–Edmonton game in Edmonton, with Ken Daniels as Edmonton host. On February 10, when Leafs were not playing and Quebec was in Montreal, the Montreal crew became a mixed powerhouse of five top men: Cole, MacLean, Bowman, Irvin and Cherry. After that one, MacLean and Cherry fled Montreal fast to join Neale and Montreal's usual host Chris Cuthbert in New York the following day for one of Hockey Night in Canada's rare Sunday games — Calgary playing the Rangers.

Summing up, the top Hockey Night in Canada on-air people during the first months of 1990 were Cole and Irvin on playby-play, Bowman and Neale as color men, and MacLean and Cuthbert as hosts. Plus Cherry. Cuthbert, Steve Armitage, Don Wittman and other CBC-cum-Hockey Night people, although away at the Commonwealth Games in New Zealand late in January, were close to the leaders in terms of national telecasts over that period. Former Ranger goalie John Garrett,

Edmonton's Bruce Buchanan, Montreal's Scott Russell, Scott Oaks of Winnipeg, and others worked regional telecasts from Vancouver, Calgary, Edmonton, Winnipeg or Quebec.

A color man is supposed to add, well, color, and the only one from among these crews who has been able to rival Cherry's popularity — for vastly different reasons — is Harry Neale. When he and Bob Cole are in the broadcast booth, collectors wait for Neale's special twist to what from some commentators would be routine. In the first few months of 1990 this was a partial harvest:

In March Ed Olczyk of the Leafs took a stick in the face and lay in pain against the back boards for a few seconds, with Cole and Neale both reviewing replays of the check that had felled him. When Olczyk slowly skated to the bench fingering his bruised and cut mouth and a camera picked up the shot, Neale remarked, "Looks as if Olczyk is going to be all right, although he might not be able to whistle tomorrow morning."

When Sergio Momesso of St. Louis Blues, coached by tough ex-player Brian Sutter, made a bad check that led to a Toronto goal and was skating to the St. Louis bench, Neale commented, "Momesso needs a lot of nerve going back and facing Sutter after that check."

Once in the last minutes of a game when Detroit was defending a slim lead against the Leafs: "Look at Detroit, lined up four of them across the blue line. The only thing they aren't doing is joining hands."

Shawn Burr had been playing very well for Detroit in that game: "They sent him down to Adirondack for three games early in the season to catch his attention, and I think it did."

Veteran Red Wing defenseman Mike O'Connell, during a Detroit power play, mesmerized the Leafs by stickhandling around near the boards just inside the blue line until most of the Leafs were there with him. Finally the last Leaf to be decoyed, Dave Hannan, left his check, Steve Chiasson, near the other boards, whereupon O'Connell passed to Chiasson, who shot on the net. Bernie Federko tipped it, and it was in. Neale, analyzing this evidence of Leafs' lack of patience: "They

Who Gets on the Air?

should've let O'Connell stickhandle around until his arms got tired."

One late-season sensation occurred when two Montreal Canadiens stayed out after curfew in Minnesota and were suspended for the following game. As Neale noted, some years earlier Rick Vaive, then with the Leafs, had been punished for something that happened in Minnesota; so had Borje Salming on another occasion. "Minnesota," mused Neale, "can be trouble for people with something more than hockey on their minds."

When Jim Korn of New Jersey Devils hit Brian Curran from behind, starting a rhubarb that ended with Korn banished for the rest of the game and Curran for two minutes, the Harry Neale report was: "Korn has started more fights with sucker punches than any other player in the league. Now he can watch the rest of the game on TV — that is, if they have TV in the police station."

In a New York game between the Rangers and Edmonton Oilers, Neale, on Kevin Lowe's refusal to wear a mask: "Kevin says he wants everybody to see his pretty face."

In the same game Esa Tikkanen of Edmonton had been penalized and was shown in a two-shot skating toward the penalty box with the referee and talking a mile a minute. Most broadcasters don't like chronic complainers. Neale made that point with: "Tikkanen knows all the refs well, spends a lot of time talking to them, with very little results."

Again in that game with only minutes to go Rangers got a goal to go up 3-1. The camera swung to show Ranger coach Roger Neilson while Neale commented, "He's already phoned down for the snow fence."

And finally, one night in Toronto that winter a veteran linesman, Bob Hodges, somehow got his crotch in the way of a heavy whack with a stick during a mixup behind a net. He went down writhing. When he got shakily to his feet he was in obvious pain. "Looks as if he's okay," Neale commented, "but he may be talking a little higher for a while."

This came not long after popular and outspoken host Dave Hodge had been banned from Leaf games by Harold Ballard over a comment Ballard considered derogatory to the Leafs. Neale reflected, "Maple Leaf Gardens has been tough on Hodges lately."

Like that one, his best lines always seem to be right off the cuff, but he confesses that he constantly watches for good lines when he's reading books, newspapers, whatever. If he sees something he likes and laughs at, or thinks of a crack that might fit into a play sometime, he'll make a note and file it away.

"I wait for the time I can use it and I have stuff that I haven't been able to use for two years, waiting for the right incident to happen. I'd like to tell you that they're all originals of mine, but I find them in all kinds of places and then apply them to hockey. The Hodge one wasn't. It just came out of the blue."

No one has done better in describing Harry Neale's essential style than Dick Irvin did in his entertaining book of memories entitled *Now Back to You Dick*:

> When Harry was coaching (Vancouver and Detroit), he was king of the one-liners, and the media loved it. He was told the Canucks didn't like his practices.
>
> "That makes us even," Harry replied, "because I don't like their games."
>
> We were working a Montreal–Boston playoff series when the camera took a shot of a Boston sub, Kraig Nienhaus, standing near the Bruins bench in civvies. He was sporting a punk-style hairdo, with much of it standing straight up.
>
> "There's Kraig Nienhaus," Harry said. "Looks like he combs his hair with a hand grenade."
>
> "Another time, he wanted me to ask him, on the air, how many goals he thought Rocket Richard would score if he were playing hockey today. So I did.
>
> "I'd say about 25 or 30."
>
> "Only 25 or 30?" replied his straight man.
>
> "That's right, Dick. But don't forget, he's 64 years old."

Harry Neale has a million of 'em, but he came up with by far his best, and most quoted, when he was running the lowly Canucks and his team was in the throes of another terrible slump.

"We're losing at home and we're losing on the road. My failure as a coach is I can't think of anywhere else to play."

Whatever the individual preferences in who calls the plays, who provides the wit or color, whether a fan prefers the fastest-skating teams or the hardest-hitting teams, or one star over another, each night when game time comes near, several million Canadians will have geared their evenings to the moment when once again the puck is dropped and, in its sixth decade, Hockey Night in Canada is on the air.

Chapter 4
Big Deal on a Little Golf Course

> *When Jack MacLaren first suggested that we would get money for hockey broadcasts, it was then I believed the story about manna from heaven.*
>
> — Conn Smythe,
> Toronto Maple Leafs founder

It's a long leap backward to the summer of 1929 when two men shook hands in the middle of a fairway on a little old summer-resort golf course and got it all started. "This was the year of The Great Golf Game," declared a summary of that year drawn up by the advertising agency that later became known as MacLaren's. "The month was June, the place was Orchard Beach golf course on Lake Simcoe. . . ."

One of the men was Conn Smythe, a short and cocky item in his early 30s, part owner and total boss of a hockey team he'd acquired two years earlier and whose name he'd immediately changed from Toronto St. Patrick's to Toronto Maple Leafs.

The other man in the handshake was Jack MacLaren, a few years older, who was in charge of a half-dozen people in the Canadian office of an American-owned advertising agency, Campbell-Ewald Limited, based in Detroit. MacLaren, in his own way, was as fast off the mark as Smythe, but more polite. It was not difficult to be more polite than Smythe.

There was a third golfer with Smythe and MacLaren that day — Larkin Maloney, general manager of Canada Building Ma-

Above: Foster Hewitt: first and greatest. (*Alexandra Studio, Toronto*)
Right: Raspy voiced, friendly star of the commercials, Murray Westgate. *Below:* Hot Stove League, 1945: *left to right,* Elmer Ferguson, Wes McKnight, Bobby Hewitson, Harold (Baldy) Cotton.

"And now, tonight's three stars...." After a game in the late 1950s, Hockey Night's Bob Gordon shows Gerry Ehman, left, and Bob Pulford where to take their bows.

Hot Stove League, late 50s: host Jack Dennett, Scott Young, former Leaf captain Syl Apps, Boston chief scout Baldy Cotton. (*Jack Mitchell Photography, Toronto*)

Above: Keeping up morale: Foster signs autographs during WWII. *Right:* Three generations of Hewitts, two of them broadcasters, *from right,* Foster, son Bill, and grandson Bruce. (*Toronto Telegram*)
Below: Cyclone Taylor on the shovel and Foster Hewitt as host turn the first sod for the Hockey Hall of Fame, May 1960.

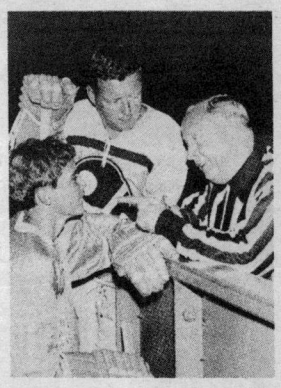

Hockey Night production meeting, Leafs v. Montreal. George Retzlaff on the window sill, Bob Gordon, Frank Selke, Jr., MacLaren's Mike Wood. *On the couch:* La Soirée du Hockey's Gaston Dagenais, director; Louise Tardif, script assistant; Jacques Berube, producer. (*Jack Mitchell Photography*)

Montreal on-air and production people, 1969 or 1970: Jacques Berube, producer; Dick Irvin, color; Danny Gallivan, play-by-play; Madeleine LaFrance, script assistant; Ted Darling, host. (*Bellamare Photographe*)

The man in charge of the
Leafs: Punch Imlach behind
the bench, February 1967;
Leafs on the way to the
Stanley Cup. (*McFadden*)

The man in charge of
Hockey Night: Ted Hough,
MacLaren Advertising
vice-president, and
president of Canada Sports
Network. (*Dick Loek/
Hockey News*)

George Retzlaff, *far left*, host Ward Cornell, producer Bob Gordon. (*Hof Richter/Photoport, Port Credit*)

Meanwhile, in Vancouver: executive producer Ralph Mellanby, color man Babe Pratt, play-by-play's Jim Robson. (*Gagephoto Service*)

Before Imperial Oil's 1976 crisis-causing dropout; Hough with Don Twaits, Imperial's advertising manager. Inset: The man who first tied it all together, Hugh Horler.

Corridor script conference: Hockey Night's and CFRB's Jack Dennett; Retzlaff's assistant, Audrey Phillips; La Soirée du Hockey director Michel Quidoz; Retzlaff; and Bob Gordon. (*Dick Loek/Al Stewart Enterprises*)

A decision at the top: Frank Selke, Jr., vice-president and general manager Roger Mallyon, Ted Hough.

Big Deal on a Little Golf Course 39

terials. All three owned or rented modest summer cottages on the south shore of Lake Simcoe, an easy drive north from Toronto. They frequently met on Orchard Beach's undemanding course and customarily went around the nine-hole layout twice.

Maloney was a racetrack crony of Smythe's. He'd been a believer and investor two years earlier when Smythe was beating the bushes for money to buy the St. Pat's. In later years, when Maloney got even bulkier and Smythe's sharp tongue as boss of the Maple Leafs and Maple Leaf Gardens had become an international sports legend, they owned horses together, and at the racetracks were known as Lumpy and Grumpy.

The Smythe-MacLaren common denominator was ambition. The Leafs played their home games in an old building called the Arena Gardens on Mutual Street in downtown Toronto, which Smythe intended to replace with what he'd say, not modestly, would be the best hockey rink in the world, to be called Maple Leaf Gardens.

MacLaren's ambition was more or less parallel: he wanted to own the best advertising agency in Canada. Campbell-Ewald had entered Canada in 1922 with three employees, one being young Jack MacLaren. He'd been scrambling ever since to build it into something he could eventually take over and put his own name on. He had an idea that Smythe's ideas and his own might have some kind of a date with destiny — although at that moment, the size and scope could not be foreseen by either of them.

This day on the golf course, the Gardens existed only in Smythe's head. What Smythe had that MacLaren coveted was Leaf radio rights, which included the services of Leaf broadcaster, Foster Hewitt. In 1927 when the Leafs were born, their games rarely filled the Arena Gardens, with its seating capacity of 8,000. Smythe had put together the money to buy St. Pat's, but was by no means the club's largest investor. Major decisions had to be okayed by his much less adventurous board of directors.

One of these decisions he had to fight for was to have Foster Hewitt broadcast the last part of every Leaf game live from the Arena Gardens. Many directors were opposed, arguing that people would stay away if they could get the game free on radio. Smythe had the opposite idea: that the broadcasts would fascinate fans into storming the ticket windows so they could see the action live. He won that battle, at first only on a trial basis. Hewitt did the rest. He had been broadcasting hockey from Ontario Hockey Association amateur playoffs on up since 1923, starting out working from three rinkside ice-level seats (to give him room to maneuver) paid for by the *Toronto Star*, where he was a news reporter. A telephone installed at his elbow carried his play-by-play back to the *Star*'s own radio station.

As the broadcasts built a following, Foster refined the operation. First he tried a glass booth built at rinkside, but the glass fogged up so much that he could hardly tell the players from the referees. His next move was to a perch in the rafters above the crowd. When Hewitt began calling the Leaf games Smythe made no charge for broadcast rights. He was just happy to get the publicity, and he was right. Soon all 8,000 seats were filled, and sometimes another thousand crowded into every morsel of standing room. Hewitt's broadcasts had become a local sensation. Jack MacLaren's interest was not far behind. He'd always had a sharp eye for anything he might sell to a sponsor.

Smythe's regular caddy on summer days back then was a boy in his early teens, Warren Reynolds, eventually to become head of his own advertising agency. His family rented a cottage nearby. Part of being a good caddy is to stay close when there's a shot to be played. That is how, one day in the summer of 1929, Warren happened to hear something that stuck forever in his mind.

Fifty-odd years later in a letter to a friend he recalled the occasion. It was a very laid-back pleasantly warm day, the course almost empty, no need to rush:

"From time to time they would stop and talk about matters not related to golf. In fact, it was usually about hockey, which is

Big Deal on a Little Golf Course

what I expected with Conn Smythe. It was about the sixth hole the second time around, and I was right there when Mr. Smythe and Mr. MacLaren stopped in the middle of the fairway and shook hands. I didn't know what it was all about but remember Mr. MacLaren saying, 'It's a deal, I'll have an agreement drawn,' and Mr. Smythe saying [no doubt in his usual rasp], 'You have my word and we shook hands! What more do you need?'

"Later [actually close to two years later] when it was announced that games from the new Maple Leaf Gardens would be broadcast and that the agency headed by Jack MacLaren had arranged sponsorship of the broadcasts by General Motors, I realized what the handshake had been all about. But what I remember most is how impressed I was, at a young age, that these two important men could trust each other on the strength of their word."

Although some accounts have placed The Great Golf Game in 1930 or even 1931, an article written for *Maclean's* magazine a few years later by Montreal writer Leslie Roberts, while all the principals were still alive and could be interviewed, set the date: 1929. He declared that the handshake between Jack MacLaren and Conn Smythe that day "was beyond doubt the most important deal ever made in Canadian radio, and probably in Canadian advertising."

At this distance it is difficult to know how far down the road Jack MacLaren was looking at that time, sewing up radio rights to the Leafs two years before he actually used them. One possibility is that a condition from the beginning was that the handshake would not count until Maple Leaf Gardens was ready.

At the time, the Gardens existed only in theory and Smythe's attempts to raise enough money to get started. He did have a few investors interested, but a few months after the historic handshake, the stock market took its 1929 dive. Immediately, some of those who had encouraged him originally changed their stance. To build a kind of cathedral to hockey in the state the country was now in was seen by what Smythe called "those lily livers" as much too wild a scheme. Prudent investors tended to cross the street when they saw him coming.

Among his remaining backers was Larkin Maloney. In his business Maloney knew a lot of the people who put money into construction projects. What was needed, the two men realized, was somebody big — an investor on the highest level of legit who would give credibility to the idea of investing in the Gardens. Maloney had a connection with a firm of Montreal architects, Ross and MacDonald. The firm had been involved in building the Royal York Hotel and other major projects in Toronto. Thus it happened that late in 1930 this odd couple, bantamweight Smythe and heavyweight Maloney, went by train to Montreal looking for advice and money. Ross and MacDonald suggested they go to Sun Life Assurance Company. Sun Life listened, and with some pushing from the company's Toronto-based directors, who thought Sun Life was spending too much money in Montreal and very little in Toronto, promised to invest $500,000.

When that news got out, many of the previously wary were converted — Sun Life had no history of throwing money down drains. The rest of the money was raised, but still with difficulty. The last of it came on a dramatic day when Smythe was importuning his board of directors for more money to get the Gardens built. That meeting had been called by Sir John Aird, head of the Bank of Commerce and a Gardens director, to open bids to finish the construction. Houses and stores on the corner of Church and Carlton had already been knocked down in preparation, but when the bids were opened, the newly formed Maple Leaf Gardens Limited found that it was still short. Frank Selke, Sr., working as Smythe's assistant at the time, had mortgaged his house and bought $4,500 in Gardens stock. It was still not enough. He and Smythe then had an idea — could they cut labor costs by persuading the men already at work on the site to take part of their pay in Gardens stock?

It happened that day that the Toronto Trades and Labour Council was holding its weekly meeting. Selke, as a longtime member of the electricians' union, had a strong voice in the council. He has said since that he ran all the way to the Labour

Temple to make his pitch. The stakes were high: construction was almost at a standstill and if the Gardens project had to be halted, many men would be thrown out of work. Business managers of the various unions finally said they'd go for it if their members would agree.

Selke ran back to the Bank of Commerce meeting and reported the news to Smythe. When Smythe went back in to the directors' meeting with that announcement, Sir John Aird said, "Well, in that case, our bank will pick up the rest." On June 1, 1931, steam shovels arrived at the Gardens site to begin work.

As Smythe wrote in his 1981 memoirs — *Conn Smythe, If You Can't Beat 'Em in the Alley* — "I don't know how you would built Maple Leaf Gardens today in five months, but partly it was accomplished because the men who built it believed in what they were doing. After all, they were going to be shareholders, weren't they?" He also mentioned that among the shareholders doing the building was only one dissident, a member of Selke's own union. That man's protests eventually led to a fistfight, one on one, the dissident versus the union's business agent, Cecil Shaw. "I've always thought maybe it was the best fight ever staged in Maple Leaf Gardens," Smythe recalled. "At the end Cecil Shaw was on his feet and the other guy was on his back looking up at the sky. The Gardens didn't have a roof at that time.... I realize now that getting the Gardens up and clean, painted, well lighted, with ice in and the bands marching out on the ice before a cheering crowd, all done between June 1 and November 12, was amazing." The bands were from the 48th Highlanders and the Royal Grenadiers. What they played was "Happy Days Are Here Again."

And that was the night Foster Hewitt called his first game out of Maple Leaf Gardens on what was known as the General Motors Hockey Broadcast, the forerunner of Hockey Night in Canada. That summer the two-year-old handshake on broadcast rights had finally borne fruit.

There had, of course, been negotiations in the meantime involving General Motors. MacLaren led the agency team, but one story has it that the GM deal really was started by Einar Rechnitzer, who'd been hired a year earlier by MacLaren to handle the General Motors account for Campbell-Ewald. One night, this version of the story goes, strictly by accident Rechnitzer had tuned in Hewitt's hockey broadcast from the old Arena Gardens.

The game had preempted Rechnitzer's favorite musical program, and (this already sounds as if written by a romantic ad-agency copy writer) when he tuned in and got hockey instead, he did not throw the radio out the window — he *fell in love with hockey!* Dreamed all night about Foster Hewitt's voice! Soon thereafter, in the normal course of his work on the General Motors account, mostly involving the print media, Rechnitzer was asked what was available on radio for sponsorship. Rechnitzer suggested hockey. It is not certain to this day whether he knew at the time that MacLaren had already sewn up the rights, or whether he found this out when he discussed the idea with MacLaren.

Well, it could have happened like that.

Of course, rights were one thing, but finding someone to pay for using them was another. General Motors was only one candidate. At the time, according to Smythe's memoirs, not only the agency, but also Hewitt and Frank Selke were out beating the bushes. Hewitt was said to have had one other company — British American Oil — interested. Or maybe that's what they told General Motors to help negotiations along on the financial side. At any rate, soon the agency had in its pocket the first-ever long-term deal for live hockey broadcasts — a five-year contract with General Motors to put both Toronto and Montreal games on local radio in those cities in their league openers on November 12.

That summer, with the Gardens roofed but otherwise far from finished, Smythe told Foster, "I want you to figure out where you want to broadcast from and tell the architect."

This launched an event that, in the realm of oft-told Leaf tales, ranks second in the charts only to the one that launched Conn Smythe's philosophy on how to win at hockey: "If you

Big Deal on a Little Golf Course

can't beat 'em in the alley, you can't beat 'em on the ice." The short form of the story of the hunt for the ideal broadcast position is that Foster toiled up and down the stairs in the old Eaton's Annex in downtown Toronto, looking at crowds from every floor until in his third or fourth time past the fifth floor he stopped, possibly from exhaustion, and said that was where he could see the best. Turned out he was 56 feet above the sidewalk. He gave that specification to the builders.

Later he wished he had also specified how he would get to his new workplace — rather than by a catwalk with no safety railing, which is what he got. The first time he started across the catwalk, he made the mistake of looking down, and finished the trip on hands and knees.

A little later Foster was in the Gardens one day with C. M. Pasmore who, with Maurice Rosenfeld as co-director, ran the agency's radio department. When the two men stood looking across the rink at the long and slender-looking tube hung in space, Foster's broadcast position, Pasmore mused, "Why, it looks just like the gondola on an airship." The gondola it was, from then on.

Inside, the gondola was spartan. A photo shows Foster on an ordinary wooden chair facing a hefty microphone. The mike is on a ledge alongside the night's program listing the players. The wooden wall is strung with wires and cables. There was no provision for giving him information or direction by earpieces or a phone. If anyone had to communicate with him, it would be when the microphone was off for commercials, or a note could be passed to him silently.

Three radio stations had been booked for the opening broadcast. On paper everything about the production looked fine. Rupert Lucas, a well-known broadcaster then and later, would do the General Motors commercials for their line of the time — Chevrolets, McLaughlin Buicks, Oldsmobiles and Cadillacs — alongside Foster in the gondola. Radio station CFRB would provide someone — eventually this was CFRB's young Wes McKnight — to handle announcements from an ice-level studio. A piano duet had been hired to play live in a studio at radio station CKGW, for simultaneous transmission on the other two stations during intermissions. Foster was in good voice. Pasmore couldn't think of anything that hadn't been checked in dry runs.

The one hitch he couldn't have foreseen: CKGW, designated the key station for opening night, was owned and controlled by the Westinghouse radio network in the United States. At virtually the last minute somebody in the U.S. Westinghouse head office was on the phone to CKGW exclaiming, "What the hell do you mean, a hockey game? What you're going to carry is our network show!" The game was simply bumped from CKGW, and the change in plan was unknown to anyone in the gondola for more than two periods. To get the word up there Pasmore or somebody would have had to make the arduous climb. Thinking of the catwalk and his serious shortage of substitute manpower, Pasmore made a command decision: why did the gondola need to know, anyway? He simply sent a taxi to pick up the piano players at CKGW and race them to one of the other first-night stations, which also had a piano.

All of which might be a hint that technologically, the hockey-broadcast situation in Maple Leaf Gardens at the very beginning was somewhat Stone Age — but only by today's standards. In 1931, procedures for covering sports events were being invented as they went along. The procedure boiled down to: Got trouble? Fix it!

For instance, at the end of a period when Foster had finished his wrap-up — he worked alone; color men had not yet been invented — the gondola operator was supposed to pass this news along to the ice-level control room. Not by voice, there were no phone links, but by throwing a switch. The control-room operator, when and if he noticed that Foster was finished, would call or signal this news to Wes McKnight. Wes then would throw to whoever was providing the intermission musical entertainment for all those folks out in radioland. No matter how quickly the exchanges between gondola and ice level were made, a few seconds of dead air ensued — which Pasmore eliminated within a game or two by having headphones and audio hookups installed so that cues went directly back and forth, cutting out the middle man. Even inventing the wheel had to start somewhere.

The only thing Smythe, Foster and the crowd didn't like about that first broadcast from the Gardens was the game result: Chicago 2, Toronto 1. Smythe immediately concluded that with his total absorption in getting the Gardens ready for the big night, he hadn't been keeping a close-enough eye on the team. It looked flabby to him, and he said so loudly — but not quite as cuttingly as once, years later, when he described shaking hands with a rather woebegone Leaf team as like shaking hands with a bunch of jellyfish.

Naturally, in the custom of owners and managers from time immemorial, he blamed the coach, Art Duncan. A few days later Smythe did something about it. The previous spring in the Stanley Cup playoffs, a 37-year-old one-time amateur star, Dick Irvin, had coached what Smythe considered to be an inferior team, Chicago, right through to the final before losing to Montreal Canadiens — and then had been fired. Five games into the season when Leafs had no wins and two ties, Smythe fired Duncan and hired Irvin. At the time Irvin's son, another Dick Irvin, later to be an all-star broadcaster with Hockey Night in Canada, had not yet been born.

Duncan was not the only victim of opening night and Leafs' subsequent losing string. The original piano duet didn't last long. Soon McKnight's throws were to the bandstand at a dance hall called the Silver Slipper, where a nationally known actor named John Holden, a real smoothie, was master of ceremonies. "And now, for your dancing pleasure . . ." Holden would intone, as the leader struck up the band. It is not entirely impossible to imagine that at least some hockey fans within reach of the music then got up, grabbed the nearest lady and danced. After two or three numbers, Holden would throw back to McKnight who would send it back upstairs to Hewitt; the puck would be dropped, and away they'd go again.

Meanwhile, Smythe didn't always spare Hewitt, either. As Smythe once said, "Foster and I are friends, but we're not married to one another." Whatever difference marriage might make was not specified. But if Foster said something on the air that Smythe heard and didn't like, they'd have words. Smythe found that Foster, for all his mild demeanor, was not easy to push around.

From the Smythe memoirs: "One time I criticized him for repeating one of the things that eventually made him famous, the line, 'He shoots! He scores!' I thought he should learn four or five more words in the English language.

" 'Aw,' he said, 'there's no use trying to please you.'

" 'That's an unfair statement,' I said. 'You have been pleasing me.'

" 'But there's no use!' he insisted. 'You always want something better than is being done.'

"I took that as kind of a compliment. And he isn't the first guy I've liked and admired but still tried to move up a notch or two."

While the Toronto broadcasts were being fine-tuned, the broadcasts of Montreal games were going through the same process under Pasmore's direction. At that time there were two Montreal teams, Canadiens and Maroons. Originally, Canadien games were carried on Quebec stations entirely in French, Maroon games in English. So with Rangers at Canadiens and Chicago at Toronto on November 12, 1931, it seems that neither of our official languages can claim a first — but the dead heat made French first in Quebec, English first in Ontario. Some things don't change.

As the first General Motors season went along, on certain nights when one of the Montreal teams played in Toronto, Foster's English play-by-play was piped back to Montreal. From the beginning of the second season, 1932–33, when either of the Montreal teams played Toronto, the games got that treatment. Games involving these two Canadian cities against any other teams in the league — Ottawa, New York

Americans, Detroit, Rangers, Boston and Chicago — usually were carried only in the host city.

In the 48-game season, with nine teams, each club played six games against each opponent. Because the Montreal–Toronto games were the only ones being carried in both cities it is very likely that this arrangement contributed centrally to one of the great hockey rivalries, one that still exists.

While the kinks were being worked out of the first season or two of broadcasting, on the other side of his job Pasmore worked hard both winter and summer to extend the broadcasts far beyond the original local stations in Toronto and Montreal. The small per-game fee (amount not known) that the agency paid to Smythe was set, so the more stations who bought the broadcasts, the better the return, both financially to the agency, and in a sales sense to the sponsor. On January 1, 1933, when a limited national network of 20 stations began to carry games from both Montreal and Toronto in English, a telephone survey a few weeks later indicated that each audience for a regularly scheduled game could be estimated "at just under a million listeners." Canada had a population of less than 10 million at the time, and radio sets were found by no means in every home, so the listener level was already surprisingly high.

One of Foster's most severe tests came on the famous night of April 3, 1933. Leafs and Boston had been fighting through a very tough best-of-five Stanley Cup semifinal for the right to meet Rangers in the final. Rangers had had an easy time getting there. Boston and Toronto had split the first four games, three of them in overtime. But the worst was still to come. Whoever won the fifth and final game on April 3 had to catch a train for New York and start the final against Rangers the following night!

Foster was in good voice, making himself heard above the tumultuous crowd of 14,500. The first two periods were scoreless. Between periods he summarized what had been happening and then shared the intermission commentary with announcer

Gordon Castle, who also did commercials. Near the end of the third period Castle left to go downstairs so he could interview players as they left the ice. There was again no score in the third period, so with Castle gone below, Foster did that first overtime intermission alone, still showing no strain.

The game had started at 8:30 and the broadcast at 9:00. At 1:25 a.m., still with no score, still alone, Foster had been talking steadily through play-by-play and intermissions for four and a half hours. Some fans had left. Some who left and got home to hear the game was still on, turned around and went back. Others who had been listening to Foster from the broadcast's beginning, reacting to the realization that this game would go down in hockey history, got into their cars or boarded streetcars to get to the Gardens. When some said they'd thrown away their ticket stubs and others said they'd never had tickets in the first place, Smythe instructed the doormen, "Let 'em all in free."

Occasionally Pasmore would puff up the stairs and along the catwalk to the gondola with notes on what was going on below. During intermissions, one of his notes read, players were lying on their dressing-room floors, exhausted. "I wouldn't mind doing the same," said Foster hoarsely. Down below, the league president, Frank Calder, was conferring with Smythe and Boston's Art Ross about the chances of postponing the New York opening of the final series for one day, on the grounds that whoever won shouldn't be penalized by the idiocy of scheduling a game in Toronto one night and in New York the next — never mind the added factor of overtime.

Calder called New York. The Rangers refused to postpone. The first game of the final would start in 17 hours.

In the fifth overtime period, Foster noticed that his eyesight blurred from time to time when he tried to focus on the game below. His speech was thicker, the pauses longer. Once, Pasmore, listening on earphones in an adjacent room in the gondola, jumped up and dashed in to where Foster was, just in time to see him teetering back, about to fall. Pasmore got him upright again and immediately leaned out of the gondola and

Big Deal on a Little Golf Course   51

bellowed to Castle, who was at ice level still waiting for a hero to interview.

Castle heard the shout and raced upstairs. He got there just as the fifth overtime period was ending. Foster silently handed him the microphone and later, perhaps in sheer relief at being able to shut up for a few minutes, said that Castle for the next 15 minutes delivered the most brilliant ad-lib commentary he'd ever heard.

At 1:45 a.m., the sixth overtime period began. Foster was ready to go again. Late in the fifth minute out of radios across the country came Foster's voice: "There's Eddie Shore going for the puck in the corner beside the Boston net! Andy Blair is on for the Leafs now — he hasn't played as much as the others and seems a little fresher than some. He's moving in on Shore in the corner. Shore is clearing the puck — Blair intercepts! Blair has the puck! Ken Doraty is dashing for the front of the net! Blair passes! Doraty takes it! He shoots! He scores!" The game, 164 minutes and 47 seconds of playing time, had ended an overall five hours and 30 minutes after the opening face-off.

Foster took a taxi with some of the Leafs to a sleeping car waiting for them at Union Station, slept until four in the afternoon when the train pulled into New York's Grand Central, had dinner, took a cab to Madison Square Garden and broadcast the game. Leafs lost. At 11 p.m., April 4, seven hours after Leafs had reached Grand Central, their sleeping car was hitched to a train pulling out for Toronto for the next game. There was not much sleeping done on the road home.

The Leafs eventually lost the series. Foster figured they would have beaten the Rangers and won the Cup if it hadn't been for the marathon on April 3, the overnight train ride and another game 17 hours after Doraty's goal.

Incidentally, Foster Hewitt's longest-game and longest-broadcast record lasted just three years, until, with Charlie Harwood calling the play-by-play, Detroit beat Montreal Maroons 1–0 after 176 minutes and 30 seconds of playing time in the 1936 playoffs. The only goal was scored by Winnipeg's

Modere "Mud" Bruneteau. When Foster heard that his record had been broken, he laughed. "That's a record they can have. I hope I never break it."

Chapter 5
Goodbye General Motors, Hello Imperial

> *Before the broadcasts did go west, I can recall tuning in, in Regina, to CKOK, Windsor, now CKLW . . . [There was] a lot of static but I was able to pick up most of the play-by-play.*
> — Lyman Potts, radio pioneer,
> later head of CFRB

For a couple of years, Foster did not have an opposite number in Montreal — someone who really owned the play-by-play job. In the summer of 1933, with the prospect that Hockey Night soon would be carried coast-to-coast on a mixture of public and private stations, a competition — these days it would be called an audition — was held to try out announcers, English for the Maroons and French for the Canadiens. Those who applied were the best around, sensing big opportunities. That same summer General Motors of Canada had bought broadcasting rights from both Montreal NHL teams. In the U.S., sportscasters were already becoming famous, in some cases rich. There was the feeling in Montreal that these could be plum jobs. Hockey broadcasting bigdomes of the time, mainly from General Motors and the ad agency, gathered for this competition at the studios of Associated Screen News.

What they did was to screen a game film and let the candidates go to it. The first segment was for "play announcers". They came in one by one to describe the action on the screen. In an adjoining room the jury listened and made judgments. Two, one in each language, stood out and were asked to come back a couple of days later to do it again, a check to make sure the first judgments stood up. The second segment was for "summary readers", an end-of-period commentary. Thus were born today's color men.

Out of those competitions, Phil Lalonde, director of radio station CKAC, owned by *La Presse*, became the Montreal French play announcer and Roland Beaudry, a sports editor, the French summary reader. Charlie Harwood won the brass ring as the first play announcer for Montreal English games, with Elmer Ferguson, then sports editor of the *Montreal Herald*, the first English summary reader.

At the beginning of that season, a total of 24 stations across the country were carrying hockey, including five in Quebec. Five months later the total had risen to 33. The 1933 listener poll had estimated that there were just under a million listeners. A year later a General Motors promotional pamphlet stated that in the new season more than a million people would be listening to their hockey games on the GM network.

Lyman Potts, a radio pioneer from Regina who later headed CFRB in Toronto, clearly remembered the extension of the General Motors Hockey Broadcast network to western Canada. "It was an ad-hoc network, the stations being chosen by the agency and the lines rented from CN.... Before the hockey broadcasts did go west, I can recall tuning in, in Regina, to CKOK Windsor, now CKLW.... [There was] a lot of static but I was able to pick up most of the play-by-play."

But big changes were on the way by then, one relatively low profile and the other still controversial 54 years later. Jack MacLaren bought out Campbell-Ewald's Canadian operation and renamed it MacLaren Advertising. That was to have a long-range impact, but did not exactly stir the country at the time.

The other came a few months after the marathon Detroit–Maroons game. General Motors' five-year contract to broadcast hockey from both Toronto and Montreal ran out and was not renewed; a new president of General Motors Canada, just in

Goodbye General Motors, Hello Imperial

from the United States, told MacLaren that he did not believe hockey would sell cars.

There are various versions as to how Imperial Oil moved in to take advantage of this somewhat unprophetic decision. One is that a member of the Maple Leaf Gardens board, Victor Ross, suggested that Imperial Oil would be an ideal successor. At the same time, Hewitt was dickering again with British American Oil. But while that company once again dawdled, Imperial didn't. On this point, the footnote to history that somehow sounds most likely is the fact that MacLaren's Einar Rechnitzer and Imperial's Frank Prendergast, assistant to that company's president, were friends.

Prendergast's portfolio included advertising and public relations. According to Prendergast's son Walter, when the General Motors contract was nearing its end, his father asked Rechnitzer to call him immediately "if the hockey sponsorship ever comes loose." If there was a courtship of Imperial by Maclaren's at all, that was it. When the time came, Rechnitzer was first to know.

He phoned Prendergast and said, "Frank, she's loose. General Motors is dropping out."

Prendergast: "Sold!"

Only then, the story goes, did he tell his boss and Imperial's board of directors what he had done. That might all be true. But the way it appears in various correspondence files doesn't mention the Rechnitzer–Prendergast axis at all. Probably it did exist, but for reasons of what today might be called covering one's ass, the official handling was strictly by the book.

On August 5, 1936, Pasmore wrote to Imperial, attention Prendergast, a letter that conveys the tone of much business dealing long ago:

Gentlemen:

We are able to offer you play-by-play broadcasting rights to National Hockey League games as may be available in Toronto during the forthcoming season of 1936–37. In Toronto we have an agreement with the Maple Leaf Gardens covering all broadcasting rights of Maple Leaf games played in Toronto. In Montreal we have the assurance of the Montreal Forum directorate that if any broadcasting rights are given for the season of 1936–37, we will have prior claim to those rights.

The total cost of scheduled games (excluding playoffs) for national coverage — including both the Toronto and Montreal franchises — would not in any event exceed $100,000, based on programme, station and other services as recommended by us. Of this total, approximately $27,000 represents bilingual coverage of the Province of Quebec; the balance representing coverage of Ontario and the remainder of Canada. Additional costs for playoffs are naturally uncertain, but are not likely to exceed $25,000.

Naturally your immediate decision will apply only to the main principle of the above proposal. Details as to radio stations, talent, etc., must necessarily be subject to later discussion. Meantime, at the request of your Mr. Prendergast, we have agreed to defer offering this service to any other sponsor prior to Monday, August 10, 1936, by which time we would like to have word from you.

One day later Pasmore got his reply from Prendergast:

I am instructed to advise you that we accept this offer as outlined in your letter. Accordingly please ... proceed with the necessary immediate arrangements on our behalf.

Apparently, in substantially expanding his hockey network, Pasmore didn't have to consult anyone except the stations involved. In 1932 the government had appointed an outfit called the Canadian Radio Broadcasting Commission, forerunner of the CBC, with its offices in Ottawa under the chairmanship of a former journalist and magazine editor, Hector Charlesworth. But when Pasmore sent Charlesworth a telegram on August 7 it was only to ask for an extra half hour or more on hockey nights from the CRBC's Montreal station,

CRCM, so that games that ran past 10 p.m. could be broadcast to the finish.

At the same time, Pasmore wrote or telegraphed several other stations. In the telegram to Charlesworth, he hadn't mentioned money. In phone calls to other stations in the Montreal area — Marconi's CFCF and shortwave CFCX (wattage at the time unknown), La Patrie's CHLP (100 watts), and *La Presse*'s CKAC (5,000 watts) — he offered to pay a $40 broadcast rate to the first two, and they accepted the same day by letter. Whatever he offered to CKAC, he wound up paying the station $88, probably because of its much stronger signal. These fees were subject to the usual commission of 15 percent paid to advertising agencies, so in the $40 cases the station would actually get $34 for its first half hour and payment at the same rate if the games ran longer.

Even that rate could be further reduced if a station agreed to what was called a serial discount, one based on frequency of the run-overs past 10 p.m. Only CFCF declined to allow the serial discount.

It's unlikely that any of the stations knew that the deals differed. Pasmore, like many a MacLaren negotiator after him, often had to tread lightly and play trade secrets close to his chest. For instance, in sales of broadcast rights, Montreal never got as much money as Toronto. Some people knew that, but it was never openly discussed. Yet the Toronto rights were simple: Jack MacLaren and Conn Smythe exchanged phone calls, confirmed by letter for bookkeeping purposes, and that was that.

In contrast, there was a definite air of cap-in-hand in Pasmore's manner when he was dealing with Montreal's T. P. Gorman, a crusty Ottawa Irishman who was one of the founders of the NHL and a Stanley Cup winner several times as owner or coach. By 1937 Gorman was in charge of the old Montreal Maroons, who were soon to sink out of sight, and also was manager of the Canadian Arena Company's Montreal Forum, headquarters for both Maroons and Canadiens. Gorman negotiated for hockey rights on behalf of both teams.

When Pasmore went to Gorman looking to do rights business, it wasn't a case of a phone call and a confirming note. On September 20, 1937, Pasmore wrote a meticulously detailed letter to Gorman, covering four pages single-spaced and full of cheerful inducements, such as bus excursions to be arranged by MacLaren's through which thousands of Imperial Oil dealers and their families would pour into the Forum. Along with that and other prizes, he offered Gorman $350 net per NHL regular-league game, $600 net per game for the playoffs, and urged that Gorman grant MacLaren's an option for the subsequent two years.

Gorman's reply came three weeks later, first by telephone, then by letter on October 12. The price, said Gorman, would be $400 — not $350 — per league game, $600 for playoffs, and that "while you have the exclusive right to broadcast these games from the Forum, we retain the right, as conceded by you, to negotiate and complete arrangements for the broadcasting of Thursday-night games in New England and in Essex, Franklin and Clinton counties in New York state."

For several reasons, Gorman added, he couldn't make this longer than a one-year deal, but might extend it under the same conditions "should we decide to continue broadcasting next year." On October 14 Imperial Oil okayed these terms. Perhaps some of the hesitation in signing a long-term deal was due to uncertainty about how long the Maroons could struggle along. They were an excellent team but had poor crowd support, even after King Clancy quit the Leafs and took over as Maroon coach to try to liven things up.

Gorman for once must have envied Toronto, where usually all that happened in the way of getting ready for a season was a June phone call from Jack MacLaren to Conn Smythe, a covering letter and let's go. What Gorman didn't know was that while MacLaren and Smythe did like to keep things simple, Imperial Oil was getting a little restive.

The problem, as Prendergast wrote to Pasmore on June 15, 1938, was the price for

Goodbye General Motors, Hello Imperial

... tieing up the hockey broadcasting franchise again for the 1938–39 season. I would like you to explore any possibility for reducing the cost of these franchises and also to study carefully the whole plan with a view to determining whether we could not cut the costs of the hockey broadcasts this year.

For instance, is there any possibility that we might be able to sell the game to some interest which would bring Foster Hewitt's description to the hometown of the visiting team?

This might apply in the cases of Chicago, New York, Boston and Cleveland, if Cleveland comes into the league.

I wish you would study the whole matter very carefully and get in touch with me at any early date.

Whether Pasmore studied the matter "very carefully" and got in touch at an early date is not known. It is certain that Prendergast might as well have been whistling Dixie — the costs did not get any lower that year and have been going up ever since. Three weeks after the Prendergast letter, on July 8, 1938, Jack MacLaren wrote to Conn Smythe, giving what one might call the bottom line, just the facts:

Dear Mr. Smythe:

Imperial Oil Limited has signed a contract with us covering the broadcast of all home games of the National Hockey League from Maple Leaf Gardens for the season of 1938–39.

It is understood that the net income to Maple Leaf Gardens will be $750.00 per game for the regular schedule, and $1,000.00 per game for playoffs.

It is understood that Foster Hewitt's services and necessary mechanical facilities and services will be provided by the Gardens as in former years.

As we have assured our client, Imperial Oil Limited, that your Executive Committee would concur with the above arrangement, your acknowledgement as soon as possible would be appreciated

While this brief look at the files might be considered by some not quite on the entertainment level of Harry Neale or Don Cherry, it seemed useful to establish the original tone. As raucous as the broadcast games became, very little that was raucous happened on the executive level. Gentlemen dealt with gentlemen.

Imperial Oil and hockey were to be inextricably linked in the Canadian psyche for the next 50 years. Even when Imperial dropped out of Hockey Night in Canada from 1976 to 1982, public perception of the heresy of Imperial's severing its link with the game was minimal, except for within MacLaren's, where it ranked somewhere close to the San Francisco earthquake. To the public, Esso simply had been too long on radio and later television on hockey nights for any mere six-year hiatus to register very strongly.

At the same time as the 1936 sponsor switch, the old ad hoc radio network put together by MacLaren Advertising was approaching its final months. The Canadian Broadcasting Corporation supplanted the previous broadcast regulator, the Canadian Radio Broadcasting Commission, and began network broadcasting on January 1, 1937.

Hockey's long involvement with the CBC began simply enough with CBC's Charles Jennings announcing, "Your Imperial Oil hockey broadcast! Bringing you . . . Foster Hewitt!" This was followed by Hewitt's distinctive voice crackling out along the network with what would become his trademark opening, "Hello Canada! And hockey fans in the United States and Newfoundland!"

No use of the phrase Hockey Night in Canada. It came later; no one is sure when.

When Leafs' hockey with Foster Hewitt went coast-to-coast on the new public network, private stations across the country still supplemented the coverage and did so for many years, in some cities — Toronto for one — giving double coverage, public and private, even where public stations existed. One element didn't change: Toronto games still went to Ontario

Goodbye General Motors, Hello Imperial 61

and the rest of Canada, except Quebec, which got the Montreal games in English and French.

But other elements were changing, and the size of the radio audience seemed to be growing boundlessly. By the end of the 1930s, each game was reaching nearly two million people. Foster Hewitt's voice and, beginning in 1939, the popular intermission discussions featuring hockey experts on what was called the "Hot Stove League" became part of Canada's social history. Millions in all provinces came to treat Saturday night as Hockey Night, one of the few bright spots in a country facing war while still suffering the Great Depression. Fans coming to Toronto for the first time trooped like pilgrims to Maple Leaf Gardens, the only Toronto institution known across Canada with unquestioning respect. The same situation prevailed in Montreal, where fans flocked to see the Forum.

Hockey greats of the future took their earliest instruction in hockey gospel from those early broadcasts — a young Maurice Richard and many others in Montreal and throughout Quebec; a young Gordie Howe in Floral, Saskatchewan; a few years later Bobby Hull in Point Anne, Ontario; and thousands of others, future stars as well as those who never made it. They laced on skates in country and city snowbanks and dreamed.

But while the Montreal broadcasts always had their devotees, it was not until many years later, when Danny Gallivan began broadcasting games from Montreal, that anyone even approached Foster Hewitt's national impact. Hewitt's artistry was founded on his ability not only to call what was going on but to anticipate where this play or that would lead. Knowing many players from as far back as their amateur days, he made them come alive: Howie Morenz, the Stratford Streak; crashing Eddie Shore from the West; crafty Frank Boucher, the Cook brothers, Nels Stewart, King Clancy, Dit Clapper, Hooley Smith; the crashing body checks of Red Horner, quiet Joe Primeau feeding flawless passes to the powerful Charlie Conacher, or speedy Busher Jackson in full flight.

Conacher told of a winter in the 1930s when the team barnstormed across the country. When they stopped at railroad stations where throngs waited to see their heroes, some fans would be looking past Clancy and Horner and Conacher's Kid Line colleagues and the rest to call, "Where's Foster?" Years later Bobby Hull said that when he was on the threshold of becoming a great star and first met Foster Hewitt "it was like meeting God."

In today's world of instant millionaires and transitory heroes, it is doubtful if anyone could ever build the national fame that Foster had. Howie Meeker, for a spell, and Don Cherry, today, probably come as close as possible. Today competent, even brilliant, hockey broadcasters are not quite a dime a dozen — but there are dozens of them. Foster, in his time, was one of a kind.

But to go back to that 1929 handshake one final time: it was a fact that for many years thereafter a deal that became worth millions of dollars had no formal contract, although letters between Jack MacLaren and Conn Smythe seemed, however obliquely, to acknowledge the old understanding.

In one 1936 letter to Jack MacLaren about MacLaren's first hockey deal with Imperial Oil, Smythe included this line: "It is the feeling of our executive [meaning the Gardens executive] that the relations that have been established between yourselves [meaning MacLaren Advertising agency], General Motors and ourselves should be continued."

General Motors, being a different kettle of fish, did have a formal contract with the Gardens drawn up in 1934 acknowledging that as sponsors they had some rights, such as to the services of Foster Hewitt and access to the Gardens for planning purposes.

But a matter to become of high importance nearly 50 years later specified that those rights were not assignable. Meaning that in any change of sponsorship — the first of these was General Motors dropping out and Imperial Oil coming in — the rights reverted to the original handshake between Smythe and MacLaren.

As time went on, exchanges of business letters between MacLaren Advertising and the Gardens were no more specific than references such as: "In all other respects it is to be understood that the same terms, conditions and privileges shall apply as have actually applied in practical operation."

Even in 1951, 22 years after the handshake, when television was on the horizon for the 1952–53 season and a different rights fee had been negotiated and dealt with in a letter to Smythe from Jack MacLaren, the only line that could be construed as contractual between the original handshakers was: "In all other respects the television franchise agreement will be the same as for the present radio broadcast."

Chapter 6
The Landing of Hugh Horler

> I'd been working in MacLaren's Winnipeg
> office a year or two when one day I got a call
> from Rechnitzer, who by then was executive
> vice president. He told me to come to
> Toronto. He didn't say what for. He just said,
> "Be on the train tomorrow morning."
> — Hugh Horler

Hugh Horler was a dark-haired and thin young man in his early 20s, when he received that summons from MacLaren's head office in 1941. He went home and told his wife, who didn't kick up a fuss. That kind of short notice was not uncommon in almost any business at the time. The boss spoke, the employee jumped. Horler packed a few things — he didn't know that he would never be back there to live — and climbed aboard the morning eastbound train, crowded with troops. Steaming through northern Ontario, at every stop where there was a liquor store and a fighting chance of making it there and back before the train left, designated sprinters in uniform got back with whatever they could buy. Liquor rationing was in its early stages at the time, but few liquor-store clerks turned down men in uniform. Still, it wasn't exactly party time on those trains. Lineups for meals would stretch back through several cars.

When Horler reached Toronto late the following afternoon, he walked out of Union Station into a typically raw and dank autumn day, looking for Bay Street. The MacLaren office was at number 372 a few blocks away. Rechnitzer looked surprised to see him.

"I got the feeling he didn't remember exactly what he'd had in mind when he'd phoned me. He drank quite a bit from time to time. Might have phoned me after he'd had a few. Anyway, there was a lot of hemming and hawing. Finally he said he didn't know exactly what I would be doing, but I'd be working for two people, Pasmore and Rosenfeld, and to report to them in the radio department."

There he learned from Pasmore that on hockey matters, he'd work for Pasmore. For anything else connected with radio — writing commercials, publicity or whatever was needed on other radio programs — Rosenfeld would be his boss.

To Horler the hockey part of the job was pure dream-fulfillment. Hewitt was one of his idols. In his hometown, Edmonton, hockey was close to being the local religion, and his father had been right in the middle of it. Jack Horler used to broadcast junior and minor pro hockey games from rinkside with young Hugh standing right beside him. Now some junior stars he'd seen play in Edmonton were in the NHL. He'd see them clumping by in the Gardens' corridors and generally had the feeling of being exactly where he wanted to be — a junior member of the hockey broadcast's production team. Pasmore, Kay Dale and Horler. Who could wish for anything more?

Kay Dale, an attractive woman in the Girl Friday mold — long before such a description went out of style, if not practice — was Pasmore's secretary, a close friend of Foster Hewitt's and a busy regular in the gondola. For at least a quarter century thereafter she was the person to call when anyone, journalist or client, wanted an answer to anything about the hockey broadcasts. She was essential to the operation because Pasmore often was not immediately available.

A few steps away on Bay Street was a fairly new hotel called the Savarin. Pasmore habitually would check in at MacLaren's each morning, pick up a pad of paper and mosey on down to a table at the Savarin where he would have a few beers and work until the place closed at six (that closing, for an hour and a half, was a wartime rule in aid of getting drinkers home for supper). Back at the other office, Kay Dale and Horler held the fort. If Pasmore was required in person, they always knew where to find him.

His job was keeping the CBC and private stations happy and helping to keep Imperial Oil, the sole sponsor, happy, as well. Horler eventually was to inherit all those tasks and more, but meanwhile, with the actual radio feed from the Gardens along the network by then pretty well a matter of routine, he wrote the "commercials" — which, in wartime, actually had nothing to do with hard sell. With gasoline and tires rationed, Imperial Oil had decided against any sponsor mention except occasionally a one-liner: "This game is brought to you by Imperial Oil." What had been commercial time was turned over entirely to plugs for various war charities, or announcements requested from time to time by the government. In that sense, Hockey Night in Canada had been turned into part of the war effort.

A prime example came soon after the devastating December 7, 1941, Japanese attack on Pearl Harbor and other disastrous losses in the Pacific that soon followed. After Pearl Harbor, an invasion somewhere on Canada's west coast seemed a possibility. Defending that coast was given high priority. Troops were shipped there, including Major Conn Smythe's newly organized 30th (Sportsmen's) battery. Coastal defenses were stretched thin. On land and sea the army and other armed services, along with civilian volunteers, patrolled lonely bays and inlets; in the air the RCAF's lumbering coastal patrols flew reconnaissance sorties. All were drastically short of binoculars.

The defense department asked Hockey Night to appeal to the public for any that people could spare. Horler duly wrote that message. The following Saturday night Foster devoted a minute or two of his game broadcast to the urgent need for binoculars and instructions as to where they could be turned in. Within days, 1,100 binoculars were handed in or sent to RCAF establishments around the country. The following Saturday night Foster told his audience, "That's enough binoculars."

The Landing of Hugh Horler

Besides writing such announcements, one of Horler's weekly jobs was "writing the 'Hot Stove League' scripts and giving the guys a call so they could prepare their ad libs." The "Hot Stove League", invented by Pasmore in 1939, is long gone now, and many oldsters would say, "Worse luck!" It was absolutely the best in the business at keeping the nation arguing and laughing through hockey intermissions. Fergy, Wes, Baldy, Bobby — say one of those names in any beer parlor in the land and everybody knew whom you were talking about. Working from a tiny room near the Leaf dressing room, the early "Hot Stove" regulars included Elmer Ferguson, sports editor of the *Montreal Herald*, who had done the end-of-period summaries on the first hockey radio broadcasts out of Montreal in 1933; the *Toronto Telegram*'s Bobby Hewitson, CFRB's Wes McKnight and former NHLer (Pittsburgh, then the Leafs) Harold "Baldy" Cotton. Free-lance actor and broadcaster Court Benson was the first host. CFRB's Jack Dennett was to join up much later. Over the years, some "Hot Stove" guests were well-known enough to have a recognition factor almost equal to that of the regulars. One was Father Athol Murray of Notre Dame College, Wilcox, Saskatchewan, known across the land, as he was in his home province, simply as Père. Witty sportswriter Jim Coleman was the only one of the lot without a nickname. He was simply Coleman.

Whether these garrulous wits really followed Horler's scripts was a moot point. Their sessions usually sounded strictly off-the-cuff. But due to wartime regulations obeyed to the letter by the CBC, every word on a hockey broadcast apart from Hewitt's play-by-play was supposed to be scripted. At the time, a government censor had an office in the *Globe and Mail* building at King and York. His job was to head off any media disclosure of what could be remotely interpreted as useful military information.

As a result, nobody on the broadcast could even say a hangover was due to a farewell party for good old so-and-so off to the war zone, or mention individuals in the armed services at all except in the most general way. While newspapers operated under the same bans, radio was deemed a particularly important risk. But if enemy shortwave listeners did learn anything from the Hot Stovers, it was probably about back-checking, how Sweeney Schriner kept his hair slicked down through thick and thin, or the merits of Beehive Corn Syrup. When they did stray from the script for ad hoc jokes or comment, they knew enough not to get the censor on their necks.

Horler's scripts were typed on thin sheets of paper called flimsies with four or five carbon copies, one to be delivered to the CBC for checking and, if necessary, the censor's okay. After the top copy, typed in hunt-and-peck style by Horler, the flimsies were just barely legible, if that. So if the silver-tongued orators of the "Hot Stove League" sounded a little stilted from time to time, it was because they couldn't read the faint carbons. It didn't matter; few people needed less prompting than the "Hot Stove" regulars.

By the time Horler arrived in Toronto and the hockey-broadcast scene, the game had overcome many of its early image problems with an impatient war-supporting public.

Canada's declaration of war on Germany in early September 1939, followed quickly by dispatch of the Canadian Army's First Division to Europe before Christmas that year, had emphasized that this was real, this was earnest — and many argued that if the First Div was over there, why wasn't every big strong athlete at least in uniform? In the war's first year, professional hockey was attacked for continuing with business as usual. The *Globe and Mail* trumpeted that young hockey players should be shooting rifles instead of pucks. An Ontario judge was more specific: "When I read the sports pages I see great Goliaths of men in the wrong uniforms."

However, high-level support for both amateur and pro hockey and the broadcasts came swiftly. As "the most popular sport in Canada," one senior army officer said, "the hockey broadcasts and games are of the utmost importance to morale both at home and abroad." Letters from servicemen in England

The Landing of Hugh Horler

soon backed up this opinion. Indeed, one beef often was that a few units with powerful shortwave radios could pick up the hockey broadcasts live, get the scores and win bets against men of less fortunate, or more trusting, units. Letters were addressed to Imperial Oil, to Foster Hewitt personally, to Conn Smythe, his assistant Frank Selke, Prime Minister Mackenzie King, Leaf coach Hap Day or anyone else who might have some influence. The pleas had one main theme: why couldn't the hockey broadcasts be shortwaved to Britain and carried by the BBC?

The idea was considered. A full broadcast was deemed out of the question. But, someone suggested, how about a shortened version? Imperial Oil said they'd bankroll such a project.

From then on the Saturday night Leaf games were recorded in full, and minutes after the game ended Foster Hewitt, Hugh Horler, Kay Dale and a technician from the CBC would go straight from the Gardens to a CBC studio. They'd listen to the game recording and select highlights — especially plays leading to goals or fights or whatever seemed most interesting. Some of the earliest cut versions, re-recorded into a continuous half hour, were flown to England and the BBC by the RCAF. Soon they were being shortwaved instead and rebroadcast on BBC shortwave. Canadians listened on watch at shore batteries, searchlight sites, in ships at sea and in aircraft aloft. Foster Hewitt's familiar voice with its familiar subject was a reminder of their home country and all there was in Canada, including hockey, to go back to.

For the rest of the war Foster received letters from all over the world, wherever Canadians were serving.

"Dear Foster," one letter read, "I have just been listening to the hockey game that was played last night in Maple Leaf Gardens. It was the most enjoyable time I have had since I left home."

And another: "I was walking past a servicemen's hostel near the Tottenham Court Road tube station and I heard this voice, your voice, coming through the blackout curtains, and I ran in there and it was the hockey broadcast. I damn near cried."

Foster used to spend most of his Sundays answering letters. For years after the war he was stopped by strangers with tales of the trenches, bombers, fighters, ships, or wherever they'd been while listening to what, for some, was their favorite war cry, "He shoots! He scores!"

As the war went on, hockey broadcasts actually maintained a quality higher than the watered-down game itself could manage. More and more NHL regulars joined the armed forces, either by their own inclination or pushed by public pressure that the physically fit, especially those with high profiles, should be in uniform. Talented young players who in normal times would have been moving into the NHL as rookie stars gave up that chance, and what might have been their best hockey years, for the duration.

Foster Hewitt watched from the gondola and described with the same "He shoots! He scores!" fervor the play of the many men in their place who, under other circumstances, never would have made the NHL. Or would not have made it without years of seasoning in the minors. Or would have retired from the game long since.

Whatever Foster Hewitt and his listeners along the network and abroad thought of Ted Kennedy of Toronto, 16, Don Gallinger of Boston, 17, Hy Buller of Detroit, 18, Andy Branigan of New York Americans and Joe Bell of New York Rangers, both 19, playing alongside real NHLers or an assortment of refugees from senior hockey, these boys and men did keep the game going. With dozens of stations across the country now carrying the games, an end-to-end rush by little-known Tommy "Windy" O'Neill of Toronto or Johnny Chad of Chicago sounded via Hewitt not that much unlike a rush by the more familiar stars of the prewar game.

So Hockey Night in Canada went on, the tradition uninterrupted. On the working side, the MacLaren group of Hewitt, Pasmore, Horler and Kay Dale wasn't really affected by the diluted brand of hockey that persisted, which, though a little weaker every year, also produced the fiery Maurice "Rocket" Richard and his 50-goal season in 1944–45 and some of the league's enduring stars, such as Bill Durnan, Butch Bouchard and others.

Hewitt loved The Rocket, but in praising him he didn't knock wartime hockey. He broadcast the best way he could with what he had. And in a time when Boston Bruins one year invited 16 teenagers to training camp, there were still some fine last hurrahs from the likes of Sweeney Schriner, Babe Pratt, Flash Hollett, Syd Howe, Herbie Cain and others.

This period also produced the only occurrence of outside interference with the hockey broadcasts. In 1944 when Conn Smythe was invalided home with wounds suffered in Normandy, which were to plague him the rest of his life, he was furious with the government's persistent refusal to conscript men for overseas service. Servicemen wounded as many as three times were being sent back to fight because of the shortage of reinforcements.

On reaching his army hospital bed in Toronto, Smythe immediately launched a bitter pro-conscription publicity campaign, front-paged by the *Globe and Mail* and other newspapers and heavily supported by other officers who had also seen firsthand the results of the chronic shortage of fresh fighting men. Smythe demanded time on the hockey intermission, normally "Hot Stove League" time, to take the fight to the country. For the first time ever, the CBC, which normally only had a representative "around somewhere" (Horler's phrase) intervened, very upset because conscription, or lack of it, was the prime political issue of the time. The CBC felt it could not possibly take sides, through its hockey broadcasts, by letting Smythe have his say.

The situation was finally calmed down, but not without a fight. Smythe could go on the "Hot Stove League", but the restrictions demanded by the CBC were so drastic that for the first time ever the usual Saturday pregame meeting was held in Jack MacLaren's office.

"Everybody was there," Horler said. "Smythe, the CBC, us, Imperial Oil. Smythe was livid, but he was literally tamed into agreeing not to say what he really wanted to say — which was basically that 'all those dirty cowards out there' should be in uniform. The questions had to be thoroughly scripted, which they were. Wes McKnight was the interlocutor for the 'Hot Stove League'. Smythe stuck to the script. It was a miracle."

It was not long after that "miracle" that the war in Europe ended. When the wartime-only players went back to senior hockey, business and civilian life, a golden age of hockey and its broadcasts followed. In the late 1940s the Toronto Maple Leafs were winning three Stanley Cups, Detroit's dominance was looming, Canadiens were always hot contenders. And Hugh Horler, as the man in charge of Hockey Night, was being recognized as one of those most essential to seeing that the quality of the broadcasts equaled the newly recovered excellence of the games themselves.

This was done without any changes at all. "Everything pretty well stayed the same," he said. "Foster, the Hot Stovers, everything else. There was no imperative to bring in new voices, no motivation to change anything. No money was being spent."

But then trouble did loom. The elder Frank Selke had left the Gardens in May 1946, after a simmering feud with Smythe. Smythe felt that in some ways Selke, in charge while Smythe was away, had undermined him with the Gardens directors. Smythe thought it was time he was named president of the Gardens. When he sought Selke's voting support, Selke turned him down. Smythe told him he was going to be president, anyway, "and if I get it without your help, or vote, then it would pretty well prove that I don't need you, wouldn't you say?" The past, when Selke had helped get the Gardens built in the first place, apparently no longer was a factor.

This split probably was a good thing for the NHL. Selke, a strong man in his own right, then moved to Montreal, and the Canadiens, to found a dynasty there. But soon, according to Horler, "our biggest problem at Hockey Night involved Selke. He knew exactly what power radio had. He often told the story about an exhibition series Leafs and Canadiens played across the country in the late 1940s. When Canadiens skated onto the ice

The Landing of Hugh Horler

at Calgary they were booed. When Leafs came on they got a standing ovation. The same thing in various forms had happened when Leafs toured with Detroit Red Wings and another time with Chicago Blackhawks. Calgarians hardly even knew the Canadien players, but they all knew the Leafs, because it was almost always Leafs on Hockey Night in Canada. In Calgary Leafs were the heroes and Canadiens the villains. And Selke decided he had to do something about that."

What he did was get in touch with Spence Caldwell, an energetic and talented broadcaster who at the time headed the CBC's second network, the Dominion (the first was the National), and later founded CTV. Selke and Caldwell worked out a plan to give Hockey Night in Canada some competition across the country by broadcasting Montreal's midweek games on the Dominion network. The complications with broadcast rights looked staggering, yet Horler managed to put together a second hockey network very fast.

"That is really what forced Smythe to share the Saturday shows," Horler said years later. "Selke and Jack MacLaren were good friends, but when the proposal to broadcast midweek games was put to MacLaren, he and his staff turned the whole idea down.

"Smythe and Selke then, between them and with MacLaren's involvement, made a deal that rather than have two separate broadcasts, they'd share the Saturday nights," Horler recalls. "We had to sell Smythe on the idea. We put together a great board, a map of Canada with lights that went off and on that impressed the hell out of Smythe.

"The deal was that Maple Leaf territory, so-called, would always have the Leaf games. Same with Montreal, and they alternated in going national. French radio, of course, would remain the same as it had always been with MacLaren, strictly for Quebec. The only one who was screwed was Caldwell and his Dominion network."

This arrangement lasted a long time, and still is the basis for Hockey Night planning. Pasmore died suddenly in 1949, with Horler left in full charge of the broadcast product. The games by then were going out to a maturing cross-Canada network of 54 CBC and private stations, 13 of them broadcasting in the French language, the total audience more than three million Canadians every Saturday night. Television was just around the corner.

In a MacLaren's official company record of those years, Horler is described as providing "aggressive leadership" to Hockey Night in Canada. The adjective "aggressive" didn't seem to suit the actuality of Horler, who struck most people as quiet. But in managing the switch to television — undoubtedly the greatest change since hockey had first gone out over the airwaves in the 1920s — he quietly got his way most of the time. Two other men, George Retzlaff of the CBC and H. M. "Bud" Turner, Jr., eventually chairman of MacLaren Advertising, were soon to join him as major figures in hockey broadcasting's television revolution.

There's no doubt that Turner's background aimed him straight at the kind of job he first filled at MacLaren. He had worked for General Electric in Schenectady, New York, for a year or so, where he was the company rep for "The Fred Waring Show", sponsored by General Electric.

Waring liked to do one live commercial per show. Each week, Turner says, "I always had to take a spare something along to the show in case Waring dropped the toaster or whatever he was plugging." Turner's year of Thursdays to Sundays with Waring wasn't much in the way of television experience, but it was more than most in Canada had at that time. Turner started at MacLaren's in 1951 in the media-checking department and moved to Horler's Radio and TV group a year later, mainly to act as a liaison with Imperial Oil.

The work-up to televised hockey began in 1951. From the beginning there were two main points of contention. One was camera placement. The other was centered around what kind of play-by-play commentary should be used when television did finally arrive.

Deciding where to put the cameras caused disputes that are somewhat amusing now — if only because placing cameras in the earliest stages of hockey television was akin to inventing the wheel. Conn Smythe insisted on his own ideas against those of Horler and Turner. George Retzlaff, later as executive producer and eventually head of CBC Sports the recognized genius on such things, was a lowly cameraman at the time, overhearing the arguments but never asked for his opinion, let alone given a vote.

Smythe's opening edict was that the cameras must not interfere with the view of anyone who paid to get in. That meant, he ruled, or attempted to rule, putting them behind the cheapest seats in the Gardens, the grays.

"Might as well be watching the game from Etobicoke," Horler, Turner and CBC people muttered to one another.

At one point it seemed eminently sensible to some to place a camera in the gondola. The argument was that it would have the same point of view as Foster when he was calling the play-by-play. Should be great. So a camera was placed in the gondola. The picture made all the players look as if they were skating uphill, and another great camera-placement idea bit the dust.

Smythe fought on. When he finally conceded that one camera should go on one side a few rows of seats up from ice level, he argued that there should be a matching camera at the other side.

Turner: "When I pointed out the dizzying effect this would have on viewers if the picture showed a player from one side and then switched in midrush to showing him from the other side, Smythe growled, 'What's the matter with all the young men today? All they do is say no! I'm surrounded by people who say no! Doesn't anybody say yes anymore?'"

But nobody said yes to that one, so one camera was placed at midrink and another behind each goal. Switching between them also was disorienting to the viewer. The battle went on.

Meanwhile, Smythe's position on what form the commentary should take was much less complicated. He would listen to other ideas, but he really put most of his faith in Hewitt. At MacLaren's, the Gardens, Imperial Oil and in Foster's own head there had been long arguments as to what kind of commentary would suit the new medium best. In Britain and the United States, where televised sports had been part of the scene for a few years, the most common style was to let the pictures tell their own story, with only low-key interjections identifying players or occasionally explaining a play. No use having pictures, exponents of this style claimed, if you're also going to call it in the go-go style of radio. Namely, Foster's style.

One line of thought, which had some supporters both at MacLaren's and Imperial Oil, was that Foster would call the games on radio only, with someone else handling the TV play-by-play. Whether Foster saw that as a potential demotion over the long term, no one can say. But he knew both styles inside out, an expert at one and an unofficial graduate student of the other. He'd had a television set in his home from the late 1940s, and on the road often watched sports, including baseball, where low-key commentary was the norm. At one time he predicted to writer Trent Frayne that hockey broadcasting would be revolutionized by television. By the time the cameras were actually on the horizon (no offense to people who like watching hockey from the grays), he'd changed his mind. The low-key stuff had put him to sleep, eliminating a lot of the excitement he knew he could generate on radio.

In the end he contended adamantly that his play-by-play would be as good for television as it was for radio, and therefore there was no reason not to use the same commentary, that is, his own, on both radio and TV.

Horler in the agency, some people at CBC and Turner in his role as an adviser to Imperial, thought the same.

That debate was still in progress in the spring of 1952, only a few months before television would make its Canadian debut. A Memorial Cup series for the junior hockey championship of Canada was being played at the Gardens. On Horler's initiative, MacLaren's borrowed a mobile two-camera television unit for a closed-circuit broadcast of one game. Foster called the game in his usual style for a select screening-room audience of those most concerned with launching hockey TV that autumn.

At game's end, he'd won his point by a landslide. It would be Foster on both radio and television. He not only won the battle for himself, but set a style followed by hockey broadcasters everywhere from then on.

There were two oddities before the first puck was dropped for television in Maple Leaf Gardens. One was that Montreal managed to do its first televised game on October 11, three weeks before Toronto's debut on November 1. The reason, according to several Toronto accounts, is that Montreal's operation didn't have as many great brains arguing about camera placements, style of commentary and so on as Toronto. In Montreal they just did it. In Toronto, in addition to getting any ideas past the brain trusts at MacLaren and at Imperial, the producers had Smythe to deal with, which took a bit of time. In this case about three weeks longer than Montreal.

The explanation for the second oddity went back to when Imperial first came in as sponsor in 1936. Over the ensuing years, Smythe had began to feel that he'd made a bad business deal; had been too undemanding for his own good.

"With both Jack MacLaren and Imperial soft-soaping me, I made a financial deal that was easier than I should have made," he grumbled. It was not always easy to follow Smythe's thought processes, especially what grew out of that one. If he thought he'd been stung in 1936, wouldn't it have been reasonable to expect that he'd try to get even in 1952? Instead, when he gave television his go-ahead, his money demands were staggering — in reverse. He sold that first season of hockey television for $100 a game! Again, the reasoning was pure, perverse, but indisputably Smythe.

He wanted time, a whole season, to make his own judgments on whether television could do the job as well as radio had. The ludicrous $100 a game for the television rights was his hedge. Locking himself into large television fees, he thought, might make it more difficult to change his mind if the first televised season was a flop. On the other hand, while some at MacLaren's also wanted a year to look at the new medium before signing for the long term, others didn't want to find that they'd put all that brainstorming into a project with financial terms that would certainly have to be renegotiated into something they couldn't even guess at — but knew would be a lot more than $100 a game! That's exactly what happened. After the first year, which got rave reviews, the television rights to Maple Leaf games cost Imperial $150,000 a year in a three-year contract.

That didn't end it. For years Smythe worried all his broadcast-rights decisions like a dog with a bone. In the mid-1960s he contended that the deal he made even after the first season of television was still far to low.

"To me, again, the money was manna from heaven! It was always my contention that professional hockey, properly presented, as it was due to Foster's artistry, was one of the most exciting spectacles in the world . . . and of the greatest value to the Gardens. My belief was still, how could anyone in their right mind, with a good product [he meant hockey] to sell, turn down all the advertising they'd get from the broadcasts." For that reason he considered himself a pushover. He never backed off that contention. He was never famous for praising others who made better deals than he did, but years later he said frankly, "It wasn't until my son Stafford was president of the Gardens in the early 1960s that we really got the price into the right range."

By that time Stafford had bought out his father's controlling stock in the Gardens and had taken in as partners John Bassett, chairman — his stock share the largest — and Harold Ballard, executive vice president, third man on the totem pole. When Conn Smythe's final TV contract ran out in the early 1960s, Stafford negotiated a contract that called for the Gardens to be paid nine million dollars over six years for the rights. That's a million and a half a year (or more than $21,000 per game) for what Conn Smythe at first had sold for a piddling $100 a game.

By the time of Stafford's hard bargaining on rights, two

The Landing of Hugh Horler

other figures, who would come to mean more to the first 20 years of hockey television than anyone else, were well established on the scene. One was H. E. "Ted" Hough, a quiet man who had been around the broadcasts for many years before he had any kind of official role. In the late 1930s when anyone in the gondola wondered who he was, someone would say, "Oh, he's some kid from Imperial." Eventually he would become head of Hockey Night in Canada.

The other, George Retzlaff, started as a young CBC cameraman and, on a rising curve roughly parallel to Hough's, became head of CBC Sports. For the first nearly 20 years of hockey television, these two essentially ran the hockey broadcasts.

Chapter 7
The First Masters: Retzlaff and Renaud

Training for hockey television, I especially loved the camera work. . . . Once I was assigned to a drama show on one of three cameras. I ended up doing the whole show by myself because the other two cameras conked out. I had that instinct — show 'em!
— George Retzlaff, producer, Leafs' games

I remember The Rocket had heard from his friends about how we had shown one of his goals, a super goal. Once when he was hurt and couldn't play he asked me if he could come into The Truck. I gave him a small chair, it was very cramped in that place, and he stayed there for one whole game, impressed with how it was produced and the different shots cut together and put on the air.
— Gerald Renaud, producer, Canadien games

In Winnipeg when George Retzlaff was four or five years old and home radios were rare, his parents had a crystal radio set with a headset. They got him to put it to his ear and listen to music. He remembers that as the beginning of his fascination with broadcasting. When he reached high-school age during

The First Masters: Retzlaff and Renaud

the middle 1930s, he played football and a little hockey for Daniel McIntyre Collegiate and worked in a warehouse during the summers.

He was not through school when his father lost his job and couldn't find another, as was a common sad case, especially in the West, during the depression years. The people he worked for in summer, hearing about his dad, gave George a full-time job so he could help out at home. That ended his formal education, but at night he took drama lessons from later CBC greats Beth Lockerbie and Esse Jungh and through Jungh got a job in the control room of radio station CJRC. There he learned to be an operator, and he loved to work football and hockey games with the hard-drinking, brash and witty Jack Wells, just in from Moose Jaw, a man who became a friend for life.

Once, Foster Hewitt, visiting Winnipeg on an Imperial Oil promotion trip, called play-by-play for one period of a hockey game; Retzlaff was excited to meet and work with the man he always listened to on Saturday nights. It gave him a taste of what was to come.

First came the move east, almost mandatory for Winnipeggers of that time if they wanted to make money and be somebody. He got a job at CFRB, control-room operator on a lot of live shows. He married, became a father, but couldn't find a decent place to live in a crowded Toronto, a time when landlords wouldn't even answer the door if they saw through the window an eager young couple carrying a baby. The housing situation sent him back to Winnipeg and a job for CBC as an operator doing mostly music programs — but missing sports.

His break came in 1951. The CBC, organizing for television, sent personnel people across the country to conduct interviews at CBC stations. The purpose was to get willing and able people representative of all the regions, but without denuding any one area of its best. Retzlaff was one of the two people selected from Winnipeg to go to Toronto for training.

When all these hopefuls assembled in Toronto, there were

two groups — production people, among whom was the later famous film director Norman Jewison; and technical people, mainly unknowns. The two groups took instruction courses separately in the mornings, Retzlaff among those at the Ryerson Institute of Technology (which became the Ryerson Polytechnical Institute). In the afternoons the two groups would assemble for joint training sessions in the CBC building now called Studio 7, on Jarvis Street.

In a 1990 interview Retzlaff described the process. "What they'd do is try us all out on different jobs. One day you'd be a floor director, one day you'd be an audio man, the next day you'd be a cameraman. You'd find out what you liked doing and they'd find out what you were good at. One day I was working on a camera. Everybody was taking a break, but I started playing around, using the camera as a zoom camera and trying to keep the focus. At the same time, everybody who was on break was watching — and I knew that! You have to do things to sell yourself; you've got to make somebody take note of what you're capable of doing. They're not going to ask you. But you can sure show them.

"And that's how I got into camera — because of something I was doing on my own time. I loved the camera work, especially when something went wrong and what had started out as fairly routine suddenly was a challenge. Once I was assigned to a drama show on one of three cameras. I ended up doing the whole show by myself because the other two cameras conked out. I had that instinct — show 'em! Be aggressive. That's what I believed in those days and still do."

When the matter of camera placement was being settled at the Gardens before the first televised hockey game went on, Retzlaff didn't have any official say at all in the dry runs. He was simply manning one of the cameras. He and Horler had known one another in Winnipeg, so when Retzlaff had ideas he sometimes could pass them on. But mainly it was again a matter of showing them; and along the way taking advantage of the CBC management situation at the time.

In charge of all CBC's so-called "outdoor activities" was

The First Masters: Retzlaff and Renaud

Sydney Newman, which made him head of CBC Sports and producer of Hockey Night in Canada. He was an experienced broadcaster and filmmaker well qualified for any production job — except, apparently, hockey.

The season started in early October 1952, a few weeks before hockey television was to begin. Watching an early game with all the other most-involved agency and sponsor people in the gondola, Newman, so the story goes, exclaimed ecstatically to Foster, "This is going to be easy! It's just like ballet!" Foster's reaction was one of shock. He and Bud Turner exchanged what Turner later called "a look I'll never forget — we knew we had a dilly."

Retzlaff's attitude toward Newman was milder: "I respect Sydney Newman — but he didn't know too much about hockey." That was a major drawback. As producer, Newman's job during a game was to sit in The Truck facing the array of camera images and call to the switcher what shots he wanted to go on air. That takes not only split-second reaction time, but an expert and intuitive feel for the flow of the play — what would happen next, what the next shot should be. If the producer hasn't that hard-earned instinct, the on-air picture is always too far behind what is happening. There was one possible solution: a super switcher who could keep up with the play without being told. Because of Retzlaff's camera work in various work-ups and dry runs, Horler gave him that job.

Retzlaff: "So that's what I started at, switching. Sydney was sitting there, but I had pretty well free rein. Sydney got mad at times because I was sometimes doing things he didn't like — you know, I appreciate that — but what the hell, I knew what had to be done, and also had a feeling that Sydney wasn't going to be long in sports at the CBC. Somebody had to do it who knew what he was doing. I wanted it to be me. Right from when I came to Toronto to train for television, I wanted it. I wanted to produce hockey." Others — especially Horler — could see that, as well. After half a season or so, a move was made. Newman went on to other things. Retzlaff became head of CBC Sports and producer of Hockey Night in Canada. He was just a little older than 30 at the time.

He didn't entirely realize it then, but his new role had many elements of pioneering. The relationship between the CBC and MacLaren's was changing. In radio, if a company sponsored a show, basically its advertising agency was in charge. The CBC representative normally said little. This went for all the major shows at the time — such as Buckingham Theatre (plugging a brand of cigarettes) and Ford Theatre. But the CBC saw television as such a powerful new medium that it didn't want an ad agency to have final control. So in hockey, although the MacLaren's broadcast team under Horler actually produced the games for Imperial Oil and had the star, Foster Hewitt, and other on-air people under contract, the CBC was demanding much more say than ever before, determined to resist abdicating to sponsors and ad agencies.

Hence Newman, a respected senior man, as well as his eventual replacement, Retzlaff, had to answer — sometimes instantly — for anything on the broadcasts that CBC did not like. That meant Retzlaff had to be capable of throwing his weight around; otherwise he'd be massacred by the CBC, or MacLaren's, or both. He developed the facility. For many years there was to be tension between the CBC and Hockey Night. One reason the relationship never came unstuck was that Retzlaff, although carrying the major responsibility for what went on the air, also could see the agency's point of view — even when he had to overrule it. At the same time Horler, while hanging tough at protecting the agency and sponsor interests, also was very good at understanding the CBC's side.

Retzlaff eventually wound up placing the cameras not quite where he damn pleased (Smythe still had to be considered, but he had mellowed some — about cameras, anyway), but generally, with frequent experimenting, where they would give the best coverage.

His crew in those early days numbered 12 in all. On game days he would tour everything that had to do with the telecast. When he was satisfied that all was in readiness, cables laid, cameras hooked up, circuits and microphones checked, on-camera people made up, lighting all set in the intermission studio, he would go out to the north side of the building and climb into The Truck, which in that era was a really primitive version of the mobile unit. At the time, he was both producer and director.

Seated before monitors that showed him what each camera was doing, he'd call instructions. Nobody ever could argue much with Retzlaff at that level; he'd been a cameraman and knew the hazards and the possibilities; he'd been a switcher, so knew that job, too. He'd call the shots to the switcher; stay with the play on one, tell the switcher where he was going next ("ready four, take four . . . ready two, take two"), call one shot while readying another, get that one and then on to the next, through goals and stops by the goalies, through whistles and fights and goofs and heroics. Thirty years later Ralph Mellanby, one of the world's preeminent sports producers — Calgary Olympics, Seoul Olympics, and Retzlaff's successor as executive producer of Hockey Night in Canada — said that many procedures pioneered by Retzlaff were still being used because they simply could not be bettered. What Retzlaff had produced in 1950s' television action was so seamless that whole generations of viewers hated to go to the toilet in case they missed something.

A modern viewer might argue that anybody could go to the toilet during a commercial. Some even contend that in the early days millions of successful Canadians were toilet trained by dashing away when a commercial began and hurrying back still doing up their rompers.

But in Retzlaff's early years there were *no* pauses for commercials during play. All advertising consisted of simply running messages telling about Imperial's dependable service or great products swiftly across the screen with the action going on as background. That was a luxury lost forever when cutting away for a filmed commercial a set number of times during a period when there was a stoppage in play became standard procedure. These *pauses* for commercials, of course, affected the flow of the game and at first were protested vigorously by fans and hockey people alike for that reason. You've got a great spurt going and the whistle blows and if the occasion is used for a commercial break you stand there losing momentum — that was the theory, anyway. Even now, people seeing hockey live for the first time must endure, as do the players, the dead air while everybody waits around for a beeper to sound in a linesman's pocket to signal that the commercial has ended — drop the puck.

Fans with long memories remember fondly more than the old commercial messages superimposed on the action without interrupting it. Intermission commercials were produced live, in the studio, during the early Horler-Retzlaff years, and somehow seemed more appealing that way. There in the studio was the swift little George Feyer with chalk and a blackboard, drawing funny cartoons to get across the sponsor's message. Or there, in his Imperial Oil cap and uniform was homey believable Murray Westgate — perfect casting — extolling with rasping voice and neighborly friendliness the virtues of Esso's latest products and old-time dependability before delivering his enthusiastic, totally convincing closing line: "Always look to Imperial for the best!"

Westgate was so good in his role that many viewers believed that he really did have a gas station in Toronto somewhere. A line overheard one Saturday night was: "That gas-station guy is really a good actor!"

Which Westgate was and is, but the Esso gas pumps followed him around long after his live commercials were replaced by film. His counterpart in Montreal French broadcasts, Philippe Robert, made a similarly friendly impression.

The problem area in early TV intermissions had little to do with commercials. It was much more basic: what to do during the nine or 10 minutes of television time when the commercials weren't on. Player interviews? The clubs weren't in favor of players giving up their intermission rests. Film? Well, but what?

It was a problem that never had afflicted radio, from the earliest live dance music from orchestras led by Joe de Courcy and later Luigi Romanelli ("And now! For your dancing pleasure!") to the 1939 birth of the "Hot Stove League" when listeners across the land could imagine a room with four or five knowledgeable guys standing around a stove getting warm between periods and simply talking about the game. The bantering, irreverent tone was very much like what went on in thousands of hockey rinks many nights a week in winter. Now Horler and his group had to find something that would work as well on television.

The first attempt, initiated by Horler, was to have a TV "Hot Stove", as well as the radio one. He had a set built that looked like a country store, the kind of place where the local experts and fans might meet to watch the game and chew over what had been going on out there on the ice.

Sharing a TV set in a store or home was common in those days. Some towns had only two or three TVs, whose owners tended to have a lot of people drop in on game nights. So this "Hot Stove" set had rocking chairs, shelves stacked with country-store props, an actual stove around which the Hot Stovers would assemble in full view of the nation.

The radio version went on more or less as before, with a much vaster audience than television could draw. Although Wes McKnight and Jack Dennett stayed with radio, they lost some of their former cohorts to the TV version, which in comparison was painful to watch. One of Leafs' great former captains, Syl Apps, self-consciously would shove a stick of wood into the stove and someone else would jiggle the handle that was supposed to clear the grates. A more recent Leaf captain, Ted "Teeder" Kennedy, was a regular after his retirement from the game. Baldy Cotton, who in real life wore a suit, now had a costume: a checked shirt and work pants. Maybe actors could have made it work, but the old easy ambience was usually not to be found among these hockey men. This might have been partly because the "Hot Stove" set had been built in CBC studios a five-minute walk away from the Gardens, so the Hot Stovers sometimes had to miss interesting action about which viewers might expect their learned comments.

The sum total seemed to be that in this portion of the switch from radio to TV, something was lost. They were professional experts on hockey, but acting for an audience was beyond them Everything had been so natural, easy, unstilted in that smoky little broom closet of "Hot Stove League" on radio, all these jokey favorites standing so close that somebody's cigar ashes were always getting in somebody's coffee. Indeed, once on "Hot Stove" radio Cotton had used his empty cup as an ashtray and was in the middle of discoursing learnedly on some play or other when he noticed, last one to do so, that flames were licking up his sleeve and everybody else was broken up in laughter. Now, that might have been good television. But as it was, nothing so naturally funny took place in the "Hot Stove" TV setup. It was a flop.

Along with that realization, a semblance of the modern TV intermission began to take shape. It still had a long, long way to go before Howie Meeker, Don Cherry, Peter Puck, "Great Moments in Hockey", "Inside Hockey" and the rest paraded across the screen during intermissions, but at the beginning of the 1957-58 season the "Hot Stove", television version, was replaced by a studio host. He welcomed the viewers, summarized the action, interviewed players and gave way now and again to Murray Westgate standing there at the gas pumps extolling the virtues of whatever Imperial Oil thought that week was most arresting about its products.

Retzlaff's swift rise to head of CBC Sports was the most tangible result of his imaginative and daring work as a director and producer. As it turned out, CBC had chosen brilliantly in Montreal, as well. There, Retzlaff's opposite number was Gerald Renaud, who at age 24 early in 1952 was sports editor of *Le Droit* in Ottawa and had a radio program at CKCH in Hull. When the CBC was gearing up for television, Renaud's brother-in-law, a producer at the National Film Board, was hired to produce TV drama. "They're looking for somebody to do sports," he told Renaud. "Why don't you apply?" It was a casual way for a star to be born, but Renaud got the job, the first sports producer at Radio-Canada. He had never even seen television, did not have much of an idea how to go about producing it, had none of the grounding Retzlaff had been given.

"I read whatever was available at the library, which wan't much. One was a book called *TV Writing and Techniques*, by Paddy Chayefsky, the American author and playwright. Another was a book by an American on televising baseball. I picked it up from there, talked to other producers who were not in sports and just improvised."

His first practice workout was to shoot a table tennis game on closed circuit on June 16, 1952. A table was set up in a studio, with two cameras, one long-shot and one close-up. From there he went, on July 25, 1952, to covering a baseball game.

"This was still unofficial, part of a series of experiments, because CBC-TV's birth was not due until early September that year. Still, for a week around the end of July the only thing on the air in Montreal was baseball!

"It was something else, directing a crew, ordering people around. I'd never done that before. It worked all right, except that I found you had to be polite. These guys were learning at the same time, and we were all really in the same boat. It wasn't that difficult."

One gets an idea of Renaud's cast of mind around that time in a comment he made much later when asked about which innovations he was proud of. To start with, he didn't agree that the proper term was "innovations". "You innovate on something that already exists, so innovations, there were not many. When you are starting something entirely new, a more accurate word is 'inventions'."

Quite simply, he'd been told that his job would be to get Montreal Canadien games on the air that autumn with style and flair and accuracy. At the time, only one game of hockey had ever been televised in Canada — and that on closed circuit, with only two cameras: the junior playoff in the spring of 1952 that had been a testing ground more for Foster Hewitt's ability to call a game on TV than for camera positioning or other technical considerations. Nobody had written a book, or even many memos, based on that experience.

Still, he had two positive advantages. One was that he had played the game and understood it.

The second sounds simple, but really stands up today as a statement of aim adaptable to covering any sport. During those weeks in the summer of 1952 when he was either out experimenting, or sitting in his office with a succession of diagrams representing the rink in front of him, trying to figure out camera angles and the way to shoot a game of hockey properly, he put into a few words the end result he was looking for:

"The basic principle for the camera positions I wanted to have was *an ideal seat from which to watch to game*. One, you could be close to the action; two, you could have a clear view of the whole rink; three, some places around the rink you could have a close-up view of the action, but not the overall action; all together providing the perfect spot where you couldn't miss anything and also could follow the flow of the hockey. It's quite fast and if you are too close, you are bound to miss something, and if you are too far away, also. I was only 24, but it all seemed simple enough to me at the time. I'd been a journalist and I really just went from the written language to the visual language, trying to plan so that I'd not only show what was going on but also leave a way to put in a touch of myself in the way I edited, cut and used the cameras."

Of course, in applying this principle he was mentally adding in what would be his role as director in The Truck, cutting it all together on the fly to create that "best seat in the rink".

When he had his camera positions worked out on paper, "the best spots according to what I knew then," he went to the Forum with Bud Turner and Roland Saucier of MacLaren's and Ken Reardon of the Forum to check them out practically. He got the positions accepted. Camera number two was his wide-angle camera covering the whole rink. Camera one was a medium shot. When he needed a tighter shot, it would come on camera three, placed at center ice with responsibility for some shots in both defensive zones, to the left or right of the camera, but not used when play was at center ice, because then the action would be too close.

With these camera positions okayed, an upcoming exhibition game was chosen for a closed-circuit test. Horler and Bud Turner came from Toronto to watch. After only one period, their enthusiasm and that of others among the few select viewers was close to total. That night Renaud left the Forum for home very happy.

As the years went on, there were problems ahead in both cities. Even in the simple basics of placing a camera, or moving it, or adding another, each of the two original producers had to reassure his own city's hockey brass that what was being done wouldn't be in the way of the public, that people wouldn't be tripping over cables, and that nothing would cause fire department or insurance complications. There were some permanent cable installations but mostly, Renaud said, "we drove in with The Truck and drove out with The Truck, a really unsophisticated system.

"Everything was a struggle because TV did not have the power over the owners that it has today," Renaud said in 1990. "If you wanted something at the Forum in the early days you had to charm your way through the people — Ken Reardon and Frank Selke [Sr.] — tell them how important it was for the game of hockey to have a good telecast." Retzlaff faced identical problems in Toronto. There were no precedents. Renaud and Retzlaff were setting the precedents as they went along.

Sometimes, years later, people viewing the old films of the early days of hockey TV thought they could discern differences inherent in the Retzlaff–Renaud cultural backgrounds, and probably could, but nothing that couldn't be explained in terms of two men finding slightly different ways to be the best of their time.

One of Renaud's innovations that had lasting impact came about four years into his tenure, he thinks in 1956. This was to add to his original three what is known now as the goal camera. "We put this camera at ice level in one of the corners, at the

Zamboni [ice-cleaning machine] entrance. I thought of it simply to the end of having a better telecast, giving a different angle, making the telecast more refreshing, more interesting.

"We tested that camera on the air, very discreetly at first as we went along, using it for close-ups, changes of lines and face-offs on that side of the rink, but much less often to intercut the action. The difficulty in using it to what could be the greatest effect, action around the net, was in cutting it in at the right moment. We had to anticipate, and we had to know that it *could* disorientate more than help. Sometimes you'd be lucky enough to do a cut when a goal is going in or when there is continuing action around the net, but you had to use it very discreetly because sometimes it could be a disadvantage, could make you lose the flow of the play, especially with a good hockey club." The goal camera now is common, but Renaud did it first. It was 1963 before an ice-level camera was used in Toronto, the first chance there for really good face shots during action.

The goal camera also produced a memory that Renaud still smiles about; the smile of a man whose skill had been appreciated in a way never to be forgotten. That was when Rocket Richard came to him one time and said his friends had been telling him about the way television had covered one of his goals, and could he come along and see how it was done?

"On that goal, we'd had a super close-up of him from the goal camera and also of the crowd reaction on camera three. Also the traffic in front of the goal was not as heavy as it is today — today it's like a football scrum — and sometimes if you were lucky you could have a clean shot of a play like the one The Rocket mentioned, one of his great goals. Anyway, of course I told The Rocket to come, and once when he was hurt and couldn't play he came to The Truck and asked if he could come in. I gave him a small chair, it was very cramped in that place, and he stayed there for one whole game watching how the game he knew so well and played so well was produced and put on the air."

For a time, Renaud did not leave the goal camera at its original position for an entire game. "We had some kind of an intermission studio at the Forum, really nothing like the sophisticated studios they have today. This camera — a couple of minutes before the end of a period — was dollied from the Zamboni entrance into the studio to do the English-speaking intermissions." (French intermissions usually were done in the Radio-Canada studio, away from the Forum.)

Later on, in the late 1950s, by which time Tom Foley was the regular Montreal host, a fifth camera was added that was, in Renaud's term, "slaved" to the studio. This meant that the goal camera did not have to be moved, and perhaps miss great shots — and that Foley could do player interviews at the end of a period without the race to get the goal camera dollied into place for its part-time job.

In total, Retzlaff and Renaud were talented principals in the long-running and not-always-friendly jousting between the first two Hockey Night in Canada television teams, Montreal and Toronto. Canadiens and Leafs, for many years the only Canadian teams in the NHL, were never happier than when they were beating each other. Competition between the television teams was a natural offshoot. On the ice, off the ice, the motivations were not all that different. Thirty years later it was commonplace for hockey-television people to remark that procedures pioneered by Retzlaff and Renaud were still being used because they could not be bettered.

So their shows do look good 35 years later. But at the time the reaction was not always so positive. In Toronto all hands, from the host to Imperial's advertising manager, Scott Fyfe, and MacLaren liaison to Imperial, Bud Turner, were always aware on Saturday night that on Monday morning whatever they did wrong, or even right, would be subject to rigorous second-guessing at Imperial headquarters on Toronto's St. Clair Avenue. Turner's role had changed over the years on a rising scale of importance, eventually to that of the full-time executive on the Imperial account, meaning everything that the title connotes in advertising — he had to kowtow a lot in several directions, both to Imperial's advertising department and to Conn Smythe of the Leafs.

He even conceded once that his winning smile sometimes got him into trouble: he'd smile before he fully heard what one of his ogres was proposing, and then would have to backtrack. Imperial's John Gibson was the first Imperial advertising manager he had to deal with, then Scott Fyfe, but whoever was sitting in the driver's seat at Imperial head office was very demanding, very involved. Especially Fyfe. At one time Imperial executives had earphones installed near their box seats in the Gardens so they could get on Turner's case without delay when something went wrong on radio or television. The radio side was relatively trouble-free, but Monday-morning meetings in Fyfe's office left no goof, or its perpetrator, unscathed.

Turner made notes of those meetings in a memo to himself entitled "The Early Years, 1952–58". This account seems to contain some exaggerations, but Turner claims not. Sketching in the background, he wrote that in 1952 when almost all other advertisers were pressing hard for the safety and assurance of filmed commercials that they could check in advance, Imperial went the other way.

Turner credits Horler with selling the idea of "the presence, flexibility, economy and effectiveness of presenting all Imperial Oil commercials live." What he means is that Imperial tended to change its mind a lot on what any specific night's commercial should be about. On film this would not have been easy to handle, or might have cost a mint in retakes. Having the commercials live "allowed us to take, for instance, a well-rehearsed Westgate script covering three service pitches and two gasoline promotions and replace it with four different approaches to three entirely separate branded motor oils," plus maybe a plug for the Toronto Symphony at the earnest request of the symphony's president, a senior Imperial Oil executive, Trevor Moore.

All this switching usually occurred on Friday evening after four o'clock, Turner says, accompanied by new specific directions from Imperial's television supervisor, Stuart Foster, or the company's advertising manager, John Gibson.

"This made such a hash of the first months of hockey commercials that a special six-man committee was formed at Imperial to edit the scripts and storyboards." His description of the committee members sounds like a Wayne and Shuster skit, most of them being totally new to television, including one whose career had been spent entirely at the company refinery in Sarnia. By Turner's account, nothing worked very well until Fyfe, a former naval officer, was made advertising manager and soon showed that he meant business.

"Gone was the respectful silence that used to greet Horler's pronouncements on our broadcast expertise and reliability in producing great hockey telecasts and still keep the costs within bounds. This was replaced by Monday meetings at which we were lashed for incompetence the previous Saturday night.

"At these meetings, all Fyfe's remarks were taken from the back of a package of Player's Mild. It was his habit to hunch in front of his television set on Saturday nights and make notes on his cigarette package about everything we were doing wrong — from the host to Westgate's hand movements to shots being too long or too short. With unfailing pregame optimism, he'd approach this task believing that his scathing commentary at the previous Monday meeting would have penetrated our hides...."

Perhaps because of this new accusatory attitude at Imperial, by Turner's account Horler more or less defected from the Monday meetings, usually scheduled for 9 a.m. "It would be 9:30, 10:00, 10:30. Horler wouldn't even have arrived at the agency office. Fyfe would be on the phone from Imperial every 15 minutes wanting to know where we were. Then Horler would come and we'd grab a cab, and when the meeting started, it didn't matter what Fyfe was saying, Horler would just sit there smoking and listening, not saying a word, as if he was catatonic."

It was a long and stubborn battle, Turner wrote, with deep wounds and lasting scars, "after which we agreed to a truce on the condition that MacLaren would accept Imperial's money and do what it was told."

However, apart from those trying Monday mornings, the broadcasts won for MacLaren more accolades than the agency has experienced on a single account before or since.

Through it all, George Retzlaff maintained his independence. Whatever was demanded by Imperial, through MacLaren's, usually concerned commercials or the intermissions, and didn't affect him much. He was concerned basically with the on-ice product, the play-by-play, where he brooked no interference, consistently acting on the conviction that nobody at MacLaren's or Imperial Oil or even the CBC knew, nor ever would know, as much about doing hockey television as he did. Ward Cornell, during his 11-year stint as intermission host, always contended sardonically that Retzlaff was never wrong, had never been wrong and never would be wrong.

Where possible Retzlaff avoided committee decisions, although after Hough became the other half of the two infallibles, they often met in downtown Toronto on quiet weekday afternoons over a few drinks and, without benefit of writers or anyone else, worked out that Saturday night's show. Hough and Retzlaff were friends; Retzlaff didn't have quite the same relationship with anyone else, except his crew. That was a totally different side to his character. The crew were his own folks. One veteran of The Truck under Retzlaff said his cameramen used to adore him: "They'd get shit, but with George it was creative shit, constructive, how to do this a little bit better, how to correct that mistake — God help them if they didn't."

Retzlaff had a succession of four assistant directors through the 1950s and early 60s. "He worked the ass off them," that same observer said, "but I never met one who, in the long run, resented that." Two graduates of the hard-knocks school of working with Retzlaff now hold two of the most powerful sports-television jobs in Canada: Ron Harrison, a onetime Retzlaff foot soldier who was to become top man in Hockey Night in Canada; and Jim Thompson, who became one of

CBC's top executive producers and then a vice president of The Sports Network cable operation.

Although later, near the end of Retzlaff's 20 years on the hockey broadcasts, he sometimes was accused of not changing with the times, when the job was a constant exploration he was an innovator. Like Renaud, he set up the camera positions that made the shows a success from the beginning. And these days, when instant replays are commonplace, sometimes too commonplace, shown over and over, it's a long way back to when Retzlaff first attacked that problem. As far as anyone can remember, this was in 1955 or 1956.

He'd thought about it along this line: Lots of times viewers would like to see a goal *again*. Did it go in off a defenseman's skate? Was it batted out of the air? Who was the guy on defense who goofed and took the wrong man on a breakaway, allowing the pass that was turned into a goal? If we could only work out a way to show those plays again. But how?

The only way a televised hockey game could be reproduced along the network at the time, before microwave transmission and long before satellites, was by kinescope — basically, a 16-mm film taken off the original live broadcast, usually grainy and a much less distinct picture than the original. The kinescope would be shipped by air — "bicycled" was the in-house term — to appear in other CBC cities a day or two later.

Jeff Miles was head of the kinescope operation at the time and worked very closely with Retzlaff, who was always keen to know about anything new. Retzlaff felt that the CBC seemed always reluctant to inform producers about new processes. "Maybe they were afraid we'd try to use them before they were ready — that's one of the things that all of us producers were unhappy about. One day Jeff called me in and told me about a brand-new chemical process, what they called a hot processor. He showed me how it worked. The film would take 30 seconds from the time it went in until it came out, developed, and it could be played right there and then.

"I told Jeff that I'd like to try it on hockey — you know, get back a goal as soon as it happens. I knew there'd be time, because as soon as a goal is scored they pat each other on the back and then maybe there's a player change, so you have time. I did a little of it, testing, and then one night said, 'Jeff, we're going to do it tonight.'

"Ted Hough was pretty new at Hockey Night then, maybe just a year or two on the job helping Hugh Horler. But I didn't tell Hough or Horler or anybody, didn't tell anybody except my switchers what we were going to do. I had Jeff Miles on the line, ready; the people I had in The Truck were ready. A goal was scored and I said, okay, here it is, we're going to do it. I called it in and I punched it up and it came back and it was beautiful! Everybody gasped!

"But after the show I got hell from Ted Hough. He said, 'Why did you do this? Why didn't you tell me?'

"I could understand his reaction, because though Gerry Renaud and I often tried different things, it was policy that the Toronto and Montreal telecasts should look as much alike as possible. Nobody at MacLaren ever wanted Toronto to look any better than Montreal. In other words, I thought if I told anybody in advance what I was planning they'd say, oh, wait'll we see if Montreal can do it, too — if Toronto's going to do something, Montreal's going to do it at the same time. That was against my grain. Waiting took the fun out of it and didn't, in my view, help the end product. So he landed on me about not telling him and I said, 'I don't mind if they copy me but why should I have to wait [to] do the thing? It has worked. Let's do it.'

"But I didn't. After I got hell for doing it, I just didn't do it anymore. If MacLaren's had said, it looks good, do it — I would have done it. Montreal could have done it. They had the same kind of equipment.

Hough's recollection of the incident differs somewhat. "Sure, I was annoyed. But what I was annoyed about was not the Montreal thing — it could have been done there, too — but that if we'd known about it in advance we could have promoted

The First Masters: Retzlaff and Renaud 99

it, told people in advance what they were about to see, that here was a new reason not to miss Hockey Night in Canada — that with this marvelous and exciting new process we'd be able to repeat plays almost instantly!"

Of course, there is also the possibility, or even probability, that Bud Turner, closely followed by Scott Fyfe, had landed on Hough for not letting *them* know that history was about to be made.

So Retzlaff's way was tried once, worked, and then died. Many people in hockey still think that the first try came years later in 1960 or 1961. At the time Joe Black and Sid Travis's commercial photography firm, Graphic Artists, specialized in sports. They worked every Leaf game, one of them near each goal. Their action shots would be rushed downtown to the *Globe and Mail* for use in late editions. Bob Gordon, then very junior at MacLaren, encouraged by Hough, came up with an idea. He went to Joe Black and discussed the time frame involved in getting action shots developed and printed fast enough to be shown during intermissions.

Black and Travis were fast. They usually knew when they'd got a goal shot. A studio was set up in the bowels of the Gardens, a runner would get down there fast with film, and by the next intermission there'd be several outsize prints as candidates to go before the television camera. Eddie Fitkin, who later was Jack Kent Cooke's executive assistant with the Los Angeles Kings, was handling game highlights for Hockey Night in Canada then. He would describe the play — a goal, a brilliant rush, a big check — and then introduce the photo with the line, "Here's how it looked in stop action."

The process, crude by today's standards, had the advantage of being a fresh idea, an interesting addition to the show and a way of beating newspaper sports pages to some good action shots. The sequence of developments from there on is difficult to pin down. A few months after the first use of the "stop action" photos, Hough learned that someone in Boston was working on a process by which a static television image could be stored electronically for an indefinite length of time, but once used, was gone forever. It was not an instant replay, but it was faster than running undeveloped film into the bowels of Maple Leaf Gardens and coming up 15 or 20 minutes later with a black-and-white action photo.

At Hough's suggestion, George Retzlaff and production assistant Bob Gordon went to Boston to watch a demonstration and report. They found that the machine that did this trick would cost about $150,000. The image was not as clear as the black-and-white photos they'd been using. Still, Gordon liked the idea because of the speed. Retzlaff was definitely against; the picture was not good enough for him, especially at such a high cost. His thumbs-down vote won.

It was the middle 1960s when the replay, as modern fans know it, was born. Tim Ryan, who was soon to move permanently to U.S. broadcasting, was then with CFTO-TV — the key station for CTV's Wednesday night hockey. He phoned Bob Gordon to say that they'd figured out how to do an instant replay, and would Gordon like to come and have a look? He did. "The idea was there, which was to run the tape from one tape machine through a delay mechanism and over to a second machine, and while the first one was recording the other would be on playback. They had the right idea but had a hell of a time stabilizing the picture." So they said they'd work on it and call Gordon back for another look.

Back at his office a day or two later, Gordon picked up the phone. The caller was Ty Lemberg of CBC Sports, under Retzlaff. Lemberg had the same message as Ryan of CFTO. "Bob, I want you to look at something. We could have instant replay." Gordon arrived a little later to find Retzlaff there, too. What Lemberg had in the way of technique, Gordon never could precisely describe, except that "he had tape running all over the studio." He had put the replay on a 15-second delay. It worked perfectly.

"There it was," Gordon said, "You could see it being recorded and then 15 seconds later being played back. I said, 'Is the 15-second delay fixed?' and Ty said, 'No, that's just an arbitrary time, why don't we do it in 10 seconds?' He talked to the videotape operators and they did some juggling and took away a couple of coat hangers that the tape was running through, and there it was in 10 seconds, absolutely great." The older wiser Retzlaff was never too enthusiastic about anything, but he said it was fine. So Gordon tries to set the historical record straight: "I have to say that Tim Ryan was first to talk to me about it, and had the mechanics right, but not quite the execution. Lemberg was the one who got it right a little later. About a week and a half later we used it the first time — on CFTO."

Another achievement high on any list of Retzlaff achievements is his use of the zoom lens in hockey coverage. Originally, lenses used in play-by-play cameras were standard, without zooms. If a cameraman wanted to go from a close-up to a wide shot, he had to change — "rack over" is the term — from, say, a 55-mm lens to a 90-mm one. The director had to cut away while this was being done. When the zoom lens came on the scene, Retzlaff knew exactly what it could mean — practically revolutionize the show. He carefully trained talented cameramen Don Elslinger and Art White in the use of the zoom lens. Elslinger's nickname soon was Zoom — Don "Zoom" Elslinger.

Retzlaff's use of this new tool was considered brilliant. It was one of his triumphs, giving viewers an almost face-to-face encounter with the stars on ice.

One aspect of the show that he frankly admitted he did not constructively improve was the intermissions. He just figured they weren't his business. This resulted in Hockey Night's adding a director in the mid-1960s specifically to handle the intermissions. When an intermission began, Retzlaff would leave the director's seat in The Truck and be replaced by the intermission director — at first Wilf Hayden, later Ty Lemberg. Still later, a rotating system went into effect. One week Retzlaff would direct the on-ice game, Hayden or Lemberg the intermissions; the following week the reverse. Some people on the inside saw this as a sign that Retzlaff's long tenure was winding down. The official line was that it gave Hockey Night in Canada bosses a better feeling: if something happened to Retzlaff, they'd still have someone of experience to replace him. Whatever the case, what is not in dispute is that Retzlaff would always be looked upon as the first great master of televised hockey in Canada.

Chapter 8
The Golden Era of Ward Cornell

> *Yeah, but like most owners you forgot the most important thing, radio and television positions and press-box accommodation. They're all really crappy. But it's not a bad building.*
> — Ward Cornell to Jack Kent Cooke, then owner of the Los Angeles Kings and their rink, now called the Great Western Forum

It is possible to make a case for most of Ward Cornell's years as Toronto's intermission host on Hockey Night in Canada, from 1959 to his winding down in 1972, being something like a golden age. Those were the years when color television was introduced in Canada (1966), and in one blinding flash viewers discovered that every team in the NHL did not wear black-and-white uniforms of varying designs. Danny Gallivan was going strong in the early to middle years of his long career as the play-by-play man calling the games in English from Montreal; Bill Hewitt was doing the Toronto job because a few years earlier Foster Hewitt, of his own accord, had arranged that his son, Bill, take over on TV while he stayed mainly with radio — then the biggest audience.

In one of those early years of the 1960s also, George Retzlaff walked along a CBC corridor to an adjoining office where a stocky 20-year-old named Ron Harrison, who had played some minor hockey around Toronto, was working as a clerk in the news department. Harrison had applied several times to CBC's personnel department for a transfer to sports and had always been told he was too young. He knew Retzlaff by sight, had often seen him walk by. This time Retzlaff stopped and asked, "You want to work in hockey, kid?", thus choosing without benefit of headhunters, aptitude tests or anything else, a Hockey Night top man of the future — and also one who was to cut his eyeteeth as a floor director of the intermissions with Ward Cornell.

Golden age might be rather a florid description of any hockey decade, but in Cornell's time Toronto Maple Leafs won four Stanley Cups under Punch Imlach as coach and general manager. This on-ice success was the foundation for much other good fortune, although the battles between Imlach and Stafford Smythe that eventually led to Imlach's dismissal continued at a low simmer throughout these years when Imlach had made the Leafs the best of their time. For a variety of reasons, they went into a decline immediately after the NHL expanded from six teams to 12 in one fell swoop, fueling up forever those hockey fans who live more on nostalgia than on reality. Cornell was in office when Hough, Horler and Turner became vice presidents of this, that and the other thing at MacLaren's, confirming Hough as hockey TV's top man at the agency. When Cornell finally left in 1972, that same year would see the end of Retzlaff's epochal run as the man in charge on the CBC side, while coming up fast and unstoppable through the Hockey Night pack was the next resident genius, Ralph Mellanby.

Ward Cornell began his host year in Toronto more or less out of the blue. In late 1958 and early 1959 the search was on across the country for someone who might come close to the likable and expert Tom Foley, who lived with his family in Ottawa and was well-known as a football broadcaster, as well as host of the Montreal intermissions — so good at the jobs that he tended to set the standard.

Ward was one of a half dozen called in 1959 to audition for the Toronto job. For a while Hockey Night intermissions for the Toronto regional network resembled a game of musical chairs between tryout hosts — Terry Kielty from Ottawa, and Jack Wells from Winnipeg, Lloyd Saunders and Johnny Esaw from Saskatchewan and others, including Cornell.

During these on-air tryouts, the game that was carried on the national network alternated week by week between Montreal and Toronto, but whatever the city, Foley was always the host. Each week the game that didn't have Foley was broadcast regionally, with the novice host.

Ward certainly wanted the Toronto job, but was not high on his chances. He didn't know much about hockey, hadn't even watched Hockey Night in Canada much on television. He'd been a school teacher until 1954, then joined radio station CFPL in London full-time, first in news, then as program manager and later as general manager, at the same time doing a good deal of television work. He felt it a drawback that his sports-broadcasting background was mainly in football — the old Ontario Rugby Football Union with London Lords, Sarnia Imperials, Balmy Beach and the rest; intercollegiate with his hometown University of Western Ontario going against Toronto, Queen's and McGill; and the Big Four with Hamilton Tigers, Argonauts, Ottawa and Montreal Alouettes. But he did know broadcasting, which he'd figured out, accurately, was the job's main requirement.

When he was anointed as the regular Toronto host, for a while he would broadcast football Saturday afternoons in Ottawa, Kingston or Montreal, and then fly or drive to Toronto to work the hockey game at night. Tom Foley also worked both sports. Weekends both traveled a lot.

One October while flying between cities on one of those busy two-game Saturdays, the plane carrying Ward ran into a wild storm and crashed. The newspapers called it the Miracle Crash. No one was killed. Ward walked away in his stocking feet.

Not long afterward, he was in an airport car with Tom Foley — both doing two games, hockey and football, that day. Riding along, Foley asked what Ward had been thinking in those few seconds when it was obvious the plane was about to crash. "I told him that I said to myself, 'God, am I ever glad I've got a lot of flight insurance!' And Foley said, 'You know, I'm superstitious, I've never had it and I feel that if I ever get it, it'll bring me bad luck.' "

On a subsequent night in March 1960, Foley was riding toward downtown Toronto in an airline limousine when a car coming the wrong way on a one-way ramp hit the limousine head-on. Foley was killed. Flight insurance covered ground transportation at both ends of a trip, but Foley didn't have it.

While those who had known and liked Foley both personally and as a fine broadcaster joined in his young family's grief, it now became a necessity to fill the void he had left at Hockey Night in Canada. That's when, as part of Hockey Night's reorganization to guard against the possibility of one man's incapacity throwing the whole system into a turmoil, separate Toronto and Montreal intermission crews were put together. Each stayed put, whether they were broadcasting nationally or regionally. Thus, as host of half the game's national broadcasts, Ward became a national figure. Years later Ken Dryden, the great Montreal goalkeeper, told Ward about a regular feature of the Dryden family's backyard hockey, when Ken and his goalie brother, Dave, were in their midteens. During breaks in the action they would feign intermission interviews. The interviewer would ask a question, and the reply invariably began with, "Well, Ward..."

Hockey Night's Bob Gordon, then in his early 20s, was working toward being one of the better all-rounders among Hockey Night production people. Part of his job was to work with Cornell on the intermissions. Both affable — and at the time somewhat portly — they got along well.

"From the first he was one of the best interviewers I'd ever seen," Gordon recalls. "In midweek we'd talk over who we'd have as intermission guests, who might be particularly interesting that week, and so on. Sometimes he'd take my suggestions on guests, and sometimes I'd agree with his. One of his great strengths was in the way he handled his questions.

"They were short, to the point and, most importantly, didn't give the answer at the same time the question was asked. I can't say I see many interviewers now who do that. Some, in fact a lot, take a minute and half to ask the question and answer it at the same time. Ward's eventual successor, Dave Hodge, as good as he was in a lot of respects, sometimes did that. Ward got a lot out of his guests because he let them give the answers."

To some extent Ward was effective because he took care to spend time with each of his guests before they went on the air together. Instead of the player coming in hot off the ice at the end of a period not knowing what to expect in the interview, by arrangement with Ward the guest would arrive at the Gardens a couple of hours before game time. They'd go into a little room across the corridor from the Leaf dressing room, at that time right next to the visitors' dressing room, and go over the questions Ward planned to ask.

The player's responses sometimes led to revision of Ward's original plan, but the main value was that the player had time to think about the interview and knew that Ward was not going to throw any surprises at him.

As he got to know the players individually, Ward's relationship with them was friendly, but he intentionally kept his distance. "I didn't want to be really pally with anyone, because that has disadvantages, maybe results in a treatment of one that differs from others." Interviewers who think they've died and gone to heaven when they can embarrass or nonplus a guest — or, in the opposite mode, make it a sycophantic pal-old-pal encounter — obviously do not model themselves on Ward Cornell.

Another side of his technique showed up one night when his guest was Ted Green, then a tough, hard-hitting defenseman with Boston Bruins. That night when Green came off the ice and Bob Gordon gave him a towel to stem the flow of sweat, he was obviously very uptight. Bob Gordon didn't know what to do about it, but just told him, "Hey, relax. Go on in and get acclimatized."

He went in and sat down. The show was in commercial. Ward was fumbling around with some notes in his lap. He could sense immediately how nervous Green was, hunched over, glancing around at what was going on in the studio. Right away Ward asked the floor director how much time he had. Gordon recalled, "I knew there was still about a minute and a half to go. Then I heard someone say, 'Level, please,' so they could get the voice levels, and suddenly Ward sat up and looked into the camera and said, 'Well, with the Leafs leading Boston 4–1, Cord Warnell here with Chicken Little, head of Bashers, Inc.,' and then turned to Green and said, 'Chicken?'"

As soon as Ward had started in with "Cord Warnell here," Green straightened up, thinking they were on camera. when Ward said, "Chicken Little, head of Basher's Inc.," Green just stared at him, didn't know what was coming off, and then Ward put his hand on Green's knee and said, "It's okay, we're not on the air."

Green started laughing. It was later considered to be one of the best interviews the show ever had. Instead of being nervous, Green couldn't get the smile off his face the rest of the time he was in the studio, and made his exit still laughing and shaking his head.

With all of Ward's frequent instances of aplomb (once he did an interview with basketball star Wilt Chamberlain and got some comedy out of that by standing beside the sitting Chamberlain, and still had to look up at him), routine is one thing, special occasions another. Few broadcasters are free of occasional embarrassments. There can be surprises for all kinds of reasons, but especially in situations that could not be positively planned in advance.

One of these came for Ward when he'd been rolling right along for four years as hockey TV's Mr. Imperturbable. In 1963, Leafs won their second consecutive Stanley Cup. The previous year, they'd won the Cup's deciding game away from home, in Chicago. This one was special, winning hockey's version of the Holy Grail right at home in Toronto, beating

The Golden Era of Ward Cornell

Detroit 3-1 in the fifth game of the final on the night of April 18.

Maple Leaf Gardens was bedlam when the final buzzer sounded that night. In Hockey Night's intermission studio, the heroes, management, owners, directors and others to be introduced for a few words on TV were coming at Ward literally from behind, in front and both sides.

Possibly because every major piece of print journalism written about Ward for many years conjured up his big goof of that night, Ward recalls it as if it were yesterday. "Of course, I made some great mistakes. This was one."

Bob Gordon was in the thick of it — glaring lights, milling crowds, general confusion. "It was my job to bring players and other people in. Our floor director would take each person from me and move them in to Ward. I think George Armstrong was the first, being captain, and Punch Imlach, Conn Smythe, some people from Detroit. As we got things organized after the first few, he'd do a brief interview, say, with a player on his right side, and then turn from that to his left, do that interview, turn back to his right, and so on. He finished up an interview with a guy on his left and then turned to his right, and standing there was Stafford Smythe, president of the Gardens, beaming, of course — his team had just won the Stanley Cup, and of all the people that Ward would pull a gaffe with, on national television with about three million people watching . . . Anyway, he turned to Stafford and said, 'Here we have Frank Selke, Jr.'

"I almost fainted. Smythe went white, green, stared at Ward, made some smart-ass comment that I can't remember, and then very quickly got over it, but I thought, my God, there's going to be something happen because of that . . ."

Over to Ward — he thought there was going to be something happen, too: "What the hell happened was that all those people were being thrown at me and at first it was obvious that I couldn't see who was there, so they refined it a little, the floor director would hold up a sign saying who was next, but anyway I turned and saw the next guy just out of the corner of my eye.

"I'd never met Stafford. He and Selke were about the same size and if there was a sign up, both names started with S. I made that goof, about as public as a goof could be — three million people saw it. John Bassett, owner of CFTO and chairman of the Gardens then, was right with Stafford. It was terribly embarrassing.

"Afterwards I went over to the Celebrity Club to have a drink. Obviously, I was not going to be back after a goof like that. I guess I had more than just one drink. I just hated to think about it. Of course, even in that short a time everybody at the bar knew what had happened. One of them was Bob Hesketh, who had been a sports columnist at the *Telegram* before moving to CFRB. He wasn't a real lot of help. I was going through it all again and again, and finally Hesky put his arm around my shoulders and said, 'Oh, for Christ's sake, Ward, don't worry about it. Everybody will forget about it in 25 years.' "

After he got back to his room at the Westbury Hotel, which was right next to the Gardens, Ward wrote Stafford a note: "Dear Mr. Smythe, I'm a professional and no professional likes to drop a pop fly and I dropped one. I'm terribly sorry. I'm terribly embarrassed. Please accept my apologies" — and mailed it. "I knew it was going to be a long summer for me. I didn't think I was ever going to see Hockey Night in Canada from the inside again. I know Stafford took a lot of kidding about my goof, his pals calling him Selke, and saying, 'Oh, hello, Frank', and all that stuff.

"But in a day or two I got a note back from him.

" 'Forget it.' That was all the note said.

"Four or five years later when he and Harold Ballard were in trouble and a lot of people seemed to take joy in the difficulties Stafford was in, I was never one of them. I could never say an unkind word about Stafford Smythe."

However, that is not to say that Ward was incapable of unkind words. His acerbity would sometimes surface in ways now remembered rather fondly by the men he worked with.

One came when the Hockey Night in Canada crews made their first trip to Los Angeles, after Jack Kent Cooke's Los

Angeles Kings began playing in the NHL as one of the six teams added to the league in the 1967 expansion. Cooke had built the Los Angeles Forum — he always called it the Fabulous Forum — to house his team. When the Hockey Night group arrived, a former intermission highlights man in Toronto, Ed Fitkin, who had gone to Los Angeles as Cooke's executive assistant, was conducting the hockey broadcasters through the Forum when Cooke showed up, dismissed Fitkin rather abruptly and took over the tour. It was not only the first time that Ward Cornell and Bob Gordon had seen the Forum, but also the first time they had met Cooke and saw how he sometimes treated his underlings.

This had been pretty well established in Toronto years earlier. In the 1940s and 1950s Cooke had owned radio station CKEY, various magazines, including *Saturday Night*, and an entertaining baseball club loaded with past and future stars — Toronto Maple Leafs of the International League. A lively and handsome man who worked his way to riches from a standing start selling encyclopedias door-to-door from a Model A Ford roadster, he always took great pride and satisfaction in what he owned.

Later Cooke was to become one of the richest men in sport, one item in modern times being ownership of the Washington Redskins in the National Football League, where guests in his box usually are household names in the U.S. When he was the proprietor of the Kings, Forum crowds usually were well stocked with movie stars, as well as many transplanted Canadians lining up for Ward Cornell and Foster Hewitt autographs.

With his pride in the Forum, conducting the Hockey Night tour himself inevitably became pure Cooke — an unending stream of superlatives. As he walked through the building pointing out this and that, he told his visitors in an aside that he'd like them to dine — with him, they understood — at the building's exclusive Forum Club. They'd heard about the Forum Club's celebrated food and wines. As the tour ended,

Cooke paused, expecting the usual lavish praise. "Well, what do you think?" he asked. "Isn't it wonderful, fabulous?"

Ward was the one who answered. Apparently he'd had enough of Cooke.

"Yeah," he said, "but like most owners you forgot the most important thing: radio and television positions and press-box accommodation. They're all really crappy. But it's not a bad building." It was the first time in history anyone could remember Cooke being at a loss for words. He simply turned and walked away.

They didn't see him again until they duly trooped into the Forum Club for dinner. Their first surprise was to be seated not with Cooke, but a few tables away from him. They ordered, dined and drank well, and when they had progressed to coffee and liqueurs, they got their second surprise: the bill. Recovering swiftly, Ward told the waiter, "We understood that we're Mr. Cooke's guests. He invited us."

"Oh, excuse me, sir," the waiter said, then walked over the other table, conferred briefly with the great man himself and returned to say that Cooke had invited them to the Forum Club only because they were nonmembers and otherwise couldn't get into the place.

"So," said the waiter gently, "you do have to pay for your meal." Which they did.

Despite the Los Angeles incident, all the evidence is that, with one exception, Ward never was other than amiable in his dealings with those who worked the intermission studio. He was friends with everybody, would stop and chat with cameramen, floor directors, lighting men, stagehands, the people in makeup. They liked him for not being standoffish, and if anything did go wrong that reflected on Ward, he almost invariably blamed not the intermission crew but the production crew in The Truck, which controlled the intermission studio cameras. That is where George Retzlaff held unchallenged sway. Ward is said to have never won an argument with George Retzlaff on anything. Actually, that was no surprise; none of the Hockey Night talent really ever won an argument

The Golden Era of Ward Cornell

with Retzlaff. This led to one of Ward's standard lines. When any error or misjudgment came up that might possibly have originated in The Truck, Ward was wont to smile and say to anyone who would listen: "Yeah, but it couldn't have been Retzlaff's fault — he's never done anything wrong in his life."

On the other hand, in production meetings Bob Gordon sometimes was bothered by Ward's seeming lack of interest in those parts of the operation that did not involve Ward's own turf.

"I'd be up there running through the script, what we were going to do that night, and Ward would be reading a newspaper.

"If he had a fault, it was that whatever happened on the rest of the show he didn't really care about, as long as his segment was okay."

It is probable that Ward's problem with Retzlaff and later with the much more demanding Ralph Mellanby was based on what had made Ward a success in the beginning: his broadcasting professionalism, faith that he knew what he was doing. To him that was enough. He did not take easily to suggestions of change.

Mellanby once said of him in a production meeting where the necessity of jazzing up the intermission was being discussed, "What Ward really needs is a hot poker up his ass." Tough words, typical Mellanby. He always wanted more fireworks, which was simply not Ward's style.

There were some fireworks in the intermission studio once, however. Ron Harrison has a story from long before he became Hockey Night's executive producer in 1988. Harrison was a floor director in the intermission studio during the middle years of Ward's position as host. There was one part of Ward's operation that Harrison used to bitch about, mainly to himself, because at the time he had to do pretty well what Ward wanted. What he didn't like was writing Ward's cue cards.

"I was pissed off about that. I had to write all his goddamn stuff on these cue cards. I used to come into the studio about two in the afternoon and start writing. The first one would start off: 'Good evening, everybody. I'm Ward Cornell. Tonight on Hockey Night in Canada, et cetera, et cetera . . .'

"Night after night after night! No shortcuts! He wanted everything, even his name, verbatim. I'd think, Christ, you'd think he'd know his name without a cue card. I had stacks of those things. There I was with writer's cramp at six o'clock, no dinner. I'd have to go across the hall to the old press room and get some of Mrs. Haggert's little sandwiches or I would have starved." (Elsie Haggert was the kind and motherly mother of Bob Haggert, Leaf trainer. For many years she both prepared and laid out the free lunch in the press room, treated fondly by all the hockey regulars.)

"One thing about Ward, however," Harrison continued, "he was usually very regular about proofreading his stuff. Around six-thirty or seven he'd come over and glance through, saying, 'That's fine, that's fine.'

"This one day I was writing up his cue cards — he knows his own name, I was thinking, so as a joke I wrote, 'Good evening everybody. I'm Charlie Upshot. Tonight on HNIC . . .' knowing very well that Ward's going to come over to proofread and he'll have a laugh. I don't know, we got busy, and he never came over to proofread and I forgot about it. And the stagehand is beside the camera and he has a stack of these cue cards and he's feeding them to me one at a time and in my headset George [Retzlaff, in The Truck] says, '50 seconds,' and Ward comes on and says 'Good evening, everybody. I'm Cha —' And I look at him and realize and groan Oh-h-h-h! to myself.

"For the rest of the opening, Ward couldn't say five words together without stumbling. And there's a little client room just a few steps away, different to the one we have these days, and when he's finished he gets up out of that chair and throws the mike down and goes out of there and the door slams — BANG!

"And I think, well, there goes my career, and then the phone — obviously, Ward had got through to George. George is on the phone to me.

" 'You're fired!'

"Well, I'd been expecting it. 'Okay, George. See you later.'

" 'Oh, you can't go yet! You have to wait until the game's over!' " That stay of execution is still in force.

It probably should be pointed out that Mellanby's suggested solution for altering Ward's noted laid-back style, Harrison's hatred for writing cue cards, Ward's antipathy to Retzlaff's usually supportable conviction that he was always right, and many other conflicts, some cited and some to come, were more or less inevitable, given the pressures of the job. Years later a producer in another city was quietly taken off the job permanently because of the language he habitually snarled into his microphone in dressing down any cameramen who, in his opinion, screwed up. In the heat of the moment and protected by the fact that no one outside of crew people with headsets can hear, many harsh judgments by a producer may be made and apologized for later, or not at all. The fact that the technicians on a Hockey Night broadcast always have been CBC people, but producers and directors were usually not, could result in a lot more friction than ever actually happens.

There is always the chance of conflict when you have the kind of split-second timing that requires, to give only one instance, a floor director high above the ice in the broadcast booth to be leaning over with his right hand on a play-by-play man's shoulder while the fingers of his left hand are a few inches from the face of the play-by-play man, who is talking and trying to make sense at the same time as the director is counting down by showing four fingers, three, two, one — and out to a commercial, exactly on time, or someone will complain.

Amazingly enough, few real rhubarbs occur. Teamwork is the imperative. One night in 1990 it was instructive to watch the speed with which everyone in the gondola intuitively grasped what Bob Cole meant when he had started talking about a Pittsburgh goal but had mislaid, or had not been given, a piece of paper listing the assists. In a second or two, being able to hear that Cole was talking about the goal and guessing why he was waving his left hand frantically while talking calmly, the other two in the front row of the gondola acted. Maria Maida, the statistician, grabbed that part of the summary sheet covering the goal and got it to the color man, Harry Neale, who got it all in one motion to Cole.

"Scored by, with assists from . . ." came so fast that only a witness to those two or three seconds of swift action could have guessed it had ever happened. Afterward the three of them smiled at one another. Obviously the routine had broken down somewhere or there would not have been that tiny emergency. But nobody bitched.

When Ward is talking about his own years with Hockey Night, he doesn't dwell much on the changes that eventually forced him out, his final appearances being on a part-time basis ending in 1972. In the three or four previous years Mellanby had made more demands on him than anyone had ever done. At the same time Mellanby was acting as the resident gadfly to everyone else, too, from Retzlaff and Hough on down. But Ward had other disturbing problems. For one, his first marriage was breaking up. And, as part of a general feeling that Ward needed shaking up, two writers had been hired, Morley Kells and Brian McFarlane. Kells, often seeming to Ward more interested in lacrosse than in hockey, was told to sit in with Ward during pre-interview sessions and have a hand in framing questions. Ward justifiably saw that as a lack of confidence in him. "Who the hell is Morley Kells or anyone else to be telling me how to broadcast?" He survived Kells but increasingly felt that his imminent departure was not being handled sympathetically, that a lot of things were crumbling around him. He reacted to this, not unnaturally, with what to some Hockey Night people was a new aloofness, even more separation from the overall affairs of the show, even more concentration on his own part.

The Golden Era of Ward Cornell

Near the end, Bob Gordon listened quite often to Ward's side. He was bitter, knew he was being phased out. The signs were all there — he was constantly being checked up on for this or that, overridden during meetings, hassled by Mellanby, who at other meetings, with others around, would say, "Hey, Ward! We gotta perk this thing up. We gotta do this better, we gotta do that better."

When the separation finally came, however, Ward didn't have much time for brooding about it. In the spring of 1972, the end of his last season with Hockey Night, the Ontario government, for which he'd worked occasionally as a consultant, asked him to go to England as the province's agent-general at Ontario House.

In London the ability that had been one of his values both on and off the air with Hockey Night — to charm people, make them feel comfortable, get them on his side — was valuable coin again. He accomplished much on Ontario's behalf in dealing with a wide variety of people, from prospective emigrants to customers for Ontario-made goods, was lauded officially for his service there, and when his term was over was appointed a deputy minister.

Soon any bitterness he had felt was gone. Recalling his good hockey years philosophically a few years later, he told a friend, "Nobody does one thing forever. It would be a pretty dull life."

Chapter 9
The Sayings of Chairman Ralph

He had an ego as big as Rhode Island, but the ego was Ralph, and when the man produces, you can take the ego.
— Bob Gordon, on Ralph Mellanby and his time as Hockey Night's executive producer

Rhode Island isn't big enough. How about Texas?

— Ted Hough

When Ward Cornell was having his mid-1960s troubles, relations between the Toronto and Montreal sides of the operation were in — to use a line from an old magazine cartoon — a low period between slumps. In covering game action, this caused little or no damage. The two best hockey producers of the age were at work on every game: George Retzlaff in Toronto and Gerald Renaud in Montreal. But in other areas the situation was not quite so cut and dried.

At the time of Ralph Mellanby's arrival on Hockey Night, the gentlemanly René LeCavalier was the unchallenged best in French hockey broadcasting, but changes were soon to come in English. Danny Gallivan called the Montreal play-by-play with verve and flair, but Mellanby felt Gallivan's color man, Keith Dancy, was not right for the part. This was perhaps the first indication that, personal friendships notwithstanding, if

Mellanby didn't like the way someone performed they would be on the way out. Mellanby's preferences would soon become Hockey Night's rule of law. He didn't have any immediate plans to change the Toronto on-air lineup, but that would come, as well — without any great delay.

At the time, from a fan standpoint some swore by the Montreal broadcasters. Others preferred Bill Hewitt and Brian McFarlane in Toronto. Ward Cornell in Toronto and Frank Selke, Jr., in Montreal did their jobs well as intermission hosts. Viewer debates usually split along traditional Canadian lines — Quebec and part of the Maritimes versus Ontario and everybody else.

But other parts of the operation often seemed to be in permanent disarray. Liaison between Toronto and Montreal was all but nonexistent. If Montreal, for instance, decided it wanted to shoot an intermission film feature on Toronto's Frank Mahovlich, Dave Keon or Johnny Bower, a Montreal film unit might simply show up in Maple Leaf Gardens with cameras and interviewers without mentioning the matter to Toronto at all. The same situation in reverse might happen in Montreal.

By the middle 1960s Ted Hough was worried about the persistent cross-purposes in these two main parts of his constituency. He knew the relevant attitudes better than anyone, because part of his job was to negotiate not only with the bigdomes of each club for broadcast rights, but also to negotiate pay and conditions with the on-air personnel in both cities, and production details with CBC's Montreal and Toronto operations.

One problem he had rates among the picayune eternal verities of being Canadian. That was to find the right people to fill in occasionally on Montreal English telecasts, if a fill-in was needed. "If for some reason we needed a play-by-play man or color man or host there," Hough says, "we ran into a great deal of difficulty getting one the Montreal club management would accept. They would usually consider someone from Ottawa acceptable, but heaven help us if we tried to put in someone from Toronto. In contrast, it was never a problem fitting any of the Montrealers into a Toronto broadcast."

A recent arrival from Mars might require an explanation as to why the Montreal management would object, sight unseen, to *any* broadcaster from Toronto. To Canadians with memories of longtime French-English tensions, as Canadian as the Northwest Passage, no explanation is needed. Selke and Irvin and Gallivan were Montreal residents, Dan Kelly a border person from Ottawa. No other Ontario Anglos need apply. (Later Brian McFarlane was a regular on the Montreal crew — but that was different. He had once worked at CFCF in Montreal as sports director. Also, Harold Ballard of the Leafs had kicked him off the Toronto broadcasts. That made him by proxy a good guy in Montreal.)

What the situation required, Hough decided, was a talented man, preferably one living in Montreal and with broadcast experience there, who as quickly as possible would bring some kind of order out of the current disarray. There was not a large field of prospects. But in the spring of 1966 he thought he had found the man, and he hired Ralph Mellanby. As it is almost impossible to tell Mellanby's story in an orderly manner with input from all concerned, it seems better to let Mellanby tell at least part of it in his own words:

"Apart from the fact that when I was a kid playing road hockey with my bother in Essex, Ontario, and would pretend I was Foster Hewitt calling the play-by-play, my first touch with the show came a couple of years after I was hired by CTV network to work out of CFCF in Montreal as a director for football broadcasts. That's when Montreal was a power in Canadian football. CTV didn't have any hockey then, but I was involved in a lot of other CFCF shows, some of them sports, and when CTV did get the Canadien midweek games in 1964 naturally they had to put together a production team. I was assigned to direct, with Gerry Rochon as producer.

"I remember one meeting we had not long before we were due to go on the air. There was a big guy from MacLaren's who got up and made a speech about how good we'd have to be to

The Sayings of Chairman Ralph 121

match CBC's Saturday night games. He said flatly to Rochon and me, 'If you two guys can't do it, we'll get Retzlaff and the CBC and they'll have to do it.'

"That was probably the best thing he could have said, making it a kind of kamikaze challenge. As in CBC's Saturday night games from Montreal, Danny Gallivan would do our play-by-play, Keith Dancy the color and Frank Selke would be intermission host. The only difference would be in production: Rochon and me. Selke also was public relations director at the Forum. To talk things over, get our bravery up, Gerry and I took Frank out to lunch.

"Gerry had a couple of pops [Mellanby's own slang for drinks] and so did Frank and I, and I remember Frank beefed quite a bit about the CBC. So we started to talk about how much better we were going to be than the CBC. Gerry really got going on this, we'd do this better and that better, and because directing was on my shoulders, I remember cautioning Gerry, 'Be quiet, because if we don't pull this thing off . . .'

"When we did come up to that first Wednesday night game, the broadcast start was 8:30 — half an hour after the first face-off. At 8:25 the power went out in the Forum. Suddenly, five minutes to air, we had nothing! In those days you didn't prepackage and send stuff down the line to the station. All we had at the station were opening billboards [pre-shot openings and closings for different sponsors] and a guy who would coordinate getting the commercials in. We'd even lost our intercom with the station! All I could think of when we were totally helpless was that luncheon weeks before, with all the bragging about how great we were going to be.

"With about two minutes to air the power started coming back on, a little at a time. The coordinating director at the studio called me. The phones were working again but nothing else. He asked, 'Well, what do I do?'

"I said, 'Pray, baby, pray.'

"Moments after that we came up with one camera. The billboards came on, which gave us a little relief. Then I cued Danny Gallivan and he said ringingly, 'Welcome to this historic moment!' as only Gallivan could. And there we are with only one camera. Then the other camera came up on Frank Selke in the studio. The next piece we had was video, and then in the nick of time we were okay, came on and did the game and got a lot of plaudits after. So that was my very first hockey game as a director, and doing things with MacLaren's."

Hockey occupied Mellanby for only one night a week, and he worked on a number of other programs. Eventually he tired of sports and switched to news, and then directed variety shows, still directing the odd game if a regular got sick. For two seasons he had nothing much to do with hockey.

Then one weekend Leafs had a playoff game in Montreal that, as far as the sponsor group was concerned, was not good enough, especially the intermission and the pregame show.

Mellanby: "Whether it was inadequate or not, is not important. The sponsors [Imperial and Molson with equal power, Ford by then a third regular sponsor on a slightly lesser basis] really raised hell.

"With the sponsors pushing and television changing so rapidly, having just moved from black-and-white into color and also into a lot of technical advances and with expansion just around the corner, the heat was really on MacLaren's to make some changes. At one big meeting between MacLaren's and the sponsors, somebody wise decided that they just couldn't have the same agency guys running things anymore; they needed more expertise in production. A guy from Imperial Oil, I think Jack Burkholder, said, 'What we need is someone who's in show business.' Quite frankly, without casting aspersions on Hugh Horler or Ted Hough, there'd never really been a technically trained television producer running the whole show from beginning to end."

There were several candidates. George Retzlaff was considered. And because of his experience in variety at CTV, as well as hockey, someone thought of Mellanby.

"Some time after that I got a call. 'Ted Hough here,' he said. I'd met him, but not very often — he was kind of invisible. Hugh Horler and Bud Turner, who were in the agency's upper echelons by then, had just made him the boss, the president of the MacLaren subsidiary that was running Hockey Night then [eventually to be called Canadian Sports Network]. Part of Ted's call was very funny. Ted said, 'We're looking for our first executive producer. Would you be interested?' I almost jumped through the phone to say yes, but I did hold back, pretty cool. And really, he sold the job down. He said he thought I was probably very happy doing variety with CTV, and this job might be of no interest to me, but if I wanted to talk about it, would I come to see him and Pat Di Stasio, head of MacLaren's broadcast division in Montreal."

Mellanby went to talk. He learned that the job would mean living in Montreal and commuting to Toronto. He would run the French side, too, La Soirée du Hockey, but MacLaren's would pick up the tab for a French course at Berlitz.

"We went out to the Holiday Inn to have lunch, and knowing Ted's intense loyalty to Imperial Oil, as we sat down I said, 'You know, this hotel is owned by Gulf,' and he said, 'Oh, jeez, maybe we shouldn't eat here! But we're not moving now that we're here!'

"A little later he dropped the bomb: 'I'll tell you right now that because of our salary structure we can't pay you more than $20,000 a year, tops.' I almost fell over. I never thought there was that much money in the world. [Hough disputes the salary figure. Records show it was $13,000, but Mellanby remembers it as $20,000.] I was still thinking, if they're willing to pay me that — I'll play it cool. Ted's a tough negotiator, but I knew then that I must be the only candidate, right age at the right time, or something else that had impressed the guys at Imperial Oil and Molson, so I held out for a car and a good expense account. Also I told him I'd have to think about it and talk it over with my wife.

"Janet was so mad at me for not taking it right away! We lived in a little house in Pierrefond. She wanted a bigger one.

"She said, 'You're going to blow this!'

"I said, 'I don't think I'll blow it.'

"When Ted and I met again and I said this is what I want, this, this and this, he said okay. . . .

"Then, maybe I was feeling a little seller's remorse. I talked about a lot of other ideas I had that MacLaren's could use in other shows they had — General Motors Theatre and stuff like that. Ted shook his head and said, 'We're not interested in your other ideas, just hockey.' Anyway, he gave me the mandate to be in charge, make decisions, do what was necessary.

"What we started from in that first year was rather unusual. I was walking into something, Hockey Night in Canada, that was like a religion, like church. There were sacred cows. All sorts of things. But when I met the sponsor group they made it pretty clear they wanted change. They wanted a show that was up-to-date. Still, in some of my early experiences, apart from Ted and a few other key people at MacLaren's, I didn't get a lot of support. Certainly not from the networks carrying the games.

"I think it was on my first trip to Toronto that I met Retzlaff in the motel parking lot across from the CBC on Jarvis Street.

" 'Congratulations on the job,' he said. 'Nice salary?'

" 'Oh, great,' " I said. 'I'm looking forward to it. You know, George, we've got some terrific things that are going to happen. Great ideas. It's going to be great.'

"And he just looked at me, looked at my wife, and said, 'I think the last 14, 15 years have been great.'

"It wasn't much different in Montreal. Gaston Dagenais was the French director-producer, and we had a meeting around a table and I was telling him and the others with him about the new plans and doing film profiles on players and so on.

"He replied, 'I don't care how much film you shoot, you can't shoot as much as I did last year.'

"I said, 'What if I shoot a million feet?'

" 'You can't shoot as much as I did last year.'

"That's the kind of support I was getting. He also told one of my colleagues, 'If that guy writes any more memos, I'm going to break his knuckles.'

The Sayings of Chairman Ralph

"As for Retzlaff and Gerry Renaud, I have great respect for both of them. I've looked at a lot of their old shows on kinescope, black-and-white, using nothing like the equipment we later had. Those shows were good. Even brilliant. Retzlaff was great on camera angles. He also brought better sound, he and Moe Hastie, his sound man. Retzlaff, he's the man who *made* hockey broadcasting in Canada. He should be in the Hockey Hall of Fame. So should Gerry Renaud. Gerry brought something I can only describe as a dynamic way of shooting a game. He brought in the close-up of the goalie. When the puck was around the net he'd go to the net shot, which was a big thing. He shot a game with a kind of French joie de vivre.

"Maybe because MacLaren's influence got them the best people, maybe because of their pride — whatever the reasons, these two talented guys deserve the credit for the early years of Hockey Night in Canada. If you compare their work to other sports, other things that were being done on television at the time, their work was twice as good as anything else."

But new technology was appearing rapidly; new styles of broadcast journalism were coming into vogue, and there was growing competition from other sports for sponsors' money.

"I looked at the shows from previous years and it was a learning curve for me. I talked at length to MacLaren people, got their ideas frankly on things that had been done, the people who had done them, who was good and who wasn't and why. I looked at the talent first and knew that changing things there would be the most dramatic move — but also knew that the show and its people made up such an in-house organ that if I'd tried to change the talent in the first year I'd have got killed.

"So at first I did other new things, set up a features unit, made minor changes. What I was doing was stirring the pot. But a lot of small things happened in those early days. One involved Foster Hewitt.

"He was doing mostly the radio broadcasts then, but on television at the end of a game he'd come on camera with his picks for the three stars. Coming straight off radio, he used to look like a ragbag. I asked Morley Kells, one of the recently hired ideas men, 'Why isn't Foster wearing a Hockey Night in Canada jacket? Hasn't anybody talked to him about that and the way he looks?'

"Kells replied, 'Nobody talks to Foster. He's a law unto himself.' "

Mellanby asked Foster to lunch at the Westbury Hotel to bring up the issue. Foster said Mellanby was the first person who'd ever talked to him about how he looked — after almost 15 years in TV. "From then on I sent a makeup girl upstairs to the gondola to do a fast retouch on Foster before he did the three stars, got him a Hockey Night jacket, and he came on Wednesdays and Saturdays looking terrific, with lots of aplomb. When he went out to speak at functions he always wore the Hockey Night jacket."

Mellanby does a fast forward to an event 15 years later. "I was the one who arranged for him to go out on the ice on the fiftieth anniversary of the Gardens in 1981. Some accounts, including Foster's own biography, say that Harold Ballard invited him to do that. But I know that Ballard really didn't want it. I talked him into it. When I argued that he had to, that Foster was a national treasure, he said, 'Okay, you call that sonofabitch. . . . Well, he's got the treasury, all right.'

"That's why Foster walked out on the ice on his own in 1981 wearing his blue Hockey Night in Canada jacket and crest and got a long ovation. When he came off and we were walking down the corridor he said to me, 'You know, that's the first time I've been on the ice since opening night.' Fifty years before!"

Mellanby had been around Hockey Night for 15 years by then and very little surprised him. As the new boy in 1966, commuting between Montreal and Toronto, he was not as skilled at preventing his jaw from dropping open. As in once when he'd been asked to organize a function at which the sponsors would be dazzled with the agency's plans for the coming season. He, Brian McFarlane and an Imperial Oil man were in the Hot Stove Lounge at the Gardens talking over how to do it when the Imperial Oil man said excitedly, "What you do is rent the Gardens! Get one of those big screens and show your presentation that way!" Mellanby thought about it, imagining the Gardens thronged with Imperial Oil dealers, Molson reps, everybody involved. Then he thought of the money involved — it would have to come out of his budget — "and if we were in for $20-25,000, jeez, I didn't know . . . I asked the Imperial Oil guy, 'How many people are we talking about here?'

" 'Oh,' he said, 'seven or eight . . .' and he's counting on his fingers, 'Don Twaits, the advertising manager, and —'

"I broke in. 'You're going to rent Maple Leaf Gardens for seven or eight guys at center ice to look at a big screen?' "

They didn't do it, instead had a nice party in Montreal, a venue that he used often for such matters to try to assuage the frequent misgivings there that Montreal was always playing second fiddle to Toronto. "Both English and French Montreal crews always felt inferior, Toronto-controlled, defensive. This was because of Foster's longtime national fame and a lot of other things. That's also why, when I took the job of executive producer, Ted wanted me to stay in Montreal. I did a lot of commuting for three or four years before I moved to Toronto."

At first, Mellanby also had other puzzling matters to contend with. Ted Hough, normally his backer, often complained that the play wasn't close enough, would ask plaintively at the Monday meetings, "Why are we shooting from so far away?" This one was solved when once in Hough's house Mellanby asked where he kept his television set. Hough showed him a little 10-incher in his den. Light dawned. "No wonder you can't see the puck!" Mellanby exploded. "Everybody has 21-inch sets but you!"

During Mellanby's first year or so, whatever changes he made were relatively minor: creating a features unit with Brian McFarlane and a cameraman shooting here and there and editing the stories at CFTO; starting something called "Countdown to Face-off"; doing a lot of things he'd been accustomed to seeing on American networks. "If I'd been the age that I am now and I had known what I was up against, I'd never have done some things. I just charged ahead like I've always done, called meetings and said, 'This is what we're going to do.' All the time, I had no idea that people were hating my guts. I guess I just didn't understand." But even doing what he did do, he always had the feeling he was just putting off the inevitable — tackling change in the on-air talent. When he did move on that, he said years later, "I knew I had control on the talent side when Keith Dancy, a guy I really liked personally, was let go after my first season. That was me. There was nobody else responsible." Dancy had been working then since 1960 as color man with Danny Gallivan, and both wanted to keep it that way. But Mellanby felt differently, that Danny was dominating the telecast, and that not only the show but also Danny's career would be helped by upgrading the man beside him, getting it closer to the Toronto situation where Brian McFarlane was in great form working the gondola with Bill Hewitt.

To fill the gap, Mellanby called open auditions for someone to do the color with Danny. "When I walked into the audition room I found 20 guys, including Keith Dancy. When we went to work, two stood out, both experienced, young and fresh. One was Dick Irvin, who I'd worked with often when I was with CTV working out of CFCF. The other was Dan Kelly, who was with the CBC in Ottawa. When I told them I was hiring them both I said, 'Dan, we're going to start off with you working the color on Saturday nights, and Dick, you'll do the Wednesday games.' Both seemed happy. Then Kelly said, 'Never mind that, what's the money?' Which was Kelly's way."

After the first year with Kelly and Irvin, the immediate challenge then was NHL expansion, six new teams, lots more jobs for good hockey broadcasters. Dan Kelly was the first to go. He phoned Mellanby to say he had a great job offer from St. Louis Blues, one of the new teams. They wanted him to be their radio voice, do baseball and football, commute to his CBC job in Ottawa if he wished, and take home a salary of around $50,000.

Mellanby took it in stride. " 'What time does the plane leave?' I asked. So we only had Dan for one year, but he made his contribution, and that year was a big one in changing the look of the show. Dick and Dan and Brian were all young guys. I told Ted Hough that spring when we were reviewing the year, 'I don't want to knock down the walls all at once.' Which was true. I wanted to just drill into them, because I knew they'd finally tumble."

Mellanby came to love expansion. He felt the new teams brought a new openness to the old league. He and cameramen traveled to all the expansion training camps, getting action shots of every one of the virtually unknown players, so that the first time they appeared on television they could be shown in action: "This is what Walt McKechnie looks like. This is what Bob Clarke looks like. This is what Gord Labossiere looks like."

He met expansion's Wren Blairs and Lynn Patricks and Scotty Bowmans and Keith Allens and Red Kellys and Red Sullivans and Bert Olmsteads, and in every camp felt new spirit. "They were the second-class guys. They wanted to do things differently!" One illustration came during the Stanley Cup final in the first expansion year, Montreal against St. Louis. Scotty Bowman, who'd coached St. Louis to the first championship of the new west division, said, "Sure," when Mellanby asked him to come on TV live from behind the bench, a first. St. Louis lost four straight, but Mellanby remembers it as a good series — probably because Bowman had provided him with that "first".

Buoyed up — being sort of an expansion man himself at Hockey Night — Mellanby really concentrated on getting the show to where he wanted it. He was aiming at what he called "a more journalistic approach, a more entertaining approach, with a lot more bite."

In Montreal, when Frank Selke left his host job on the Montreal intermissions to become president of the expansion franchise in Oakland, a series of other younger people were tried for host jobs in both Canadian cities. Probably that early,

Mellanby decided that one other person to be replaced was Ward Cornell, who'd had a great run but did not fit Mellanby's image of what Hockey Night's future should be.

Mellanby's whole idea was geared partly to expansion, clubs being added every few years, all this giving the league a new look for new and more youthful fans who could clue in on young and sharp commentators.

"If something was happening in the league that people were talking about, I wanted guys who would *ask the questions* and get the answers. That old crap with a host in a player interview saying, 'What junior hockey club did you start out with?' had to go."

Dick Irvin had helped in that, a man who told things as they were, and later Dave Hodge, who had a lot of bite — as he later showed. In spades.

"Both Dick Irvin and Dave Hodge got us into trouble from time to time, but that was part of the game. We should be in trouble. Hodge certainly wasn't a house man. From the start I had a lot of trouble with Harold Ballard about him. Dick was a different type of reporter, but he was a reporter and a truthful man."

Some of the new prospects came and went fairly rapidly. One was Ted Darling, who worked in Montreal before he went on to be the voice of the Buffalo Sabres.

Another was Mike Anscombe, who did good work as host in both Toronto and Montreal before moving to the Global Television network, where he's now a senior news anchorman.

Mellanby's overall idea in those years was that the show had to get rid of the old look and still keep the Hockey Night heritage intact by mixing the new younger people in with three who were readily identified with the Hockey Night traditions of the past — Danny Gallivan in Montreal, Bill Hewitt in Toronto and Jack Dennett, who'd for years done most jobs except play-by-play on both radio and television. For the first few years that Vancouver was in the league, Dennett worked a lot of the games there.

And suddenly, Mellanby felt, "we started to come together, but I still felt we needed something else for the show, a new and provocative personality. They don't grow on trees.

"Before Hodge arrived, we used to use guest analysts. One night Red Fisher, who was then the *Montreal Star*'s sports editor, was booked for one of his fairly regular appearances with Dick Irvin in a segment later called the Red Fisher Report. Red Fisher was and still is always good, a trusted person who knows hockey as few do, and writes and speaks his own opinions. This is normal now, but Red was one of the early believers: if a franchise or a player was in trouble he'd come out and say it, when he knew what the truth was.

"This particular night when Red was scheduled, somebody mentioned that Howie Meeker was in town from Newfoundland for a convention. He'd played seven years with the Leafs, coached them in the 1950s after King Clancy and before Billy Reay, had been general manager for a few months before Stafford Smythe fired him, and knew hockey. A new voice and face.

"We paid $50 a night in those days for guest analysts. The problem with getting Howie was that Red Fisher had been booked. I phoned Red and said I'd like to use Meeker on the show but it had to be that Saturday night; he'd be going home to Newfoundland in a day or two. Red was very cooperative. All he said was, 'Oh, fine, but I want that 50.'

"So I called Meeker. He was good, a disturber from the word go. After his first broadcast I knew we had a find if we could get him to work regularly. I said, 'Would you come back in a couple of weeks?'

"He said, 'No goddamn way, I'm not coming back from Newfoundland for this!'

"I said we'd pay his way. 'For 50 bucks?' he shot back.

"I said okay, we'll give you a hundred. So he agreed to come and that started an era all of its own."

In those early days Howie was an instant hit. He outraged people, took beer-parlor hockey talk by storm. Nobody was safe, including the Canadiens. As Dick Irvin recalled in his

1988 book, once Howie loudly pointed out a mistake that a Montreal defenseman had made, leading to a goal.

"You don't do that!" Howie screeched. "You just don't do that!"

Canadiens were furious. And later he really upset Toronto. "Why would I hire that so-and-so?" Mellanby says. Eventually he felt, "Howie kind of — I don't mind saying this, I told him this, too — I think Howie became a parody of Howie, he started to *play* Howie Meeker. But in the first days and especially the 1972 series between the NHL and the Soviets, he was the most refreshing thing on television, the personality I'd been looking for. I put him under contract and did a lot of shows with him, including later when he had his own show. I hadn't been wrong about his impact on the hockey scene. I used to do my own instant research. I'd go into a pub where nobody knew me and sit with some guys and get talking hockey, and Meeker.

" 'That sonofabitch,' they'd say, and then add, 'but I always watch him.' I believed those guys more than I did MacLaren's research, and especially what I got coming back at me from the owners."

There continued to be very big opposition to Meeker, especially at the Forum. This, incidentally, was more or less routine. Once David Molson banned Red Fisher from the telecasts. It took a while, but Mellanby got him back. Ballard was always firing Hodge. Mellanby would come in to the MacLaren office and look around and say, "Hodge is fired," and everybody would look up briefly and say, "Oh, really?"

Mellanby had a principle on such firings. He couldn't prevent them at the time, because the owners had that right. But Mellanby would keep leaning on the door. Sometimes it took a year or so, but if one of Hockey Night's guys was barred by any club, Mellanby didn't fire him. He had to put his own job on the line sometimes to get a man back. If this meant playing games with the owners, so be it.

"Once Irving Grundman, when he was Montreal's managing director, barred Meeker from the Forum. I dropped this story where it would do the most good. When reporters phoned Grundman about it, he denied that he'd ever barred Meeker. 'Howie Meeker is always welcome in the Forum,' he said. So the next year I had Howie back in the Forum for a game and Irving demanded, 'What's Howie doing here! He's banned!' and I said, 'No, you said in the paper that he's not banned.' So I played games sometimes to keep men I wanted, but I did keep them.

"Funny things happened sometimes with the talent. The last time Ballard fired McFarlane, I went in to see Harold and appealed his case and maybe made some kind of an impression, but it was Dick Beddoes who really saved Brian. He did the thing with Ballard about Brian's family, his long time with the show and so on, and Ballard finally said, 'Well, okay, but I don't want him on all the time.' Finally we had to work out a compromise. Ted Hough had to go over. He got Ballard to accept it, that Brian stayed on, but would do most of his work out of Montreal and maybe other cities, but not Toronto.

"Soon after that we had a Toronto-Montreal game in Toronto, coast-to-coast, late in autumn, quite cold, and because Brian had become part of the Montreal crew I wanted him on the show.

"I told him, 'You're doing a piece outside the building, under the marquee. We'll tape it.' The marquee at the Gardens is where they always put up the names of the two teams playing — everybody's seen that marquee shot one time or another. So Brian was outside being taped against the background of crowds going in and all the excitement of a Montreal-Toronto game, and there were these two guys, and Brian heard them talking about him.

" 'That's Brian McFarlane,' one said. 'The guy with the cameraman.'

" 'Yeah? What's he doing outside?'

" 'Ballard's barred him from the building.'

"The second guy looked aghast. 'Jesus Christ! He's gonna be cold by Christmas!'

"Brian ran into the Gardens and told me that one, then went back outside."

When Clarence Campbell was the NHL president he and Mellanby were often in touch — angrily or happily. "He appreciated most of what we were doing. But when his secretary called me and he came on and started off, 'Mr. Mellanby,' I knew I was in trouble. He'd say, 'I watched the telecast Saturday night and it was a disgrace!' And he'd go on to say why, using words half the time I didn't understand. But if he came on the phone and said, 'Ralph,' I knew he wanted something."

Mellanby's role in developing Don Cherry is often lost in the lineup of people claiming that credit. But Mellanby's first vagrant thought that Cherry might be useful on television came quite a while before there was any chance of that happening. It stemmed from an incident during a Stanley Cup playoff between Montreal and Boston, where Cherry was the coach.

"There'd been a fight. Stan Jonathon from Boston beat up Pierre Bouchard. We didn't replay fights in those days, like some networks do, because of research showing that TV hockey fighting had a bad effect on children. TV made the fights unreal, something like the cartoons of characters being hammered that they were always seeing. Of course, Cherry didn't know anything about that — all he knew was that his guy had won the fight.

"The next day Cherry and his team are all watching a TV rerun of the game, and it comes up to the fight and they're waiting for the replay and there's no replay! Cherry complained loudly to Don Wallace, the senior Hockey Night guy there. And a game or two later in the same series I'm in the studio and there's a fight on the ice. This time the Boston player got beat. Next thing I know Cherry was storming into the studio. Outside, they're ready to face off the puck and there's no coach behind the Boston bench, everybody looking around and wondering where Cherry was. And here's Cherry in my room and he's yelling, 'You sonofabitch! I guess you're going to replay that one, eh? I betcha you're going to replay that one, because my guy got beat!'

"He's right behind me. I turn and say, 'No, Don, we're not going to replay that one, either.' He stormed out and got

Pros on and off the ice: Dave Hodge prepares to interview Gordie Howe. In background, Intermission's Matt Chenewski and Harold Ingham. (*Dick Loek/Al Stewart Enterprises*)

After mid-week games on CHCH-TV, Hodge presided over a lively wrap-up: here with Dennett, Howie Meeker, Dick Beddoes. (*D. Mils*)

Above: Toronto – Montreal rivalry extended through hockey teams, production teams, and play-by-play announcers. *Clockwise from left:* Danny Gallivan, play-by-play announcer; Lionel Duval and Richard Garneau, co-hosts; Gilles Tremblay, color man.
Below: Alan Gilroy, network supervisor, CBC radio sports; Ron Caron, assistant advertising manager, Montreal Canadiens; René LeCavalier, play-by-play announcer (French); Marcel Emard, network supervisor, CBC Radio-Canada TV sports. (*Graphic Artists Photographers, Toronto*)

Above: Young fan looking for autographs from Bill Hewitt, Brian McFarlane, Bob Goldham and Gilles Tremblay. (*Dick Loek*)
Right: Ralph Mellanby – for nearly twenty years the engine that drove the show.

Above: Fraternizing: NHL linesman John D'Amico, Don Cherry, referee Bruce Hood, Don Harron as Charlie Farquharson, Harry Neale peeking over Bob Cole's shoulder, Leon Stickle, Andy Van Hellemond and Hockey Night executive producer after Mellanby, Don Wallace.
Below: In 1972, George Retzlaff (*left*) was the first recipient of the Foster Hewitt Award for excellence in sports broadcasting. (*Toronto Sun*)

The good guys, early 1980s, *clockwise from top left*: Dave Hodge, Lionel Duval, Gary Dornhoefer, Mickey Redmond, Don Cherry, Steve Armitage, John Wells, Gary Arthur, Danny Gallivan, Gerry Pinder, Bill Hewitt, Gilles Tremblay, Bob Cole, Dick Irvin, Ted Reynolds, Don Wittman, Brian McFarlane.

Ron Harrison, executive producer after Wallace, in Hockey Night's background set.

Cole and Neale with Maria Maida, statistician, in the gondola.
(*Graphic Artists Photographers*)

Top on-air talent in 1989-90. *Top row:* Bob Cole, Harry Neale.
Bottom row: Scotty Bowman (*Fred Phipps*), Dick Irvin, Don Wittman.

Ron MacLean (*left*), whose job is to keep the lid on Don Cherry.

behind the bench, and the game got started again. But from that moment on I sensed that here was a guy who wanted to be involved in television, knew the impact television had, what it could do."

After Boston let Cherry go, he coached at Colorado, fought with management and got fired. That spring he and Mellanby were sitting in a hotel on Long Island after the final game between the New York Islanders and Philadelphia, the first year Islanders won the Stanley Cup. Well along in the evening Mellanby told Cherry, "If you don't get a job, come and see me."

Cherry didn't get another coaching job, and Hockey Night in Canada did get him. It wasn't long before the fun began. Cherry became a big star, but the CBC hated the way he talked. One head of CBC Sports said to Mellanby, "You know, we have a language policy here. This guy doesn't speak English."

Mellanby: "I had to laugh. They don't give a shit about entertainment. Just about grammar. I say, 'Don has become a big television star with two official languages — he doesn't speak either of them.' But next thing I know the CBC got to one of my producers, Don Wallace, who took it seriously and had a meeting with Cherry in Vancouver to tell him that from now on he had to speak the Queen's English. Cherry phoned me and said that Wallace had told him if he didn't change the way he spoke, he'd be fired.

"I said, 'Don, you speak just like you want to. You don't speak English, but you speak hockey. You speak like the guys in the bars. Keep on doing it.' So he was happy after that and I gave Wallace shit about it. But it never let up. I got a call from another CBC guy, high up, telling me the same thing, that 'we can't have this kind of speech going out over the airwaves,' and all this shit. But I lived with it, through thick and thin. Ballard was on my side. He said, 'That guy's good, keep him on. I laugh at him every week.' "

Mellanby saved Cherry several times, but sometimes did experience the same pangs that hockey coaches feel when they have to let a player go who has done a lot for the coach, has given honestly of himself, but has to be told that it's time to move on.

"I've lost friends because of it. Ward Cornell. He was my best friend on the show for a while. We loved movies, we loved theater, we had similar educational backgrounds. He was a guy I depended on in my first three years as executive producer more than anybody else. For advice, the history of the show, for how I should handle this person, and just for kinship. It was a very sad thing to see him go, but it wasn't only me in that case, it was a collection of people and pressures that said Ward had to go. But it's true that for other reasons, the show, I didn't *fight* for him. I think he knows that, and it's what bothered him at the time, and maybe does yet.

"The best guy I ever had in his reaction to being to let go was Babe Pratt, out in Vancouver. Wonderful guy, wonderful hockey background, Boston, Rangers, Toronto. . . . I had to let him go because, again, we had outgrown Babe Pratt.

"I called him up and said, 'Babe, I would like to talk to you personally, but I'm not going to be in Vancouver so I have to do it on the phone. We're going to make changes.'

"And he said, 'Well, I've been on the show for eight years and I've loved it, and I'll keep the jacket, and if you ever need a sub or anybody to help you out, I'm there for you. Thanks a lot for having me.'"

Obviously it is difficult to put Mellanby into some kind of a nutshell in an attempt to analyze his kind of overdrive. An indication may be taken from his original analysis of Hockey Night as he found it, namely, and simply, that the weaknesses were the areas between whistles.

The action on the ice took care of itself, but in his first year he had production people counting every stoppage in play and reporting on what the broadcast did during the stoppage, pressing everybody to raise those stoppages out of being just empty space.

Other nonaction segments had to toe the same line. He told his usually quite willing, if somewhat startled, troops, "Our scripts are horseshit. We've got to have strong gutsy openings, scripted and rehearsed to get the viewer's attention and hold it. You have to grab them, let them know what the game is going to be like, the *personality* of that night's show. That will hold people to watch. They have to spot right away that this is not just another humdrum sports show."

In this, scripting openings dramatically to pull people in and hold them at least for a while, he showed his understanding of the teaser technique used in popular TV, from sitcoms to drama — an opening sequence that tells the viewer what the show that night will concentrate on. He looked at each game as a show that was more than hockey; a show with major players, their strengths not only to be talked about by the on-air talent, but demonstrated by every means possible, from intelligent camera work to lightning-fast switching. He wanted his producer-directors to do big fat close-ups of the main players and of those who might be in the spotlight however briefly. He wanted wit and knowledge from the commentators. He wanted it all to fit together. If a player's speed was his forte, it had to be shown; or his shot, his bodychecking, his toughness. "If we talk about a guy being great at one element of the game, we've got to show why, what we're talking about."

He jacked up what some people call wild sound, ambient sound, international sound — the background noise behind the voices of the announcers. "When a guy is skating down the ice I want to hear the blades cutting into the ice. When he slaps the puck I want to hear it. Same when the puck hits the boards or the glass. When the puck hits the crossbar or the post I want to hear that metallic ring." Tall orders were his business, but well-placed directional microphones can do the job, and Mellanby found and encouraged the sound men who could make everything work.

Early on, he found a careless lack of communication between Toronto and Montreal that sometimes showed in the choice of player interviews. Until then Bobby Hull might be interviewed in Toronto one Saturday night, shown nationally, and interviewed in Montreal, also shown nationally, the following Saturday night. By demanding notice well in advance of program plans, he put an end to such sloppy double-teaming.

He pushed, along with Ted Hough, for the NHL to rethink club sweaters in light of color TV — so that the home team would always be in their whites, showing off the colorful contrasting garb of their visitors.

There wasn't anybody on the show he wouldn't fight with, from Ted Hough down, to get what he wanted. He deplored stuffiness wherever he found it. He hated anyone who would hear about something new and dismiss it with the argument that what they had was working pretty well. When the CBC was slow to produce a new piece of technical equipment and Mellanby knew where it could be found, he sometimes defied the budget keepers to get it; or played dirty, such as finding what he wanted in the United States and biding his time until he had a playoff game there. Then he would rent the equipment and use it to make the Canadian shows look bad by comparison, a form of blackmail that sometimes forced the hand of his nominal masters. This earned him the enmity of many people trying to find room in their budgets.

He laughed bitterly about the CBC and its committees, under no pressure except its own overloaded procedures, taking three years to design and build a new version of The Truck, while Hamilton's private station, CHCH, under pressure to match coverage from nearby Buffalo, did it in six months.

His loyalties were based on attaining an excellence that would benefit both the league and the broadcasts. One of his maxims: "If Hockey Night in Canada looks good, the NHL will also look good and vice versa." In this sense he became close friends with Alan Eagleson, the NHL Players Association executive director, and with Eagleson's help and cooperation did everything he could from a television standpoint to raise the public status of players. One of his feats was to show the NHL how to improve, vastly, certain annual ceremonies — the all-star and awards presentations — that used be done practically in private, watched by a few sportswriters not wearing dinner jackets. In the end he helped the NHL transform these into well-attended and classy, live, black-tie events shown on widely viewed television.

Mellanby was 18 years at Hockey Night. When he left, it was to take charge of CTV's host television feed for the Calgary Olympics, in which he did so well for both Calgary and the Olympics that he got the same job at Seoul's renewal of the summer games. In both jobs, he used techniques he'd hammered out during his time at Hockey Night in Canada.

Chapter 10
Bad Day in Pittsburgh

I don't care what happens, you guys are going to put a show on the air some way.
— Ted Hough, the year
of the NABET strike.

"I can remember the first inkling we had of a strike was in early January of 1972," Bob Gordon said. He was a Hockey Night producer and director in those days. On some Wednesday and Saturday nights he worked in the bedlam of The Truck parked out behind Maple Leaf Gardens, producing the televised game, and for many years of Sunday nights he'd travel with Foster Hewitt to produce out-of-town Leaf games on radio. Ralph Mellanby said of Bob Gordon once, "You can't have anybody that's more loyal on the show or works harder." He might have been thinking, among other things, of early 1972, when a long-threatened strike against the CBC by the National Association of Broadcast Employees and Technicians (NABET) seemed about to become a reality.

The union was not publicizing its strategy, but hints, rumors, winks and nudges all pointed to the national telecast of a Boston–at–Montreal game on Saturday night, January 22, as a logical starting point, Montreal being the 1971 Stanley Cup winner, and Boston looking to be the logical successor. There's nothing like striking a hockey game of that potential for getting the Canadian public's instant attention on a January Saturday night, those millions out there awaiting the opening face-

Bad Day in Pittsburgh

off, and then ka-pow! no game — the stuff a strike strategist's dreams are made of.

Enter Ted Hough and his sometimes merry men: Ralph Mellanby, Dave Hodge, Bob Gordon, Jack Dennett, Bill Hewitt, Brian McFarlane, Frank Selke, office management guru Roger Mallyon and others.

The four-decade Hockey Night tradition was on Hough's mind. Likewise, and by no means least, the unhappy possibility of lost revenue. But mainly Hough was simply determined not to give in to any bleep-bleeping strike, if he had to create his own air force to prevent it.

"That Saturday night, with the national game to come out of Montreal, Leafs were playing in Minnesota but not to be telecast," Bob Gordon recalls. "So Ted very calmly on the Friday afternoon dispatched the Toronto crew to Minnesota and changed the network around slightly, so that instead of Ontario taking the [Montreal] game as scheduled, we'd bring in Leafs at Minnesota. It might have meant fiddling around to allow for the time-zone difference, but if the Montreal game was struck, we'd push the button and put the Leafs game on the national network instead."

Even though it was a false alarm that time, the backup strategy had been established and was there if needed. A week later, when everything started to get more serious, Hough called a meeting in his office on the Friday afternoon. Those present were Mellanby, Gordon, Mallyon, Selke and one or two others. The discussion for a couple of hours centered on the possibility of a strike the next night. Hough had been talking to the CBC on one level. Mellanby had his CBC contacts, as well. Gordon had been sounding out some technical people he knew and often worked with. These varied opinions added up to a strike being possible, probably on the St. Louis–at–Montreal game.

The talk went around and around. Chicago would be playing in Pittsburgh, and the question was: should that game be covered so that if a strike hit Montreal, Pittsburgh could be shunted on to the network?

Pittsburgh didn't have a local telecast at that time, so it wouldn't be simply a matter of pushing a button and picking up that game. It would have to be staffed by a flown-in Toronto crew if it was to be used at all.

A six-thirty Hough checked those present in the room to get opinions. Naturally, nobody could be sure. Gordon said that he could hire a plane in the morning and get into Pittsburgh pretty fast if the situation became clearer overnight. As the meeting broke up, inconclusively, Hough said he didn't think tomorrow was when it was going to happen, "but be prepared." Mallyon drove Bob Gordon home — they lived in the same direction. As Gordon walked through his front door the phone was ringing, his wife Barbara about to answer.

"I thought it over," Hough told him. "You're going to Pittsburgh. Gather up your crew and away you go."

"I forget who I took with me," Gordon recalls. "I think it was Jack Dennett to do commentary, Dave Hodge for play-by-play, and somebody else. Off we went. We did televise that game, using Pittsburgh camera crews and technicians and truck, but the strike didn't happen so the game went absolutely nowhere. Ted was delighted anyway because the *system* had worked. If the national game had been struck, he'd have been ready to bring in Pittsburgh, and the show would have gone on with — and this was as important to Ted as anything — no loss of revenue, no interruption in what the sponsor was paying for."

From that point Hough had crews on the road almost every Friday just in case. Mellanby would take one, Gordon another. They'd put their crews together and get into chartered aircraft on Saturday morning and away they'd go — to St. Louis, Minnesota, Pittsburgh, Boston, Philadelphia.

They flew wherever it was possible to have a telecast ready in case something happened to the game scheduled to go national. The union soon found out what the Hockey Night crews were doing and naturally didn't like it at all. It became almost routine that someone would phone Gordon's home Saturday morning and ask for him and, when told he was out of town, would ask

Bad Day in Pittsburgh

where he could be reached. The answers were sometimes quite evasive.

Weeks went by, the whole matter a standoff — and on both sides these were people who had been working together for years, so there was a certain amount of unofficial discussion. The strike was not against hockey; it was against the CBC, which privately, even secretly, was backing Hough's initiative. Someone in the union once told Mellanby that if Hockey Night would just hold still and let a strike put hockey off the air once, from Hockey Night's standpoint that would be it; the union would go for other shows. But hockey had the highest profile. Anyway, Hough would not hear of it. It seemed that the two sides trying to outwit each other every week would continue.

On March 4, seven weeks after the first scare, the union finally did act. Los Angeles was scheduled to play in Toronto. Rumors were flying, the same old war of nerves, that this was strike night. Not immediately apparent was a new union strategy, with Bob Gordon and his crew the target. How the union knew that Gordon was going to Pittsburgh that day isn't known. Perhaps the same arrangements had been made in other cities where unionists would support the NABET cause.

"That morning we landed in Pittsburgh about 10:00, 10:30, for a Minnesota–Pittsburgh game," Gordon recalls. "I had Fred Sgambati with me for potential play-by-play and maybe Dave Hodge as host and a little guy from Montreal, Neil Léger, about five foot four or a little more, as production assistant. After we checked in to our hotel Neil and I went over to the Arena to see how the phone facilities were coming along and The Truck setup and so on. When I walked inside and found the Bell installer I asked, 'How are you doing with the phones?'

" 'You the guy from Canada?' he asked. I said I was. 'You better get your ass out to The Truck,' he said. 'You got big trouble.'

"Sure enough I get to The Truck and up the steps and the truck technical director said, 'Bob Gordon?'

" 'Yes, what's going on?'

" 'We got three big goons hanging around inside the Arena asking for you. They won't let us set up any cameras. They've got the technical people afraid to go into the Arena.' All that kind of alarming stuff. So I went looking. Sure enough in the building are three big guys in leather coats. I said, 'You looking for Bob Gordon?'

" 'Are you Bob Gordon?' one asked. 'Are you doing a telecast out of here?'

"I said, 'Not as far as I know, yet. There's a game, Los Angeles in Toronto, tonight, and the only way we'll do a telecast for Toronto is if that game is struck by the technical people there.'

"The guy said, 'They're going to be off the air in Toronto. And you guys aren't going to do a telecast out of here.'

"I said, 'Yeah, why aren't we?'

" 'Because we're going to surround the goddamn Truck on you, throw stones at it, put a fire ax to all your cables, set fire to The Truck, do whatever we have to do, but that show is not going to go on the air.'

"I said, 'Excuse me for a second,' and I went to get the Arena manager, a good guy who'd helped us in the past. I brought him over, told the guys who he was, and said to the one who'd been talking, 'Would you just repeat to him what you just said about setting fire to The Truck, throwing stones, putting an ax to the cables?'

"The big guy looked at me and said, 'What're you trying to do, sonny, make up stories?'

"I guess I should have expected that. They obviously weren't going to make threats with a witness around. I was trying to figure out what to do next when little Neil Léger arrived, my backup, half the size of these guys and all set to do battle. I told him to go into The Truck, we had enough trouble.

"Then the Arena manager said to the guys, 'Look, I don't want any trouble in here. Away you go, outside.'

"So, all very polite, the three guys did go outside the building, but just far enough that they were still between the build-

Bad Day in Pittsburgh

ing and The Truck. I went to a pay phone, phoned Ted and told him what was going on.

" 'Bobby,' he said, 'whatever you do, get the show on the air!'

"I said, 'Jeez, Ted, you should see the size of these guys! And they're serious!' I told him what they'd said about what was going to happen in Toronto, no show going to air, and I said I thought we should believe them because obviously they were union people showing solidarity with NABET and were no doubt in touch with the union in Toronto and knew what they were talking about.

"All Ted said was, 'Bob, keep it going. Do whatever you can. And call me back in 20 minutes.'

"When I called him back he said he'd been talking to the CBC people, and that I should find a judge and get an injunction against these people to keep them from striking The Truck.

"I said, 'They're not going to *strike* The Truck, they're going to beat the shit out of us.'

"He was calm, as usual. 'Legally,' he said, 'let's tell the judge they're going to strike The Truck and see if you can get an injunction.'

"I got the name of a judge and phoned him. 'There's really not anything I can do,' he said. 'Best thing you can do is phone a security company and get their people out there to protect The Truck.'

"I phoned Ted back and told him the judge couldn't help, but thought we should hire a security company as protection.

" 'That's a great idea. Go ahead and do it.'

"I guess this has all taken about three or four hours. I'm getting a little itchy. Inside, the technical guys finally were setting up some cameras. I'm not feeling too good, but I phoned a security company in Pittsburgh and told the guy what the problem was. He said, 'Sir, I'll get five of my men out there in full uniforms, surround The Truck, and I'll put a man on each camera and with each cable —'

"Just as I started feeling a little better, he finished what he'd been saying.

" ' — and the minute something happens, my men are going to turn their backs, because Pittsburgh happens to be the biggest union town in the United States and they're not going to go against any union.'

"I took that in. 'Well, what do you suggest?'

" 'If I were you I'd just heed what these people are saying and get the heck out.'

"I call Ted again. He tells me to stick it out.

" 'How far can I stick it out?'

" 'Just keep with it, keep with it.'

"Okay, so I go back to the guys and said as cheerfully as I could manage, which wasn't very cheerful, 'How's it going?'

"They hadn't improved one bit. 'You're not going on the air tonight,' the one guy said.

"I argued that we were doing the game for Minnesota, anyway.

"He thought that over, but not for long. 'You may be,' he said, 'but if we get word that it's going back to Toronto, Minnesota ain't going to get the feed, either, 'cause we're cutting everything.'

"By then it was five-thirty, two hours before game time. I phone Ted again and tell him how serious it is, that the guys have upset the technical people, they're upsetting me, it seems like a dead end, and . . .

"He thought for a minute and finally said, 'Bobby, you've done what we wanted you to do. Now, assure those people that we will not do the telecast back to Toronto no matter what happens to the Toronto–Los Angeles telecast.'

"Surprised, I asked if I could really tell them that truthfully. He said he would talk to them if necessary. I told him I'd phone him back if they wanted to hear it from him.

"So I go back to the three goons and tell them, 'Look, we've given up. I just got that word from the president of our organization. But we are committed to do the game to Minnesota, and

Bad Day in Pittsburgh 147

if that's okay with you we'll proceed as planned, but the game will not go back to Toronto.'

"They looked at me. 'We'll phone the union leader in Toronto and you can tell him,' one said.

"The next thing was humiliating. The call had to go to a chap I know, Dick Large, who was master control operator in Toronto and one of the NABET chiefs at the time. I said, 'Dick, very definitely we are not going to do this game back to Toronto. That comes from Ted Hough. So if you'll call off your goons down here, no problem.'

"Dick said, 'Okay, Bob. Put one of them on.' So I did, and he talked to Dick, and when he got off the phone he told me, 'Okay, we're going, but we'll leave one guy here just in case.'

"By then it was six-fifteen, an hour and 15 minutes to game time. It had been a long hard day, but the moral, if you can call it that, of the story is that Ted kept me going all that time, on the hook, keeping those guys concentrating on stopping the game coming out of Pittsburgh, while all the time he had been making fast arrangements to get the Boston–at–Detroit game feed organized!"

When the Toronto–Los Angeles broadcast opening came on the air, it had been on only a few dozen seconds when a big handmade sign showed up somewhere in the crowd. One of the cameramen panned to it, obviously by prearrangement. The sign announced that NABET was striking the game. Five seconds later Hough had the Boston–Detroit feed coming in on the national network. When Gordon got back to Toronto and arrived for work on Monday morning, Hough told him he'd done exactly what had to be done. "All I wanted was time, keep them concentrating on you so that we could arrange to get this other game in. It all worked perfectly."

That was the first and last real crisis as Hough continued the process right through the 1972 strike. Gordon was away every weekend laying on backup games. Mellanby once flew out without knowing where his final destination was until he got to a phone in the Boston airport and Hough told him what city to proceed to next. All spring they did shows in American cities to send back to Canada. Most, if not all, wound up at a communications center in Buffalo, ready to go at the punch of a button if needed. Through those months Hough treated his office like a command post, sending the messages out: "Here's what *you're* doing, and here's what *you're* doing," and adding frequently, and with none of his normal diplomacy, that he wouldn't lose one second of Hockey Night through any damn strike, and that there was no way in the world that show was going to miss getting on the air.

Hockey Night did finish its regular schedule, always had a game and commercials on the air, always had a backup and sometimes two if needed, and went through the playoffs the same way.

There were other sides to Hough, or maybe it was all the same side with varying manifestations, adding up to loyalty to what he once called "our family".

One time in the early 1960s, when Bob Gordon had been around only a few years, in his job as associate producer on game nights he'd range busily through the few dozen feet of Maple Leaf Gardens that lay between the TV intermission studio — where the Hot Stove Lounge, bar and restaurant later was built — and the radio studio where the original "Hot Stove League" gabfests had held sway.

One night just before an intermission he saw approaching along the main north–south corridor none other than the prime minister of Canada, John Diefenbaker. It never occurred to him that he should check that sighting, and its consequences, with anybody. He simply went up to the prime minister, introduced himself as the associate producer and said, "Sir, would you consider coming on the intermission for an interview?"

The Chief, as he often was called, thought about it briefly and then agreed, whereupon Bob Gordon took his arm and propelled him into the intermission studio. Ward Cornell

Bad Day in Pittsburgh   149

shook hands respectfully, the camera lights came on, and they were away.

It is said to have been a good interview, partly about that night's hockey game and partly about Diefenbaker's memories of the sport when he was a boy: Saskatchewan, outdoor rinks, 40-below-zero temperatures at some games in his hometown of Prince Albert. No mention of politics at all.

However, as startled Liberal party speech writers and campaign advisers, some of them on staff at MacLaren's, put it, who needed politics in a situation like that? Not John Diefenbaker. He was the first Conservative prime minister in Canada since 1935 when R. B. Bennett had been slaughtered by Liberal W. L. Mackenzie King. Just being on hockey TV, displaying the sporting side of his nature to the huge television audience, was politics enough for anybody. Too much for some, it turned out.

When the prime minister was ushered out and Bob Gordon was enjoying the inner satisfaction of how successful his spur-of-the-moment enterprise had turned out, he saw Ted Hough striding toward him. The conversation was the soul of brevity.

"See me first thing Monday morning," Hough said.

Bob knew from his tone that there had been something wrong with the show. Couldn't figure out what. On Monday morning he went straight to Hough's office and was surprised to find Bud Turner there. Others concerned *had* been there. Hough, looking harried, got right to the point.

"Whose idea was it to have Diefenbaker on?"

"Mine, Ted." He explained how he had seen the prime minister coming down the hall and thought instantly that it would be good to have that prominent a figure on the show, so why not?

It simply never occurred to him as a factor to be taken into account that when the Liberals had been in power, before Diefenbaker, many government advertising and public relations contracts flowed MacLaren's way, as well as speech-writing jobs during election campaigns. Hough reminded him, also, that CBC policy forbade use of public figures in entertainment shows without clearance in advance.

Lamely, Bob said, "I thought that Hockey Night in Canada superseded all that, and that having him on would be a plus."

No doubt Hough had taken, in Bob Gordon's words, "all the shit," and now was handing it out. And, Hough said, because Diefenbaker had not been approved as a Hockey Night guest and probably never would have been if anyone had been there to stop it, MacLaren's would have to make amends.

A week or so later there on the Hockey Night intermission with Ward Cornell was Liberal Party leader Lester B. Pearson getting equal time.

But Hough wasn't above doing his own back-room planning.

In 1978 Foster Hewitt had retired from on-air work and his son, Bill, had taken over the family station, CKFH. By then Foster had been through a couple of farewells — the fiftieth anniversary of the first game he ever called on radio in 1923, and the twenty-fifth anniversary of Hockey Night's 1952 television debut. The local radio rights to Leaf games had been Foster's from when he founded CKFH, in February 1951. At the start, he paid $5,000 a year. In 1978 Foster offered Harold Ballard somewhere in the range of $45,000 to renew the rights, but this time he had competition. An all-news radio network, CKO, was starting up, needed something big and glossy for its launch, and decided that Hockey Night radio rights would do it. CKO bid $125,000, which Foster could handle easily enough, his reputation as a tightwad notwithstanding. He matched the $125,000 offer, figuring he could afford to try it for a year at that price and see if he could make money. Then CKO offered $250,000 for two years, plus one of Ballard's little extra demands: the purchase of two VIP boxes then being built at the Gardens, with their own bars and TV screens, far above the hoi polloi. At that, Foster checked out, and the enraged public got into the act, complaining in letters and phone calls to Ballard that a lot of them couldn't even *get* CKO

Bad Day in Pittsburgh 151

because it was only on the FM radio band, which in the late 1970s many didn't have in their cars or their homes. Why was Ballard shutting them out?

Which is where Bob Gordon and Ted Hough came back for another segment of their comedy turn.

CKO had had to start from scratch to put together a team to take over the broadcasts and was having trouble finding the right man. Ron Hewat had been doing the games for CKFH, but was high up in the station's management, loyal to Hewitt, and couldn't be hired away.

No doubt also there was in Hough a residual loyalty to the idea that the Leaf games on radio should at least come close to the standard established over the years. Plus the consideration that sooner or later the radio rights might be up for sale again and shouldn't be trashed in the meantime. And after all, whoever did the games as the radio voice of the Leafs would have some kind of impact on Leaf broadcasts as a whole.

Whatever the reasoning, Hough one day said, "Bob, we've got to find somebody to do the games on radio. See what you can do to help these people."

So Bob began listening to demo tapes from eager play-by-play announcers far and near. Hough would listen to the better candidates. Mallyon and Mellanby would listen. Finally there was fairly general agreement that Peter Maher was the best available. Hough passed this word along to the big wheels at CKO, who subsequently hired Maher.

At this point Bob Gordon thought, well, here it is, the first time in Leaf history that someone, not a Hewitt or Hewitt employee, such as Ron Hewat, would be doing the radio broadcasts of Leaf games. Maybe we should give him a send-off, he thought, let the public meet this man they would be listening to in their automobiles and bedside radios. He arranged for Maher to tape a brief interview for television. Accordingly, on the first TV intermission of the new season, here, with fanfare, was the new radio voice of the Leafs.

This made Ballard happy, countering some of the hot words coming his way for trading the long Hewitt tradition for a few more bucks.

"But the next day," Bob Gordon recalls, "did I get it from Ted! 'We're Foster Hewitt people,' he said. 'I'm a Foster Hewitt person and you're a Foster Hewitt person. Ballard screwed Foster and CKFH by giving the rights to CKO. Now you're promoting Peter Maher and CKO.'

"I reminded him that we had sat down and listened to tapes and Peter Maher was our recommendation. It didn't make any difference. His view was, never mind our earlier involvement, promoting CKO was a knock at the Hewitts, and that CKO — get this — also had a connection with Carling O'Keefe Breweries!

" 'We're first and foremost Foster Hewitt relatives,' " Hough told me, 'and secondly Molson relatives, and its a no-no to do any promoting of Carling O'Keefe and Peter Maher and CKO. Helping maintain Gardens broadcast policy is quite a different thing, totally unrelated.' "

All this is simply given here as an example of Hough's sometimes inscrutable loyalties. Even to Harold Ballard. But as well to Hough's own employees.

In the spring of 1969 Bob Gordon had been on the road for nearly three weeks working playoffs that did not involve the Leafs, so there'd never been a chance for him to get back to his home.

Finally one playoff series ended in St. Louis. "I was exhausted," Gordon said. Hough had been in St. Louis for the series, as well, "and at the end he said to me, 'Ah, Bob, everything's been going pretty good. How about you go home first-class?'

"I had to fly from St. Louis to Chicago and then Chicago to Toronto. I got myself a first-class ticket. Of course, that allows me to get on the plane first. I'm sitting there in first-class when on comes Ted. I thought he'd be sitting beside me, but he walks right on through first-class into the economy section with Clarence Campbell [then the NHL president] right behind him. Bob Gordon sitting in first-class and my boss and Clarence Campbell in economy! Struck me funny. In Chicago we change planes and away we go, same way — I'm in first-class and they're in economy.

"On that leg between Chicago and Toronto, Ted did come up to first-class and said, 'If you're going to travel up here least you can do is buy me a drink.' So I bought him a drink and asked, 'Do you think Mr. Campbell would come up and have a drink with us?'

"Ted shook his head, laughing. 'I think he's had enough.'"

Shortly after the 1972 NABET strike when Hough had been on the job night and day protecting his constituents, another major event in the hockey world arrived front and center: a September series between an NHL all-star team and the Soviet nationals — four games in Canada, four in Moscow. This was seen in Canada as a chance to avenge years of lesser Canadian teams consistently losing internationally to the Soviets.

It was to stand for years as the biggest event in hockey history. Many of the arrangements had been quarterbacked by Alan Eagleson, executive director of the NHL Players Association and also a member of Hockey Canada, the government-backed organization in charge of Canada's participation in international hockey. The hockey public in Canada was revved up as never before and rarely since, so one of the most important side issues was who would get the rich television rights.

On the record, Hockey Night in Canada *seemed* to have sewn up these rights early, Hough in charge, no competition.

Jack Miller, TV and radio columnist for the *Toronto Star*, led off his column on Tuesday, June 8, 1972, this way:

> September's Canada–Russia all-star series, the greatest hockey attraction ever, has been snared for TV and radio by Toronto's MacLaren Advertising agency. The deal was locked up yesterday afternoon in room 1818 of Montreal's Queen Elizabeth Hotel.
>
> MacLaren will arrange coverage through its production branch — Hockey Night in Canada. Look for the CBC and

CTV networks to be given four telecasts each, to keep peace there. Hockey Canada . . . has taken on MacLaren vice president Ted Hough as broadcast consultant. The TV sponsors which normally buy the Wednesday and Saturday NHL games every winter will get first chance to stick their commercials into this one, too — and you can bet they'll leap at it. . . .

Profits on this [the television revenue] will be shared with Hockey Canada. This is a coup for Hough and a lift for his spirits, which were drooping after his Stanley Cup coverage, when the CBC strike had been fouling everything up. . . .

On that same day, MacLaren — meaning, essentially, Hough — announced that it had acquired the rights, the Jack Miller column being the first publication of that news. But one day later another newspaper headline announced that Eagleson was denying that the rights had been sold. He had checked the appropriate people, he said, and from what he'd been told, "the television rights are still open to the highest bidder."

What had happened apparently was that an agreement was reached between Hough and Allan Scott, the business manager of Hockey Canada, pretty well along the lines of the *Star* column — but that it had not been formalized. The Hockey Night rights offer had been a guarantee of $500,000 against the profit total. Hockey Canada and the NHL players' pension fund would have received all excess revenue. In Ralph Mellanby's opinion, with the benefit of hindsight, "Hough blew it" by letting the word get out before the deal was signed, sealed and delivered. Others feel that the strain of foiling strike threats during the previous five months, including playoffs, perhaps had been a factor in Hough's uncharacteristically dropping his guard while his position was still vulnerable. But the deal might still have survived except that the president of Hockey Canada, Charles Hay of Calgary, who had been supposed to sign the Hough deal as outlined in Miller's column and make it official, suffered what was variously reported as a heart attack or a minor stroke and wound up in hospital.

Bad Day in Pittsburgh 155

Whatever the case, Eagleson was right — the way was open for that original decision on rights to be overturned if a better offer came along. Eagleson had a legitimate reason for wanting to get the most profit possible out of the series. A share of the profits was to go into the NHL Players Association pension plan, a fact that earlier had defused a strong disagreement between the NHLPA and club owners, who otherwise might have had to put up the extra pension-fund money themselves. To Eagleson, Hough's idea to limit the field to Hockey Night sponsors left a big potential commercial market untapped.

Wrangling over the rights went on for weeks. Hockey Canada spokesman Douglas Fisher was quoted even on June 22 as saying, "The production almost certainly will be by Hockey Night in Canada, but the matter of sponsors is fluid, no contract has been finalized."

The matter of sponsors was not fluid for long. Eagleson called Harold Ballard about the possibility of forming a partnership in which Ballard and Eagleson's friend and client, Boston's superstar Bobby Orr, would join bankrolls and make a higher offer for the television rights. They called various ad agencies, were encouraged by the results, and on June 26 topped MacLaren's offer by half — $750,000. Hough then declined to raise his own offer, but offered the production services of Hockey Night in Canada, regardless of who won the rights.

The Ballard–Orr offer was accepted by Hockey Canada three days later. As to who would produce it, Eagleson tried the CBC, couldn't get the guarantees he wanted, then went to John Bassett of CFTO and Johnny Esaw of CTV, who bought the package with Bassett's usual minimum of palaver, Esaw to be executive producer.

Still, the Hockey Night presence was very much in evidence when the series began with the stunning first-game Soviet victory in Montreal, right down to seven games later when Paul Henderson's goal with 34 seconds left to play in the last game broke a tie and won the game and series for Canada. For all eight games, Howie Meeker was there, loud and clear. And for the action on the ice, Foster Hewitt.

When Esaw was asked if having a man nearly 70 years old handling the play-by-play was a good idea, he laughed. "Who else is there for a series like this?"

Foster's commentary of the last minutes leading up to Henderson's goal has been played hundreds of times since, a hockey classic. Hough and Mellanby ended up going to Moscow with other thousands of Canadians, as fans.

And, claims Mellanby, "you ask most people now, and they don't know or care who had the rights or how much more or less the players pension plan got out of it, but they remember that Foster was there and Meeker was there — Hockey Night people, who else?"

Chapter 11
Goodbye Esso, Hello CBC

In 1976 when Imperial Oil pulled out and the show was in deep trouble, at one point Ted Hough really controlled the rights to Leaf games himself and could have made himself a million selling them to Carling. A lot of people would have, but he didn't.
— Ralph Mellanby

Much as I would like to assume the honor of having had something to do with rescuing the show, that version is not entirely true.
— Ted Hough

Somewhere between those contentions is the fairly complicated actuality. Mellanby said if he'd had the chance Hough had, he would have been sorely tempted — "it was the kind of deal that makes a man instantly a millionaire" — and might have grabbed it. But even entertaining the idea of turning the situation to his own profit never got a tumble from Hough. He was too busy trying to put back together the show that had consumed his loyalties for most of his working life.

The facts were that in the middle 1970s when world supplies of gasoline and other petroleum products were seriously threatened, some pragmatic people at Imperial Oil began to take a hard look at what the company was spending on advertising gasoline, oil, tires and other petroleum products that, quite simply, it might not have in sufficient stock to meet demand.

One high-profile target for a well-placed torpedo, a chance to save about $3.5 million a year in the advertising budget, was Hockey Night in Canada. The question the budget-makers asked went something like this: "Why the hell are we spending millions of dollars on that show when we can sell all the gas and oil we can get without it?" The main proponent of that argument happened to be a former senior MacLaren Advertising executive, John Anderson, who had switched to Imperial's advertising department not long before.

Ted Hough's subsequent assessment of Anderson's role was, "There are advertising people who are dreamers, like Bud Turner, who have some respect for the long view; and there are advertising people who are hard-nosed marketers and don't take much else into consideration. John Anderson was one of those. When we learned that his study of the situation was behind the crunch about Hockey Night, his name was often taken in vain around our place."

In its 45-year history, Hockey Night had never faced such a potential for extinction, the situation made more bitter by Imperial's suddenly becoming the exact opposite of its famous gasoline commercial built around the concept of a snarling "tiger in the tank." The transformation from tiger to pussycat was all the more shocking because it was so out of character. Indeed, in the late 1950s when the Molson family began chewing in a gentlemanly way into Imperial's monopoly on Hockey Night, Imperial certainly laid out no welcome mats for Molson to share the load. In fact, that era has a nice dramatic Canadiana-like ring to it.

This started with Herbert Molson, a decorated World War One colonel who became president of the family brewing company and until his death in 1938 was prominent in many good works around Montreal. One of the good works, indicative of the kind of profile he had in the community, had been pushing for and becoming involved in building the Montreal Forum in 1924.

Goodbye Esso, Hello CBC   159

In the 1950s the brewery, by then headed by one of Herbert Molson's sons, Hartland, was sponsoring telecasts throughout Quebec of Sunday afternoon Forum games featuring the senior Montreal Royals, the telecasts getting an eye-opening response from beer drinkers throughout the province. That success seems to have given the Molsons the idea of spreading their wings into a higher level of hockey broadcasting. Still, when Molson did come into NHL hockey front and center it was not the brewery, as such, but two members of the Molson family on their own. In 1958 Hartland Molson and his brother, Tom, bought a controlling interest in the Montreal Forum and the Canadiens from Senator Donat Raymond and the Canadian Arena Company Limited. In essence, this gave Hartland and Tom Molson control of part of the Hockey Night product, since MacLaren Advertising, who would sell advertising rights to various sponsors, still had to buy them first from the Maple Leaf and Canadien organizations.

"Hartland Molson was a hard-nosed and very clever man," said Hugh Horler, describing what happened next. "He made it clear that part of the new ownership situation would be a voice in Hockey Night. Which made it sort of a shotgun marriage, but all very gentlemanly, nobody holding anybody up."

Frank Selke, Jr.'s recollection of the 1958 purchase by the Molson brothers confirms that impression. "The move was in line with the family's longtime involvement with social and cultural affairs in the community, but they weren't stupid, either, and recognized that with the purchase came leverage to use the club as an advertising medium.

"In the first year they sponsored one-third of the Hockey Night broadcasts in the province of Quebec, nothing in Ontario, and over the period of about five years this involvement grew until they were sharing the broadcasts equally with Imperial, and ultimately — but not equally — with Ford."

Horler was involved with MacLaren in negotiating the terms of the five-year process.

"At first it didn't work out very well for me, from the MacLaren standpoint. MacLaren at that time didn't have any of the Molson Breweries business. Cockfield Brown was their agency, and from the Molson side it was understood that Cockfield Brown, not MacLaren, would produce the Montreal hockey games. That didn't sit very well, but there was nothing we could do about it. How that was resolved turned out to be simple — Cockfield Brown did it so badly. They didn't try to hire away any of our production talent, felt very confident they could do it themselves. They blew it. It took a season or less to convince Hartland. When the change was made back to MacLaren as Hockey Night's producer, MacLaren didn't get the whole Molson account. But at that time they were bringing out Molson Canadian, a new brand, and they gave us that to handle."

There were ownership developments later between the brothers and a group of younger Molson family members. These, after some years, sold to the Bronfmans, who eventually sold to Molson Breweries. None of the ownership changes really affected MacLaren's control of Hockey Night, but they formed the background to the crisis of 1976, when Imperial Oil decided to drop out altogether and Ted Hough had to try to put humpty-dumpty back together again.

Years later, Hough was still nettled about Imperial's targeting Hockey Night as the place to cut in 1976. Corporate advertising, public-relations-type advertising, other product advertising, all seemingly proceeded on their anointed way while the kill-Hockey-Night case sailed through the various policy levels at Imperial Oil.

When there was still a battle to fight and perhaps to win, Hough and Turner argued that some of these other Imperial Oil public-communications programs might consider hitching some of their functions to Hockey Night in Canada and save the Imperial presence in the show. No dice. At Imperial, deaf ears were the order of the day. Never mind that the company had been trumpeting for 40 years that their hockey broadcasts occupied a significant niche in Canadian social history. Never mind the truth that Hockey Night stood high in the uncrowded field of indigenous Canadian culture. Even Imperial Oil people who had been strong supporters of Hockey Night, including advertising manager Don Twaits, seemed powerless against the words-of-one-syllable message from the cash box.

And so it came to pass that one day in February 1976, the 1975-76 hockey season still on, Hough called into his office all the Canadian Sports Network people most concerned — the ones who might soon be looking for jobs elsewhere. Among them were Mellanby, Selke, Mallyon, Gordon and a few other staffers, as well as Bud Turner — who was senior vice president at MacLaren by then and headed for the presidency, but had battled for Hockey Night against friends and enemies alike for so long that he was always considered one of the Hockey Night gang.

Facing them, Hough said he had an announcement that he didn't want to make. Then he made it — that Imperial Oil had decided to bow out of Hockey Night in Canada. There was little or no chance that Molson would pick up the slack. Its product, beer, was banned from advertising in five provinces at the time and while it was sticking with Hockey Night in Canada as long as the games were there to sponsor, its present involvement was as far as it would go. This did not necessarily mean the end of Canadian Sports Network, Hough told his people, but as Hockey Night provided about 90 percent of the CSN income — a little baseball, lacrosse and magazine-type sports programs making up the rest — Imperial's decision did create a big problem.

"We'll be searching for another major sponsor to go along with Molson and Ford," he said. "In the meantime we must tighten ourselves up and be prepared next season for maybe a little different show."

In Bob Gordon's recollection, nothing else greatly untoward happened at that meeting, no cries of rage or pain. "We somehow had faith that Ted would look after it."

Which Hough indeed was working on. It had been on his mind for months. He and Bud Turner had sensed well in advance from Imperial Oil contacts well placed to sniff the wind that Anderson's review might have these drastic results.

In his assessment of how to cope if the worst happened, the arithmetic had been familiar enough. Imperial and Molson each had been responsible for one-third of CSN's commercial income, Ford for almost one-third — but only Molson and Imperial had shared equity ownership of the show, responsibility for paying the bills. So now Molson's one-third share and Ford's almost one-third share had to be built on.

Imperial's commercials had to be matched elsewhere, and one-half of the equity ownership was also up for sale, rent or barter; the faster the better.

Inevitably this was known on the street. In the boardrooms of companies big enough to take more than a passing interest, it was known that if MacLaren and Hockey Night could not find other corporate angels to go with Molson and Ford, the rights to broadcast Toronto Maple Leaf hockey games might be on the market for any company big enough and rich enough to take them on.

One potential replacement was Carling O'Keefe Breweries, headed by John Lockwood. Some years earlier, when Lockwood was president of Lever Brothers and MacLaren handled Lever's advertising account, Lockwood and George Sinclair, MacLaren's president, had known one another in a business way. Lockwood approached Sinclair and said that Carling O'Keefe would be interested in taking over Hockey Night in Canada. In Hough's words, "George Sinclair knew very little about — and in his position didn't need to know very much about — how Hockey Night was put together. Never did. So he sent me up to see John Lockwood and answer questions, which I did. Lockwood then told me that he was interested in pursuing the matter," and Hough was left to contemplate an almost impossible situation. Molson, which had had his loyalty for so long, certainly would refuse to share Hockey Night with another brewery in direct competition for the hearts, minds and beer-drinking choices of Canadian hockey fans. Yet, so far, Carling had been the only applicant.

Goodbye Esso, Hello CBC

However, Hough had a hole card. This in itself is an example of his craft, or some might say, craftiness.

Nearly a year earlier, when Imperial's contract with Maple Leaf Gardens for television rights to Leaf games was into its final year and there were rumors that it would not renew, Hough had realized that the real prize to be fought over eventually would be those Leaf rights. He reacted quietly in a way that was admired later. A clause in the Imperial contract provided that the rights could be renewed by Imperial, but *without the renewal, could not be assigned elsewhere.* Unless assigned, the rights would revert to the Gardens. Harold Ballard, as Gardens owner, then would have been free to sell the television rights to whoever would pay the most — maybe getting the kind of bidding war going that could have frozen out Canadian Sports Network entirely. This, depending on the new rights owner — such as another brewery not compatible with Molson — could have ended Hockey Night in Canada as a national network show.

So to have Imperial renew the rights was a first essential; even though when this was done the company was reasonably certain that it would not be using the rights itself. The second was to have Imperial agree in advance to assign those rights to Canadian Sports Network. Hough managed both elements — no doubt partly due to his long and friendly relationship with Imperial. A third essential was to have the Gardens agree in advance to permit CSN to assign *all except the production rights* to secure funding. It all worked beautifully. Imperial did renew its rights contract at a time when the pullout had not been fully decided upon. Then the rights were assigned by Imperial to Canadian Sports Network. The Gardens did its bit. Then CSN ultimately reassigned the rights to Molson — *except* the production rights, which were made subject to Gardens' consent. Presto! Instead of possibly being dealt out, Hough once again had a very high card to play.

That's what had been in Ralph Mellanby's mind when he said that Hough could have made a lot of money by arranging to sell the rights to Carling O'Keefe instead of Molson.

However, his very background made that kind of a move unthinkable.

His loyalty to Imperial over the years was no token thing: it had been Esso in his gas tank, Marvelube where it would be the most good — everything that Murray Westgate sold, Hough bought on his Esso credit card.

He felt the same about Molson. If he caught any member of a Hockey Night crew drinking some other brand he would, in Bob Gordon's description, "really blow his stack! He'd tell those guys that Molson paid our goddamn salaries and in return we would drink their beer, nothing else." He was not going to deal off the rights to Carling O'Keefe when such a move automatically would have shut out Molson, his corporate friend and the show's longtime supporter.

Yet, when he returned to his office in the spring of 1976 with the rights assured, he was still only part of the way to what he saw as that summer's ultimate destination: restoration of the show to financial stability by building around Molson.

Other Canadian Sports Network people remember the tensions of that time, Hough becoming, as one staff member said, "more serious about everything, if such a thing was possible with Ted." He looked at everything more closely than ever. He'd been fighting for Canadian Sports Network's very existence and he wasn't out of the woods yet. Even among companies professing themselves willing to buy commercials, none wanted to take the kind of equity position required, in effect to be one of the guarantors that bills would be paid.

During that time when he was trying to put together what turned out in the end to be a very complicated deal involving the Gardens, Molson and the CBC, Hough relied heavily on Frank Selke and VP-general manager Roger Mallyon to handle CSN's day-by-day business. Hough was away from his office a lot. Before, he'd always been around for advice if anyone needed it. Now even when he was there, doors were closed. One CSN staffer summed it up: "He worked his ass off. If we thought he'd been tough before, now he was a real bugger. But there wasn't one of us who wouldn't have gone to the wall for him."

Then, suddenly, the worst part was over. Hough ended up, he said later, "with a rather strange bedmate." The CBC finally decided that it couldn't see this flagship show disappear through lack of sponsorship. So the network decided to move in with Molson to share the equity position. CBC also would assume responsibility for selling the air time vacated by Imperial. Being the CBC, they could approach a number of different advertisers and in essence sell participation, or spots, on the show — almost enough in the end to compensate for the financial weight lost when Imperial left. But while details of the deal were being worked out, there was a new intensity at CSN: reminders to tighten budgets, do it this way, do it that way and, from Hough, "Remember, guys, CBC are our brothers now, same as Molson." His staff could see the pressure he was under, sensed a great deal of infighting going on, but didn't know the half of it.

What had happened was that the CBC had put a condition on its cavalry ride to the rescue of Hockey Night. This was a requirement that the CBC, not Canadian Sports Network, henceforth would produce Hockey Night in Canada. Here the CBC saw an opportunity to remove a longtime irritant — the production of its flagship program by an outsider, private company. The most devastating part to Hough was when he learned that Molson was prepared to go along with the plan which would, in effect, kill CSN. One must remember that, in dealing with what seems to have been a CBC-generated power play, or double cross, there had been by then 24 years of frequent jurisdictional hostility between CBC and MacLaren over Hockey Night. But never before had it been war to the death.

The rather amusing thing is that Hough still had the high cards, but the Molson–CBC negotiators did not know that. They just didn't get up in the morning quite as early as Hough. Unknown to, or forgotten by, Molson and the CBC was the fact that production rights could not be assigned without Gardens' consent. (Hough's radar mast must have been miles in the air when he had planned the "all except the production rights" line as the third essential of his maneuverings mentioned earlier.) So in effect CBC and Molson had a plan that they now found they would have to get past Harold Ballard, who did not like the CBC and did like Hough, his longtime sparring partner. When the CBC came calling with their proposal that they would produce Hockey Night games, Ballard refused, told them to get lost; he would go with Hough.

That meant that CSN would continue to produce Hockey Night in Canada and the CBC would continue to gnash its teeth on that account. Hough never felt quite the same again about Molson. CBC's dump-CSN plan, agreed to by Molson, put "paid" to his longtime loyalty.

Hough and Ballard had a strange relationship, based partly on Ballard's demanding from Hough and often getting, after mighty arguments, financial concessions or straight payments for the Gardens every time Hough wanted a new camera position or any other TV-related favor. They'd haggle, break off, haggle again — and usually Hough would get his deal, at a cost. The cost sometimes would be that if Ballard wanted something Hough could help him with (once this was a new pipe organ for the Gardens, to bridge commercial breaks in the play; another time some help with repairs to TV equipment at Ballard's cottage), they'd haggle and Ballard usually would get what he wanted.

One time they actually argued until a televised Leaf playoff game hung in the balance. That was a year when for some reason the CBC refused to telecast, even locally, the first game of a playoff series scheduled for Maple Leaf Gardens. Hough responded by calling Moses Znaimer, founder of Toronto's CITY-TV, and asked if CITY would take the game. Znaimer ran CITY without the red tape that sometimes afflicts networks. Znaimer said sure, he'd take it.

However, when Ballard heard that, he called Hough and said that if the CBC wasn't going to do it, he wanted CHCH-TV Hamilton (where Ballard owned the city's football team, the

Tiger-Cats, and was pally with CHCH bosses) to carry the game. The two of them argued back and forth. Hough wouldn't give in; he had approached Znaimer and didn't want to reneg. That's how the matter stood when the mobile unit that CSN had rented from Global Television pulled up alongside Maple Leaf Gardens at nine on the morning of the game, and Bob Gordon, who was to produce and direct, got a call from Gardens superintendent Don "Shanty" McKenzie to say that Ballard wouldn't even let The Truck park, let alone start laying cables, because he didn't want the game on CITY; he wanted it on CHCH.

The Ballard–Hough wrangling took an exotic turn that day. While Gordon stormed around trying to find Hough to get the matter settled, Hough simply avoided the phone calls. Meanwhile Ballard stood pat. No truck was parked, no cables laid.

It was close to 5 p.m. when Ballard phoned Shanty to go ahead, the matter was settled.

A few minutes later Hough phoned Bob Gordon, who'd been worriedly walking the streets much of the day. "Bob, we can put this thing to bed. We're going to broadcast."

"Is there anything I should know first?" Bob asked.

"Yes," Hough said, laughing, "You should know that the game will *also* be on CHCH."

The budget for the first Molson–CBC season on Canadian Sports Network was about $22 million. At tot-up time the following summer, the deficit was about $200,000. Not many companies today, or the CBC itself for that matter, would feel uncomfortable with a deficit totalling about one percent of income in the profit-and-loss columns of its most popular product. The CBC possibly had never seen a deficit that small before and debated its portent at length. Present incumbents in CBC Sports now find it difficult to believe that hockey on TV ever *lost* money. Hockey Night's association with the CBC as a partner rather than, as of old, merely a source of network facilities and technical personnel, has been in place ever since.

Perhaps the only matter left hanging from that year of travail caused by the Imperial pullout is what happened to John Anderson, the architect of the drop-Hockey-Night idea of 1976. Maybe in the advertising business not everybody holds grudges, and some furies are only skin deep. Eventually Anderson returned to MacLaren in a senior position. Meanwhile, with a change in advertising policy, in 1982 Imperial Oil also returned to the sponsor group of Hockey Night in Canada, and a lot of hockey fans now have forgotten that they ever left.

Chapter 12
The Good Guys and the Bad Guys

Remember, guys, the CBC are our brothers, now.

— Ted Hough, in 1976

Brothers? There's a country saying that goes, "You can choose your friends, but there's not much you can do about your relatives." For many years, there had been antagonism between the corporate CBC and individuals high and low in the various incarnations of MacLaren subsidiaries that produced the hockey broadcasts. An impartial observer, if there had been one, would likely have judged that Hockey Night in Canada as a whole had an arrogant and consistently critical attitude toward the CBC. Too much red tape. Too many dunderheads. Naturally, from time to time there was CBC arrogance coming the other way.

From 1964 on for some years Hockey Night dealt on a regular weekly basis with both the CBC and CTV. CBC had Saturdays. Key station for midweek Leaf games was Toronto's CFTO-TV (CTV). The compatibility comparison between the two networks came out with CBC a distant second overall despite the exception, the Hough-Retzlaff relationship. A Hockey Night veteran of those times said the CFTO people seemed, in contrast to the CBC, much more interested, innovative, concerned and *into it*.

This situation did not change for the better, maybe for the worse, when CBC became an equal partner instead of just the network from which air time was bought. Hough's plea on behalf of brotherly forbearance in effect recognized the antagonisms, but did little to make them go away.

We take you now to the Boston Garden on the night of May 3, 1979, about three years after the Hockey Night–CBC "brotherhood" had been declared official.

On the ice Boston Bruins and Montreal Canadiens were locked in what Danny Gallivan, calling the play-by-play, accurately described as a titanic struggle. It was the fourth game of the best-of-seven Stanley Cup semifinal. Dick Irvin, in his lively book, *Now Back to You, Dick*, called that 1979 semifinal "maybe the best playoff series I've worked" — and when he wrote that in 1988, he'd been working NHL playoffs for more than 20 years.

Montreal had won the first two games of the series at home. In the tense third game in Boston, when another Montreal win would have practically wrapped it up, Brad Park's goal for Boston in the seventeenth minute of the final period broke a 1–1 tie and won the game 2–1, keeping Boston alive. The fourth game, May 3, again was tagged as crucial to both teams. A Boston win would square the series, a Montreal win would provide a huge 3–1 lead in games, meaning they'd have to win only one of their remaining three games (two of them at home) to reach the final.

Across Canada, the usual three million or so sets — some playoff games were estimated to have been seen by eight million people — were tuned to the broadcast being put together from the output of a half-dozen cameras and at least as many voices — play-by-play, color, analysis and intermission interviews — all being funneled through The Truck.

With Leafs having been knocked out of the playoffs by Montreal in the quarter-final, the Toronto crew had been assigned to produce the Boston games in that semifinal. In The Truck, the rising Ron Harrison was director, Bob Gordon producer, Audrey Phillips of the CBC script assistant. Audrey, a sturdy blonde, was a Hockey Night regular and rather a legend. She'd worked hockey since the 1960s, starting with

Retzlaff, and always saw it as more than just a job. For years with Retzlaff and then Mellanby and others, she'd been one of the originators and moving spirits of travel-time off-day receptions for Hockey Night people during playoffs — in a big room with a drink or two, card games, something on TV, a place to keep crews together and talk shop, or not, instead of letting time hang heavy.

In The Truck this night in Boston all were intent on the very tight game, 1–1 at the end of the first period, 2–2 at the end of the second and into the third, when The Truck's business phone, distinct from production phones to various parts of the rink, rang. Audrey Phillips answered, listened for a minute and then in the general bedlam leaned over to Bob Gordon with one hand covering the mouthpiece.

"Bob," she said, "they want to do a news insert back in Toronto."

He hadn't been paying attention to anything but his multiple production functions.

"I beg your pardon?" he asked, surprised.

"They want to do an insert back in Toronto. You'd better speak to him."

He picked up the phone, still preoccupied. A CBC news director in Toronto was on the line, saying urgently, "We'd like to do a news insert as soon as possible, if you'd cue it back to us."

Gordon: "Wait a minute! What do you want to give a news insert at this point for, in the middle of a very close game?"

News director: "Margaret Thatcher has been elected in Britain."

In the circumstances, the British election that day had not been exactly at the top of Bob Gordon's mind. A newsbreak meant leaving the game entirely, without warning, in the middle of the action. His reasoning was that a major disaster, or a major Canadian story, an assassination, something in that nature, might merit breaking in. He felt, as any hockey producer in that situation would have, that a British election was not in that category. The horror in every sports broadcaster's head is having to come back after a break to explain lamely that while the broadcast was off the air something major had happened: a goal, a wild fight, the goalie's pants falling off, whatever.

It boiled down to priorities, those interested in British politics versus fans of hockey. Margaret Thatcher was going to stay elected at least until there was a natural break in the game — although few could have predicted how many years thereafter. But in the primary program, this game, whatever happened during an interruption could never be recaptured in the proper context. If CBC News had preempted the next commercial, or one of their frequent promos, that would have made sense. Meanwhile, this was shaping up as a battle of wills. Gordon still held the phone.

"Well, you're not going to do any newsbreak here," he said crisply, hung up and went back to his job, producing the game.

A little later, the phone rang again.

Audrey answered and said, "It's for you, Bob."

"Bob Gordon here."

At the other end of the line a voice said, "Don McPherson here, Bob." McPherson was head of CBC Sports at the time. "Who do you think you are, giving orders to the CBC?"

"I'm not giving orders to anyone. All I'm saying is that the middle of a close playoff game is not the time or the place to do a newsbreak. It just doesn't make any sense."

"I'm telling you, you do it!" McPherson, the CBC brother, said. "Get us a good break for this!"

"Gee, I'm sorry, Don," Bob, the Hockey Night brother, replied, "but the only person or persons that should give me orders, and really the only ones I can take orders from, are either Ted Hough or Ralph Mellanby. If they tell me, fine. I'm not doing it otherwise."

He handed the phone back to Audrey Phillips. She continued a fairly lengthy discussion with McPherson, who was pulling rank, of which he had a good deal.

Finally she leaned over again and said, "Bob, can they do a lower one-third font, is that okay? It would just be a flash across the lower part of the screen. . . ."

Gordon considered that much less disruptive idea, but before he had a chance to respond, director Ron Harrison — the man whose first hockey TV job had been to lie on the floor out of camera range and hold one of Murray Westgate's gas pumps straight during a live commercial; who had provided Ward Cornell with the classic "Hello, I'm Charlie Upshot" cue card during a live intermission opening; and who would be promoted within a few years to boss the whole show — had had enough.

Harrison had been trying to concentrate on his job of giving the game the coverage it deserved, playing the cameras the way a man might improvise on piano, anticipating each next move on the ice to keep up with or be ahead of the action, while his producer, Bob Gordon, wasn't being any help because he was involved with what he called later "this crap".

Harrison broke in loudly. "Hey, let's do it, Bob, and get the silly bastards off our backs. Give me a wide shot and tell them to put it in." Which was done and the game went on, finally won 4-3 by Boston at 3:46 of overtime on a goal by Jean Ratelle, squaring the series.

Whether that contretemps caused an ongoing break between the big wheels at Hockey Night and McPherson in his role at the CBC is impossible to pin down, but Hockey Night people later noted instances of more than random animosity. According to one of those involved, "After that there were some things said, maybe not quite nasty but at least derogatory, negative. Something might happen and McPherson would say sarcastically, 'Oh, Mellanby wouldn't like that, this guy's getting too much publicity.' "

This was a jab at Mellanby's well-publicized high profile as Hockey Night's innovative and powerful executive producer.

Or, another time: "Jeez, Leafs lost again, eh? You think Ted Hough can take that?" Thus accusing Hough of favoritism to the Leafs, which would be hard to prove in chapter and verse.

Whatever the reasons, the relationship between Hockey Night and CBC was obviously as strained as ever. A few years later when Mellanby left Hockey Night and was replaced at first by Don Wallace as executive producer, by all accounts Wallace and McPherson got along well. With mutual respect. That is, brotherly.

As time went on, the matter of the CBC's choosing its own times to break in to hockey broadcasts surfaced with occasionally dramatic results. One that came to have the most significant ramification was the incident that cost Dave Hodge his job, and thus cost hockey viewers one of the best.

There was no one better than, and apart from Dick Irvin in Montreal few could equal, Hodge as a hockey broadcaster, expert and well grounded in all areas of broadcasting and the lore of the game. In 1971 when, at age 26, he first auditioned for Hockey Night, his resumé looked like this: graduated in Radio and Television Arts from Ryerson Polytechnical Institute, wrote sports for the *Chatham Daily News*, was sports director of a Chatham radio station, called play-by-play for the Chatham junior team, then moved to do play-by-play with the Buffalo Sabres.

He did have a case of nerves, however, in that first audition and the early stages of his work with Hockey Night. Up against an audition lineup of top professionals, the "test" was to interview either Frank Selke Jr. of CSN or King Clancy, the affable old hockey star. Hodge's first try left him well behind Tom McKee, an experienced Toronto sports TV broadcaster, and Joe Mariash of CFTO News. The auditions were done at CFTO, with a taped playback piped to the boardroom at Imperial Oil where the candidates were watched by Hough, Mellanby, Bud Turner and Don Twaits of Imperial.

At the end of the first run, Bob Gordon, producing the auditions, phoned Mellanby to say that he wanted to delay a decision and have Dave Hodge try it again. His idea was that some of the others looked better than Hodge right now, but that with experience he might develop into the best.

He sent the others on a break and told Hodge that he'd looked nervous and should be able to do better. Hodge was given a few minutes to think about it, went through the interview again. Then Gordon left, with the final decision up to the group in Imperial's boardroom.

The next morning at the office he asked Mellanby if there'd been a decision.

"Who would you pick?" Mellanby asked.

"I'd hope it would be between Dave Hodge and Joe Mariash."

A little later Mellanby relayed the decision: "Dave Hodge will be our new Ward Cornell."

In broadcasting, very few people hit top form in a new job without some seasoning. Hodge's first live on-air interview was with the former great Leaf coach and manager, Hap Day. Again, Hodge was nervous, looking somewhat in awe. His nerves showed in what seemed to be an involuntarily movement of one hand to his face and mouth.

Gordon pointed this out while showing Hodge tapes of the show. Once was enough; it didn't happen again. At first Hodge took advice because he knew he needed it. Within a year or two, Hodge was being spoken of by viewers, critics and broadcasting insiders as close to *the* best in the business and getting better. As years went on, it wasn't long before he was giving as much, or more, advice to others on the show as he was receiving. He'd watch and listen in the client room a few steps from the studio when he had time free of his own duties. He would call The Truck to complain if he saw or heard something on the broadcast he didn't like. "Why did Bill Hewitt say that? Why didn't McFarlane pick up on this?"

It's difficult for an ordinary nonprofessional viewer to know exactly why one performer is so much better than another. It's an analysis that requires expertise. Not even counting play-by-play, which Hodge could do anytime he was needed but rarely did after intermission hosting became so obviously his true métier, the word on Hodge went something like this: when a team came in for a Toronto game he invariably knew more than anyone else in the crew the specifics of what that team had been doing lately; in short, he did his homework.

This would sometimes lead him to decide whom he wanted to interview, where his mining for information and opinion and color would be most likely to strike gold. He quickly learned not to be in awe of anyone. No matter what a player or executive had done or not done, Hodge quickly came to treat all as simply people to be interviewed, equals, no more than he was and no less.

His knowledge of all sports, and at the same time of politics, entertainment figures and just generally what was going on in the world was always up-to-date and tended to make his segments somewhat broader in scope than is normally expected of hockey broadcasters. That was the ammunition. Using it effectively was another strength. On camera he was faster than almost anybody at dealing with the unexpected. There was rarely, if ever, an egg-on-the-face situation with Hodge. He had a good instinct for getting at the questions viewers wanted answered — something perhaps stemming from what was going on right then that might otherwise have been passed over in an interview. When he asked a question and the answer included a response that should prompt another question, he'd ask it. Not all interviewers do. If there was nothing to pick up on, only then would he go on to his next question, deftly relating it to the previous answer.

Producers and directors in the hectic atmosphere of The Truck particularly admired his on-air aplomb, speed, confidence, adaptability. If he was told on his earpiece that he'd have one minute for a segment of the show and then The Truck, having made a mistake, had to come back five seconds later and say, "Sorry, Dave, we've got 20 seconds," he'd throw the cue in 20 seconds. He'd be fuming when he got off, but so professional in getting out that nobody could tell that he was harassed or harried.

Yet his producers and directors in The Truck had to be sharp *for* him, too. If Hodge referred suddenly to some piece of equipment, an ankle guard or something, that a player was wearing, a camera had to get a shot of the thing within seconds after he mentioned it.

If not, he'd blast them. "I talked about the ankle guard and you guys didn't show it! What's the use of talking about something if you don't see it?" That kept directors on edge, watching for things Hodge might want to mention — a wrist band, a splint, something a player might wear that was different. All that adds up to Hodge as perfectionist, part of why Mellanby at the height of his frequent disputes with Hodge, would say — and still does — that if he was starting anything in sports broadcasting of major scope the first man he would go for would be Hodge. Their egos frequently clashed, but the sparks they struck almost always enhanced the show.

Then there was the off-air and sometimes difficult Dave Hodge. During the 1972 NABET strike he was with Bob Gordon on the first of those standby skeleton crews, flying to Pittsburgh in a small chartered aircraft to be there just in case. At the time, it was only a precaution, nobody knowing whether the national game would be struck and the Pittsburgh game needed as a fill-in.

Bob Gordon decreed that they should go on and do the game exactly as if it were being broadcast, whether or not it would ever be needed. Even at that early stage, only a few months into his Hockey Night tenure, there was never anything automatic about Hodge's obeying a producer.

"Why don't we wait until the decision is made about using this game?" he argued.

Bob Gordon replied that if the game had to be moved to the network without notice, there would be no time for someone in Toronto to get on the phone and warn them; what the viewers would see was a game in full swing. The voice, he said, should be right there at the same instant with something like, "Now we welcome viewers in Canada to the game in progress between Pittsburgh and Chicago, with the score such and such. . . ."

Which was done as ordered, but Hodge didn't like it — especially as the game really did, in the end, go nowhere.

On the financial-negotiations side, he eventually progressed to the point where he was fairly big trouble. Most of those involved in pay negotiations on talent contracts had Hodge high up on their bleep lists.

In this he didn't follow the lead of his close friend and, for some years, CFRB radio colleague Jack Dennett, who despite his calm mien was nervous about a lot of things, with fingernails chewed to the quick to prove it. Ted Hough always said that Dennett was the easiest to deal with, invariably getting off the line that he'd do the games for nothing if he had to, but if they wanted to pay him that was okay, too.

The tougher ones included Montrealers René LeCavalier and Danny Gallivan. Both, along with Dick Irvin, usually fought the good fight, according to Hough: tough but fair. Negotiations with others in both Toronto and Montreal ranged somewhere between the poles of that nice Jack Dennett and that difficult Dave Hodge.

Hough preferred Mellanby or Frank Selke to do the negotiating, but as the court of last resort, where the buck stopped, Hough often had to referee. Eventually Hodge decided there was no use dealing with anyone else. In his judgment, as the final word had to come from Hough, he might as well go straight to Hough. Even then, there could be friction. Hough admits that too many times Hockey Night came right up to the opening of the season with some contracts still unsigned. Hough's reason — or excuse — was that it was not until almost the season opener before he knew his own budget total, which would guide what he could pay his on-air people. That didn't cut any ice with Hodge. The operation should be more efficient.

So Hodge and Hough had their annual battles, more or less on schedule. One that was not on schedule was one of the biggest of all. CBC offered Hodge a sports-broadcasting job. With Hodge apparently liking the idea, the CBC then informed Hough and went blithely on to say that, of course, even with the CBC job Hodge would still be able to work for Hockey Night.

Hough, generally thought to be unflappable, was capable of exploding. This was one of the times. Partly his annoyance went back to earlier days when he was in full charge, with Imperial and Molson to back him up.

Hockey Night's inflexible policy always had been one of exclusivity: Hockey Night people could not appear on any other shows. Hough saw this as a required individual loyalty to Hockey Night and its sponsors for everybody, with none of them ever to be seen on any other sports show. If Hodge was under contract to CBC, like other CBC talent he'd have been bound to appear on any show with any sponsor, including breweries such as Labatt and Carling O'Keefe in direct competition with Molson. To Hough, the orange blazers of CBC staffers were simply not interchangeable with the distinctive blue blazers that bore Hockey Night crests. Accordingly, Hough intervened hotly with CBC's offer. The CBC backed off. This caused the major ruckus between Hough and Hodge and didn't really leave Hodge much leeway, except to stay — and maybe sometime get even.

One of those times came long after, only a few days before the start of the 1986–87 season. Hodge held up, for contract reasons, doing voice recordings for a group of Hockey Night billboards. Most Hockey Night people were accustomed to doing billboards and other odd jobs as an unstated part of their overall contracts, which Hough thought were generous enough to cover these extras. When Hodge met Bob Gordon that day at the studio where the audio tracks were to be done, Hodge asked, "Have you got a letter of agreement with you?"

"Letter of agreement? What do you mean?"

"I talked to Frank Selke and told him that under no circumstances am I going to do billboards unless you have a letter of agreement covering extra payment for me to sign and it's already been signed by Frank or Ted."

Bob Gordon phoned Selke, outlined the situation and then turned the phone over to Hodge. He and Selke talked for a few minutes. Selke said he would call back.

One of Bob Gordon's worries was that the studio had only been booked for an hour. He suggested to Hodge that they get started anyway and at least have something done before Selke called.

Hodge: "Let's wait for the call."

They waited. Drank coffee. Finally the call came and Hodge got his verbal guarantee that he'd be paid extra for doing the billboards. The "extra" for billboards was a first, and last, for Hockey Night.

That stand by Hodge was certainly technically his right. Hockey Night's tardiness with contract offers had annoyed everyone, including Mellanby, who had to take the first wave of bitching when contracts were late. But Hodge was the only one to act at that time. ACTRA (Alliance of Canadian Cinema, Television and Radio Artists), the union to which most Hockey Night in Canada talent belongs, was not involved in the dispute over billboards or indeed in much else involving Hockey Night, apparently seeing no need.

The relationship between Bob Gordon and Dave Hodge had its ups and downs. One of the downs came after Harold Ballard had brought Punch Imlach back to the Leafs after he'd been let go by Buffalo. Almost immediately Imlach was in the middle of his well-publicized power struggle with Leaf captain Darryl Sittler, Lanny McDonald and others in the dressing room.

One night a few hours before a game, Hockey Night sought Imlach's okay to have Sittler interviewed by Hodge during the intermission. Imlach refused.

Bob Gordon, often the front end in such matters, then tried for another player.

Imlach said, "Okay, but I want to talk to you first."

At 5 p.m. that day Gordon, Hough and Selke met Imlach in the client room across from the Leaf dressing room. Imlach said, "You can have the other guy, but I don't want any questions asked with regard to the Darryl Sittler situation or the Lanny McDonald situation." McDonald, a very popular player before and for many years thereafter, had just been traded by Imlach to Colorado, causing public protests and a media storm. Imlach spoke angrily about what he considered to be the Sittler-led dressing room's defiance of his authority. Hough and

Selke acted as appeasers. Imlach had the power; if they fought him openly they'd be in trouble, then and later. In the end, Bob Gordon had to pass the word to Hodge that Imlach insisted that the player interview not get into the Sittler or McDonald situation.

Hodge reacted with anger. "How can I go on and not talk about the major story?"

Bob Gordon made a rather crafty argument in the circumstances that maybe the player substituting for Sittler would not want to be the guy who blew into the open the whole Imlach–Sittler situation as it was seen in the dressing room.

He also mentioned such known factors as who ran the club — the owner, Harold Ballard, was backing up Imlach and castigating Sittler — who ran the league and who, in effect, allowed Hockey Night to be in business. In those circumstances, "We've got to be very careful."

Hodge was not impressed, saying he must not ever be put in the position of being ordered not to mention certain things. If ever he was told he couldn't say this, or couldn't say that and the press came to him and asked if he had been censored, "I'm going to tell them yes, I was."

Gordon said he wasn't ordering anything. "Hell, I can't control you when you're on the air, anyway. I've tried and it doesn't work. But be smart enough to consider the other factors."

Hodge was furious with Bob Gordon for being the messenger, and furious with Imlach — whom he didn't like anyway — for sending the message. But the show went off without sweat. Hodge didn't stay away from the issue, but he kept it under control, avoiding the in-depth approach that no doubt he would have preferred, if he could do it without hurting himself and Hockey Night.

Sometimes in such an operation as Hockey Night there is a kind of zaniness. An example was Ward Cornell's gag on Ted Green to put him at ease. Then there was from time to time a cameraman who would spot a voluptuous woman in the crowd shot and pan lovingly up from her ankles and across the revealing miniskirt and somebody in The Truck would be saying, "Don't stop now," and somebody else in The Truck would be laughing, "Okay, guys, some camera get me a male hunk now so we don't get charged with sexism."

Then there was one Christmas special. As long as Bob Gordon was producing the intermissions, he always planned a Christmas show aimed straight at the warmth and goodwill of the season. To play Santa Claus he'd bring from Montreal one of the most censorable after-dinner speakers in the country — Red Storey, broadcaster, raconteur, 1930s Grey Cup star with the Argonauts and one of the great referees of the old six-team NHL. The studio would be decorated with Christmas trees and lights and garlands and bells. In rehearsing the intermission program, Hodge of course was no problem. Storey, being an amateur at this kind of acting, was.

So the Christmas intermission openings would be rehearsed and rehearsed and rehearsed until Storey was letter-perfect in whatever the script called for (once the opening showed Hodge sitting on Santa's knee). Then it would be taped to ensure that it could be shown hazard-free.

One night, the opening had Hodge standing by the Christmas tree extolling the traditional warmth of the season and the happiness Santa brought to children and then, on cue, calling in Santa with a ringing, "Ah! Here's the old fellow now!"

The rehearsals had been going so well that the last time Storey was sent out of the studio to await his cue, Bob Gordon in The Truck decided it was ready to be taped. The order was given in The Truck: Everybody in place. Silence, please. Roll tape. Cue Dave.

Hodge, knowing it was a tape, one planned to go to air later but still a tape, didn't let anybody in on his plan. He went into his opening monologue, Santa was cued, and as Santa walked into the set booming his ho-ho-ho's, Hodge turned to him and said, "Well! Here comes the guzzling old red-faced prick now!"

That tape is still around somewhere. Red first stares aghast at Hodge and then blows up completely, can't stop laughing.

Hodge is laughing so hard that tears are running down his cheeks. The tape can't show the tears of laughter in The Truck. Everybody needed time to compose themselves before they could do another, the real one. That keeper tape, done later, was loose and happy. A lot of laughing. The viewers never knew the joke.

Hodge was much more often a critic of the show than a cheerleader, but there was one memorable exception. The crew was in Minnesota, with Bob Gordon producing and Ron Harrison supposed to fly in from Los Angeles to direct the game. About two hours before face-off Harrison phoned. He was still in Los Angeles. In Harrison's absence Gordon would have to direct, the production's most pressure-filled job. He had very little time to prepare. He knew what had to be done — he'd been sitting in the producer's chair beside the director's for years. But watching and doing are not alike. Openly nervous, he called the crew and talent together and told them what he was up against.

Hodge immediately spoke for those present. "We're all with you, Bobby. If there's anything I can do to help, just ask. I'll do anything I can. We'll get through it together, don't worry."

At game's end, Bob Gordon walked out of The Truck exhausted, walked into the Met Center and went around and thanked each crew member as they were striking the cameras. "I figured we'd done all right, but maybe I'd never really know. Then I walked across the street to the hotel and walked through the lobby and was going past the bar when I heard a call, 'Hey, Bobby!' and saw Hodge breaking away from a group there and coming my way. I didn't really have time to wonder what was happening. Too numb.

"He shook my hand and said, 'I just want you to know that you did a hell of a job tonight. You gained my respect.' I appreciated that, believe me, especially coming from Dave Hodge!"

During Hodge's years with Hockey Night, Saturday night games were only part of his workload. He worked all CTV-CFTO mid-week Hockey Night games, and in 1977 when

CHCH-TV picked up mid-week rights, Hodge was along. For 16 years he'd worked in radio at CFRB, much of that time broadcasting Toronto Argonaut football games, whose radio rights had been bought by CFRB. Eventually his acerbic comments about a rather feckless Argo club of the time had caused the station, on a hefty push from the Argos, to take him off football — an open lack of support from his employers that disenchanted him with CFRB.

In 1986 he quit CFRB to accept a lifetime contract as sports director of Vancouver's CKNW and moved with his wife and their two children to British Columbia. This meant spending at least 10 hours in the air every weekend to fulfill his Hockey Night commitments, usually in the east. Most people would think he was overworked, but the picture that emerges has other elements: besides his prodigious energy, Hodge was a consummate professional, a perfectionist, one who insisted on calling things the way he saw them and did not suffer with equanimity anything that he thought hurt any show he was on, football, hockey or whatever. He was also heavily anti-CBC. Yet his parting was more than a buildup of frustrations over the years. As with any explosion, his required a fuse, a dynamite cap.

This came on Saturday, March 14, 1987, which turned out to be a bad day for any CBC-TV sports fans in Canada who wanted to see every game through to its finish.

That afternoon the CBC was televising the semifinal round of the Canadian Curling championships. Some Hockey Night people, including Hodge, Bob Cole and a few others, had gathered in the client room at the Gardens to watch a particularly close match between Newfoundland, Bob Cole's home province, and British Columbia, Hodge's home province.

There's a clock on the wall. When it ticked over to 6 p.m., with only three rocks to go in the game, and all those present following every shot with cheers or jeers, CBC cut away and, for *most* CBC stations across the country, joined coverage of a New Democratic party convention in Montreal. *Most*, but not all: in Edmonton curling fans sitting on the edge of their seats awaiting those final few rocks suddenly found themselves screaming with rage at an episode of "Star Trek."

When the curling vanished from the screen there was a moment of stunned silence, then an anti-CBC outburst, not only from Hodge, Cole and others in the Gardens client room but from coast to coast. For 90 minutes CBC stations from Vancouver to St. John's were bombarded with angry calls from curling fans who had watched all afternoon and then been robbed of the climax.

The reaction should have burned CBC ears. Whether it had a discernible impact on anybody in authority is a moot point, something not to bet the farm on. But that was part of the buildup to the next CBC national network sports show two hours later, Hockey Night in Canada, Dave Hodge, host.

It had been a bad season for the Toronto crew, the Leafs going nowhere. Hodge had been having strained relations with executive producer Don Wallace. When the Toronto game that night ended at 10:35, Hockey Night went to its backup game still in progress, Philadelphia at Montreal.

One CBC rule, known to Hodge and everyone else at Hockey Night, was that whatever was happening in a hockey game at 11 p.m., the network would cut away to news unless whoever was in authority for the CBC that night ruled otherwise.

In this case, just before 11, the Montreal game, tied at 3-3 and heading for overtime, went to a commercial after which overtime would begin immediately. Toronto cut in to cover with its own commercial. Somewhere in there Hodge inquired whether the game — with only the mandatory five-minute overtime remaining — would be seen to its conclusion. Someone at the CBC could have so ruled. This had even been done a couple of years earlier, CBC carrying a U.S. Open tennis semifinal to a conclusion on the grounds that "what you start, you finish", thus knocking half of an Argonaut-Edmonton football game off most of the network. But Hodge was told no, news was next, and that he was to announce that due to network commitments it was goodbye overtime.

He made that announcement and then addressed those viewers who might have thought they were going to see the rest of the game from Montreal. His message was that the powers that make these decisions had done it again, and something to the effect of "That's the CBC for you!" And he flipped his pencil disgustedly into the air.

In the client room, those who had been waiting for the rest of the Montreal game were stunned. The news came on. Bob Gordon wondered if he should go in and speak to Hodge, but thought not. "He was obviously so hot that anything said now would just light the fuse." Others involved with the show began to straggle into the client room, saying little, all knowing what had happened.

Finally Hodge burst in, angry but also obviously disheartened. "It's typical of this goddamn network!" he said. "They have no idea of what they're doing!"

Then he grabbed his hat and coat and left.

The following day the CBC announced his suspension and temporary, which soon became permanent, replacement as Hockey Night host and as Don Cherry straight man by Ron MacLean. For some weeks the palavering went on, well covered by the media.

With an apology, Hodge could have been back in business, but that isn't his way. He did take pains to make clear that this was not, as some contended, a sports type arguing for more sports at the expense of news.

"If it were the reverse, a political convention interrupted 10 minutes before the final vote, I'd be even madder. But the fact is that if you're covering something that doesn't always end in a certain time frame, you have to build in some flexibility. Don't start something you can't finish."

The CBC having done exactly that twice in one day, Hodge's "That's the CBC for you!" was about right.

All the same, and perhaps inevitably in the time-honored tradition of how monolithic corporations deal with outspoken individuals, Hodge had worked his last game for Hockey Night in Canada. Two and a half years later, still banned by the

The Good Guys and the Bad Guys

CBC but back on hockey as host of Global's NHL coverage, mostly games involving the Leafs, he made a mildly cutting but quite accurate remark about the Leafs that offended Harold Ballard, who demanded — and got — his removal from those games, as well.

Chapter 13
Memories, Memories . . .

> *If Hockey Night in Canada wants to cut
> costs, I have this great idea. Chris Cuthbert,
> the young Edmonton broadcaster, can replace
> Ron MacLean, Dick Irvin, Bob Cole and
> Harry Neale* — all by himself.
> — Ken McKee, TV and Radio sports
> columnist, *Toronto Star*, April 20, 1988

During the NHL playoffs in the spring of 1988, Chris Cuthbert of Edmonton of his own free will ignored the old army dictum: Never volunteer. The idea is that if something needs doing, but is so nasty one way or another that the commanding officer doesn't want to order it done, he can call for volunteers — some eager beaver might step forward and solve the problem. Hockey broadcasting is not war, but . . .

In April 1988, Hockey Night in Canada came up a little short-staffed in handling several sets of Stanley Cup playoffs. In Montreal on Monday, April 18, Montreal and Boston were squared off to begin their Adams division final; as were Washington–New Jersey in the Patrick division, at Washington's home ice in Landover, Maryland. The Montreal game was tabbed for national television, with Washington–New Jersey the backup.

In Calgary the next night, Calgary and Edmonton would start their Smythe division final on the national network.

Hockey Night, needing someone who would go standby in Landover to do brief update inserts for the Montreal game, thought the right man for the job was Chris Cuthbert, a rising young host very popular in the West. CBC Edmonton, however, insisted that Cuthbert not be snatched off the Alberta series. The tug-of-war was settled by Cuthbert himself. He figured out that it was possible to do *both* jobs — fly to Washington, drive to Landover, voice 15-second updates and game-coverage inserts, which would be produced there and fed into Montreal's national show by Hockey Night producer Jim Hough, Ted's son and a busy free-lance TV sports director and producer in his own right. Then Cuthbert could drive to the airport, fly to Calgary the next morning and host the game there that night.

Having figured this all out, as he said a day or so later, "I was dumb enough to volunteer. My wife thinks I'm crazy. I think Hockey Night people do, too."

When he teamed up with Hough at the Capital Center at Landover they found that although advance arrangements had been made, there was no room in any of the normal broadcast positions, which were full to overflowing. He found a table and had it set up in front of an exit beside a section of crowded seats while Hough had the requisite camera, telephone lines and technical facilities installed, then retreated to his command post in The Truck. The game began and had been on for a few minutes when well to the north of Landover something happened that drastically changed what they had thought would be a pretty undemanding assignment. A massive power blackout hit Quebec, leaving all of Montreal and much of the province in darkness. There was no power for television transmission. The national broadcast then switched smoothly to the New Jersey–Washington game, where the first period was just ending.

That switch was about the only smooth part for Cuthbert that night. There he was at his table in the crowd, Hough in The Truck. They hadn't been counting on doing more than an insert or two and a couple of minutes of play-by-play at most during intermissions in the Montreal game. They now knew that they were on the network but at first didn't know why. When they did find out they figured it was just another of those Quebec blackouts or a satellite problem and would end soon; they always had before. Chris was on the air with no action on the ice to help him make the transition from a lone backup fill-in to the only guy on the Hockey Night network, a 15-minute intermission to fill, no guests lined up, no script to signal commercial breaks, knowing little or nothing about what was going on in Montreal or how long he'd be on the air or anything else. His only link was Jim in The Truck on the phone to Montreal's Truck to find out what was going on.

"That first intermission was terrible," Chris recalls. "A straight fill. The Caps TV crew had assigned a floor director to help us out. The floor director was an apprentice, about 20 years old. She and Jimmy Hough — working from The Truck by phone with the help of the Washington crew — finally scooped up a couple of guests. George McPhee was one of them, a New Jersey player not dressed that night. They hustled him up. Hough thought his name was Mike and said that to me on the intercom just as George asked me what my name was. This was just at the point when Jimmy was saying 'Mike' and somehow in the confusion all George heard was the name Mike, so he called me Mike all through the interview.

"Also, I was still trying to figure out why we had become the national game. At the same time I was being handed scores from Montreal, so I knew they were playing and couldn't figure out why we weren't showing it. I was giving Montreal scores on the air thinking that the listeners must think I'd gone crazy and thinking that if the Montreal game was still going on, why were they seeing pictures from Washington? It wasn't until well into the second period that Jim told me what had happened and that we would be on for the rest of the night.

"If that wasn't enough, the fire marshal sent people in during the second period to remove my table! The floor director was doing her best trying to hold them off. I was calling the game with this uproar in the background. They actually moved the table a couple of feet. Fortunately the crowd where we were was very friendly, and that helped get us out of that one."

There was another matter, but this one carried some luck with it. Because Cuthbert had thought he was going to that game mainly for updates to the Montreal game, he hadn't done his usual eight-hour pregame preparation.

"But about three hours before game time I got guilt pangs and did sort of a cram, as if I was cramming for a exam. If I hadn't, I might have been in real trouble. A lot of what I'd crammed, about players and everything else, helped give me something to talk about. For instance, Sam McMaster was Washington's assistant director of player recruitment. Normally I don't cram up on people in that kind of a job because I never expect to need it. But for some reason in my cram that night I had read Sam McMaster's bio in the Washington media guide. Lo, he turns up as an intermission guest, and when he walked up I say, 'Sam, how are you?' as if we'd known one another for years."

In total, Cuthbert talked nonstop — except for commercials — that night for 155 minutes; play-by-play, intermissions, arguing with fire marshals, taking Jim Hough's cues on commercials.

The shots of him, in retrospect, were funny. With no proper lighting, sometimes he looked like a sort of worried guy talking like mad in a coal bin. But his face and voice became known across the hockey world that one night in a way that can only be compared to an immersion course. By the time he ended with an absolute tour de force, when you think of it, a 30-minute wrap-up, everyone watching playoff television across Canada certainly knew the face and voice of Chris Cuthbert and could not help but admire how he had coped.

Still, he says, "I think I screwed up the very last line on the air. I wanted to end it by saying, 'The power failure in Montreal prevented us from bringing you the Montreal–Boston game.' But when I started to say that, I couldn't think of the word 'prevent' I was so exhausted. So instead I just kind of smiled and shrugged as if to say that's it, and we went off the air."

When he got to his hotel in Washington, there were a lot of calls from people in the business. He was still so fired up that he couldn't really get to sleep. Then it was time to climb out of bed and catch the early-morning flight west. In Calgary he just wanted to get to bed, have a little nap before doing his host job in the Calgary–Edmonton game. Instead, there were 15 or 20 phone calls, which he answered.

"Then I got to the rink and actually for the only time in my life found myself the center of attention. Even though the Calgary and Edmonton teams were right there, ready to start their series, everybody was coming over to talk to me.

"Eventually I kind of hid out in the studio and thought that if this is what these guys go through, guys that play the game every day, maybe I don't like it — nice to hear, but overwhelming."

* * * * *

*Could you tell me whatever happened to
Billy Hewitt, and what he's doing now?*
— question to a CBC Radio sports show

To answer the second half of the question first, the easy part, Bill and his wife, Barbara, live near Sunderland, Ontario, northeast of Toronto, on what he used to call his farm but now is more properly described as a country estate. After a lot of renovation they have a lovely home, pool, well-tended rolling acres, a pond where ducks and geese drop in and stay awhile. Even though the Hewitts and visitors usually leave the pond undisturbed, Bill can always tell you how many mallards and teal and whatever else is flying are in today, because the pond's closed-circuit television camera pipes the constant action to a

Memories, Memories

screen in Bill's family room. He has a small memorabilia-filled office in a separate building and seems to enjoy the role of country squire. He scarcely ever sees any of the people he worked with for a quarter century on Hockey Night in Canada; often invited to various functions, but rarely accepting. This is by choice.

The first part of the question, what happened, takes longer to tell.

Billy Hewitt was born in 1928. From when he was six or seven years old he used to plead with his father to take him to the games on Saturday nights. The famous Foster would set some small job that a small boy could do to earn going with his dad to Maple Leaf Gardens and sitting with him in the gondola, literally growing up with the Leafs always in his life.

Beginning in 1936 when he was eight, he always called the play-by-play over the coast-to-coast radio network for a few minutes on what was called Young Canada Night — a time around Christmas when season-ticket subscribers were urged to bring their kids or, anyway, somebody's kids, to the game. He always knew his career would be in broadcasting.

Once in 1985, a few months after his father's death, he told a friend, "I read all these books by people who can't wait to tell about what jerks their famous parents were. Mine would be a little different — about how to grow up in the shadow of a famous father and love every minute of it." It was in the late 1950s when Bill, by then experienced in calling junior hockey and occasionally filling in for Foster on Leaf games, succeeded Foster on Hockey Night television.

Inevitably there were comparisons. The two voices were almost identical, but there was debate about which was the better. In the mid-1960s Peter Gzowski, long before he had perfected his own broadcasting technique of constructive stammering, wrote in *Maclean's*: "Bill Hewitt not only fails to improve the game with his commentary — he makes it slightly less interesting." If Bill was stung by this he never showed it. After all, it could have been worse. He remembered that 25 years earlier another eventually famous Canadian, writer Ralph

Allen, had complained that there were two games at the Gardens every Saturday night, the one on the ice and the one Foster broadcast.

The Billy Hewitt that most people on Hockey Night got to know in the later 1950s, through the 1960s, 1970s and into the early 1980s, was not an enigma. He was not what some people call "deep". He was more interested in talking hunting and fishing than talking art, politics, writing or broadcasting.

He had an open and friendly manner with players and with most of his colleagues, but these were mainly surface relationships. He tried, but couldn't seem to get close to others on the show. That might have been one reason that friends outside of hockey altogether sometimes traveled with him on trips, in turn lessening his direct personal contacts with the people he worked with — although Brian McFarlane, his color man, was an exception. One of Billy's frequent traveling companions was a policeman. On the road he spent a lot of time away from the normal hockey crowd. When his first marriage broke up he is said to have been shattered, feeling lost, showing what one called "a terrible personal anguish." He increased his drinking for a while, but never missed or fumbled a broadcast. For a while before his second marriage, his fiancée, well-liked, often traveled with him.

One assessment was that he constantly had the image of his father to try to follow. His conversation fairly often was Dad this, Dad that, natural enough in the circumstances. On the show he also tended to have elders to whom he deferred — Ward Cornell and Jack Dennett among them. Ted Hough was very close to his father, best friends from beginning to end, so Hough also was a kind of father figure. It seemed to some that Bill couldn't take a step anywhere within the bounds of Hockey Night and be outside his father's control.

Despite this, when it came to his job, play-by-play, people who regularly were charged with breaking down each telecast and reviewing the play-by-play work of Danny Gallivan, Dan Kelly, even Foster, felt that nobody was as good as Bill at anticipating a play and seeing what actually happened. In many instances where he described a play in a way that others disagreed with they'd check the replay in slow motion and most often confirm his version.

"Nine times out of 10 he'd be right and us wrong," one colleague said. "Maybe we'd seen it differently in The Truck, or Brian McFarlane right beside him had seen it differently. Billy somehow had the eagle eye, which together with his keen sense of anticipation, made for very few actual game mistakes on the air."

This was especially true in his first 10 years, when Hockey Night was covering the old six-team league. In those days it was easier to get to know the players. From skating styles, hairstyles, the way they wore their pants or sweaters or shoulder pads, picking up names was routine. This changed somewhat with the NHL's 1967 expansion. One criticism was that Billy simply did not apply himself successfully to learning the names of 120 or so new players. And habits he had formed earlier didn't help. He didn't like attending pregame meetings, and when he did he would disappear immediately afterward. If a meeting ended at, say, five-thirty — where today's play-by-play men and color men usually sit down for two hours, sometimes in the broadcast booth, to study their notes and refresh their memories on characteristics of the players they'd be seeing — Billy would disappear back to his nearby apartment and not show up again until around seven-thirty when the teams came on the ice for their pregame skate.

Many broadcasters find The Truck's constant stream of orders and advice and commercial inserts they get in their earpieces to be a distraction. Danny Gallivan sometimes turned off his headpiece entirely and also liked to grip a dead old-time hand mike while he worked. This resulted in the oft-told story about the time that Gallivan, when he had to cough, held the dead hand mike away from his mouth and coughed right into his headpiece mike, blowing listeners in The Truck and elsewhere off their chairs. In contrast, Billy loved his earpiece and would say so.

He wanted to know everything that was going on in The Truck, what camera shots were being called for, what replay had been ordered. "Gee, you guys are busy down there," he'd say. The general assessment was that the earpiece, the sense of being in on everything, helped him and for a while seemed to make him more responsive in other ways.

It might be too easy a judgment to say that many of Billy's problems were personal. The breakup of his first marriage was one. The pervasive influence of his father was another, plus his sense that some people on the show actively didn't like him. Dave Hodge customarily saw him as a nonperson. Ralph Mellanby saw him as one of the show's elements that had to be improved or replaced. Ted Hough was devoted to Foster and therefore protective of Billy's status, so whatever his situation with the show it was not going to be ended as long as Hough was in charge. Whether Billy thought of his situation in those terms can't be accurately assessed. Whatever the situation, as time went on he became more withdrawn. Once there seemed to be a break, what one associate described in these words: "This was a time when Billy almost broke out of his paternal handcuffs."

The occasion was not directly related to Hockey Night, except in what it did for his general outlook on his life. He signed up for flying lessons at Buttonville Airport just north of Toronto, intending to get his private pilot's license. All hands at Hockey Night were surprised. Those who cared about him personally said it seemed to change and enliven him, bring a measure of maturity, give him a sense of purpose that few could remember him having previously.

One day Bob Gordon, trying to get in touch with Billy, tried the airport and was put on to Billy's instructor, Gordon Clark.

"How's he doing?" Bob Gordon asked.

"He's coming along fine," Clark said. "It'll take him a while but eventually he'll get it."

Then in a casual conversation between Bob Gordon and Foster, the flying lessons came up. "I don't know whether it's the right thing for Billy to do," Foster said doubtfully. "Seems silly to me, Billy learning to fly."

Time passed, a couple of months, and one day Bob Gordon asked Billy how the flying lessons were coming. "Great," he said firmly. "I'm enjoying it immensely. I'm going to get my license."

His flying lessons had gone on for maybe eight months, during which time many on Hockey Night had mentioned how the flying experience had perked Billy up, made him more outgoing, more involved with the show and its people than he'd ever been.

"You must be proud of Billy," Gordon said to Foster. "Looks like his flying lessons are really a good thing for him."

"It doesn't show a great deal of responsibility," Foster said.

Still, Bob Gordon continued to believe what he believed — that the flying had been a wonderful thing to happen to Billy from a morale standpoint. Then he had an idea. In filmed intermission features on Hockey Night people, they'd never been able to find a good human-interest peg for a piece on Billy, something that said what he was like privately and what he did in his spare time. Gordon suggested to Brian McFarlane that they get a crew and go up with Billy, do a story on his flying lessons, an interview with the instructor, shoot film from the air and on the ground and use it on an intermission.

Brian thought it was a good idea. So did Billy. One can imagine the shot list: Billy arriving at the airport, talking to his flight instructor, being briefed on the weather, inspecting the aircraft and then taking off, the flying instructor beside him and Brian and the cameraman packed into the rear seat.

They shot what they thought was a good show — including Billy bringing the plane in to land and Brian getting out and kissing the ground on his safe return, with Billy laughing uproariously. They edited the film, put music to it and a voice track, plus an old film clip that Brian had dug out — something right out of an old Keystone Kops comedy showing a stunt pilot flying a 1920s-era aircraft through a barn. The voice track reported kiddingly, "That is the kind of thing Billy did before he got his license."

A few weeks later Billy did get his license and the piece was used on the next intermission. Everybody thought it was great — except Foster. He was furious, thought flying was too dangerous, anyway, and thought that the comedy bit at the end had made Billy look foolish. The general opinion was the opposite: that in the feature Billy had shown a personality, a human look.

A week later before another game Bob Gordon asked Billy, "When are you going to fly again?"

A very dour Billy said, "I can't. No more. My dad's made me stop."

Gordon was incredulous. "Your dad? Made you stop?"

"He got me over to his place and said that as second in command of the Hewitt family and eventual successor to him it was very irresponsible for me to fly, and he forbids me to do it anymore."

Billy was 45 at the time, being forbidden by his father to do something that he had done on his own, carried out successfully with an eagerness that he never quite recovered. He carried on for years, doing parts of his job as well as ever but still bugged by the fact that with continuing NHL expansion he was finding more difficult than ever his job of trying to keep on top of new players, new names, new conditions.

At the beginning of the 1981–82 season when he was 53, he was calling an exhibition game for CHCH-TV when he became very ill, could not distinguish one player from another. He had been losing weight for weeks and was to lose 50 pounds in total before the weight loss was stopped. Some reports were that, at this beginning of one more hockey season, having never missed a hockey assignment in his life, he had suffered a form of breakdown. The exact nature has never been identified publicly. For that entire season Ted Hough held his job open for him while others — Dave Hodge, Dan Kelly and Danny Gallivan — took up the slack. But eventually it was up to Bill to decide what to do about going back to hockey.

He'd had a lot of time, that whole year off, to think about his life and what he'd like to do and was able to do and should do. One gets the impression that he'd pretty well made up his mind, but before he made his decision known he went to talk to his father. Reading between the lines in later conversations, Billy dreaded ever going back, but might have if Foster had said so. Foster heard him out and then said, "Bill, if you want to retire now, if you've had enough, that's fine by me."

So he retired. He has put on weight since. He laughs a lot, but does not reminisce anything like the way old hockey people often do. It might be Goldie (for Bob Goldham) this or Brian (for McFarlane) that, mentioning people he is fond of, but mainly he'd rather make a visitor a good cup of coffee and turn on his closed-circuit television to show at that very moment a new flight of mallards, flaps down, slip-sliding in to splash into his pond. He and Barbara go to Florida for a few weeks in the roughest part of the year, and to their cottage in northern Ontario for a few weeks in the summer for the fishing. He never goes to a hockey game.

* * * * *

> *The Leafs, Foster Hewitt and Imperial Oil; the team, the broadcaster and the sponsor. A Holy Trinity.*
>
> — Jack Batten, writer

In 1976, a few days after Imperial announced its withdrawal from Hockey Night's sponsorship, Jack Batten, journalist, broadcaster and novelist, wrote the following in the now defunct *Canadian* magazine:

> As a boy, I had arrived at a series of beliefs that were pure, immutable and utterly comforting. Take my father's role as

volunteer Second World War air-raid warden. I believed that on practice raid nights, when he went into the darkened streets with his steel helmet, arm band and special flashlight that shone a red beam, he was personally protecting our North Toronto neighborhood from the threat of the Luftwaffe. I felt secure. I also thought that the people and values that were acting as silent and all-powerful protection for me included Joe Louis, punctuality, dentists, George Formby, always wearing a hat on school days (in my case a navy-blue cap with a tiny precise peak), Cordell Hull and earmuffs. I had strange gods and a lot of misinformation. I believed that only one company in the whole world made and sold gasoline. Imperial.

That last belief, the one about Imperial, held on the longest. . . . I remained loyal to Imperial even after I discovered the existence of Shell, Texaco and Sunoco. When I bought a car, I stopped at the Esso sign. My first credit card was Imperial's number 251 332 456 2. I figured I owed the company a lot.

Announcer: "Your Imperial Oil hockey broadcast, bringing you Foster Hewitt."

Foster Hewitt: "Hello Canada and hockey fans in the United States and Newfoundland."

For millions of us, those two lines spoken into the radio at nine o'clock Toronto time every winter Saturday night, held more promise than any other in the English language. The promise lay in more than just the Leaf hockey game, described by good old Hewitt in his nasal, flat, accurate style. There were also our other friends, Jack Dennett and the "Hot Stove League", to reassure us that all was well in middle Canada. Jack Dennett talked about Imperial products in weighty tones that probably should have been used exclusively for the announcement of D-day. We respected him though, the way you respected your minister or Winston Churchill, and we revered the products.

The men of the "Hot Stove League" seemed wiser than members of Mr. Mackenzie King's cabinet: Bobby Hewitson,

the chirpy little sports editor of the *Toronto Telegram*;
Elmer Ferguson from Montreal, heavy with years and
erudition; lovable Harold Cotton, a scout for the Boston
Bruins. Wes McKnight was their moderator, impartial, even
kind of distant. Once on the show, between periods, he asked
Hewitson a question. Hewitson answered at length.
McKnight said thanks, and then asked Hewitson the same
question. I guess he lost his place in the script. We didn't
mind. We didn't mind the fussing that Fergy went through
when he named the three stars at the end of each game. Why
three stars, by the way? Why not two? Or four? Because
Imperial happened to peddle a brand of gasoline called Three
Star. That was okay, too.

When the program went on television Hockey Night in
Canada was ruined. The TV people moved the "Hot Stove
League" onto a studio set complete with potbellied stove,
grocery counter and lovable Harold Cotton in a funny plaid
shirt. It lacked dignity. They shouldn't have done that to
Cotton.

And a new element entered the broadcasts — controversy.
Nobody disturbed us with controversy on radio, but a few
years after TV arrived, a Leaf owner, John Bassett, had one of
the broadcasters, Scott Young, bounced off the program. It
seems that in his *Globe and Mail* sports column Young had
suggested the proposed sale of Frank Mahovlich to Chicago
for $1 million was a lot of bunk. "We told the program,"
Bassett said, "that (a) what Scott had written was detrimental
to hockey and (b) he was an inefficient television personality.
At the end of the season, I guess they saw our case."

Inefficient? In the radio days we considered inefficiency a
virtue.

* * * * *

> *Olmstead said he wouldn't do it for $500.*
> — Bob Gordon, negotiating
> an Esso commercial

"This would be 1961 or so, I guess, when Bert Olmstead was one of the backbone players on the Leafs heading for their run of three straight Stanley Cups. He had a big working farm out west, and Imperial asked me to be the intermediary in approaching Olmstead to do a grease-gun commercial using one of their products. This was going to be a one-minute commercial on Bert Olmstead showing how to use Imperial Oil grease guns on farm equipment, and I'd been told I could offer Olmstead $500 to do it.

"When I broached the subject he said, 'No, I won't do it for $500.' I said, 'Well, what would it take, Mr. Olmstead?' He said he didn't want the money, but would do it for a year's supply of grease — I can't remember how many barrels that was — and 10 free grease guns. Olmstead was the first ever in my knowledge to negotiate with Imperial and win his point.

"I went back to Imperial and they were delighted."

* * * * *

> *We are first of all responsible businessmen.*
> — Clarence Campbell, one night in St. Louis

Until 1964 when Leafs won the Stanley Cup in a game at home on April 25, the playoffs never had lasted that long. The norm was more like April 14, 15, 16, 18 — in 1956, April 10. Later in the 1960s the playoffs began getting into early May, middle May, late May, in 1987 ending May 31.

In the mid-1970s when Clarence Campbell was still NHL president and playoffs were running progressively longer, one night in the St. Louis pressroom Frank D. Selke, then near the end of his second decade in hockey but fairly new with Canadian Sports Network, asked Clarence Campbell a question. The conversation was not recorded, but eyewitnesses remember it going pretty well this way:

Selke: "Clarence, the playoffs are getting later and later. How late can you possibly let these things go?"

Campbell: "Frank, you yourself know that if a hockey team is successful and winning and has a chance at a championship, the interest is there and there's no reason why it couldn't go on for a long time."

Selke: "But you're getting into the summer market. It's late spring now."

Campbell: "It doesn't really matter. When you have a city with a market of hockey fans, whether an arena is air-conditioned or not, it doesn't matter that there are only two teams left to go for the Stanley Cup. Those two cities, if nobody else, will be keen. The arenas will be filled. You could take it to the middle of July. The interest would be just as high in July for those two teams to play off for the championship as it would be in April of May or even June."

Selke: "You mean you can really see something like that happening?"

Campbell: "As long as the interest is there, I can see anything happening. We are first of all responsible businessmen and responsible businessmen will do all that they can to sell their product, and to sell your product you've got to have a winner, so it can go on as long as it takes to get a winner."

So now you know.

The next morning, however, was an off-day, and some of those who had been listening to Campbell in the pressroom after the game the night before — Selke, Dennett, Gordon and Tim Ryan, all television people — finished breakfast and ambled out into the hotel lobby. There, as usual, before people scattered to go to the Arena to watch the morning skates, or do interviews, or write columns or whatever, the hockey crowd was talking up a storm about this play and that play the night before, or about who was winning elsewhere in the playoffs, or what was the betting on what would happen next.

It was a nice day outside. St. Louis can be very pleasant in early May. Selke looked around and said to the world at large, "This is all bullshit, let's go out and look at what everything is really all about."

Someone said, "Where do you want to go?"

Selke: "Let's go to the zoo."

These four headed out to the St. Louis zoo at 10 in the morning and paid visits to every animal and bird and sat on benches, relaxed and easy, eating hot dogs and drinking coffee or soft drinks. Time seemed to pass very quickly before six o'clock came and they returned to the hotel, not having said, as far as anyone can remember, one word of hockey all day.

* * * * *

> *Babe Pratt was like the Don Cherry in those days, except he did it right to the players' faces.*
> — Ron Harrison, then Vancouver producer for Hockey Night in Canada

"In Vancouver in 1970," Harrison recalls, "the club's first year, CBC had to expand in sports to handle NHL hockey. No problem with the talent — Vancouver had experienced people. Ted Reynolds would be host, Jimmy Robson play-by-play, one of the best ever, still is, but declines to leave Vancouver. And Meeker would be there sometimes.

"But production was another thing. Jobs were open. Retzlaff told me I should go. The way he put it was that since nobody had produced hockey out of there I'd get lots of experience, do things it might take years for me to get to in Toronto. So I went. A few times at first, Retzlaff, then Mellanby sometimes, then

Don Wallace, would come out and produce and I would direct, which means I was breaking in directing hockey with some experience beside me.

"And then there was Babe Pratt. He had the title of assistant to the vice president of the Canucks at first, later, publicity assistant, but when I was there he was supposed to do our highlights. He was sort of like Don Cherry: he'd been in hockey, in tough as a player, and hadn't changed much. He was a piece of work.

"In this antiquated little Truck we had then he'd sit watching the screen and in those years Vancouver didn't have a good team, they'd get blown out, they'd play terrible. Babe would sit there screaming and yelling and swearing at the TV; he had a mouth like you wouldn't believe. And before they renovated the Pacific Coliseum, when the teams would come out they'd pass right by The Truck and Babe would walk out and call them everything in the book right to their faces. He did that every night. Every night."

* * * * *

The first time we tried color at Maple Leaf Gardens a lot of players complained about the bright lights, and some of them went out and put on black makeup, smudged charcoal on their cheeks under their eyes.

— a recollection

In the middle 1960s everybody in hockey knew that color had to come eventually, even though in Canada color sets in private homes were as yet uncommon. The only time color had even been tested on a hockey broadcast had been in the U.S. Ted Hough and others found out all they could about the necessity for much brighter lights and other technical matters, such as what the hot lights would do to the ice. In Toronto the chosen date for the first test was March 25, 1965, for a midweek game between Montreal and Toronto that would be handled by CFTO for CTV, with the color going on closed circuit only within the Gardens, while being shown in black and white on CFTO and the CTV network.

MGM in the United States was one of the few independent television outfits with a color truck. Hough rented it. The show took three days to get ready, starting on the Monday evening before the Wednesday game. The color cameras were huge, weighing about three hundred pounds each. Hough and Bob Gordon from Hockey Night met with Stafford Smythe, Harold Ballard and Punch Imlach to make decisions on such thing as camera placement and whether the lights had to be considerably augmented and the ice colored a light blue. On Tuesday with the lighting and camera installations going on all day, Leafs did their morning workout elsewhere.

After most of the cameras were in, there was one left over. Hough made what later was found to be an inspired choice. He suggested that a good place for it would be at the south end of the Gardens right behind the goal for close shots there. The Gardens agreed to build a platform for it.

One problem was that in adjusting the ice-making to allow for the heat of the lights, the ice had been made so cold that it was cracking. Accordingly, the temperature of the ice had to be changed. Still, in the morning skate that day, Kent Douglas, a Toronto defenseman, decided that with the ice so brittle and the lights so bright, he was going to flip pucks up into the air all night. The ice was less brittle by game time, but Douglas stuck to his plan and one of his airborne flips almost fooled Charlie Hodge in the Montreal net.

But one element of luck — Hough's placement of the end-zone camera — gave the game a fillip that could not have been foreseen. Late in the game a penalty shot was called, Montreal on Toronto, whose goal was at the south end right in front of that camera. The sight of Montreal's Yvan Cournoyer skating in on Johnny Bower in the Toronto net for "He shoots! Bower saves!" could not have been improved if Hough and Bower had written the script themselves. Hough would have been too busy, anyway. He'd spent the intermissions arranging studio shots of various Molson and Imperial brands so that his favorite sponsors could see their products in living color.

Color tapes of that game were taken to New York for a major presentation in the Plaza Hotel to show U.S. networks and advertising agencies the look of hockey's near future. The hope was that seeing what color did for hockey would help sell the game. The MGM color truck was required in those days just to play tapes, so it was brought in from New Jersey for the event, cables laid into the Plaza and television monitors spread around a ballroom.

Comedian Johnny Wayne, well known to U.S. audiences through Wayne and Shuster shots on the Ed Sullivan show, was master of ceremonies. It was a big deal, well done. There was no immediate flood of U.S. networks clamoring for hockey, but the throng of potential customers did get a good game, good drinks, good food and a sight of the kind of hockey that, although nobody knew it then, was to saturate cable systems and communications satellites 25 years later. At the end Clarence Campbell, on behalf of the NHL, thanked Hough: "Ted, you've served hockey well again, and I appreciate it."

Chapter 14

The Molson-ization and CBC-ization of Hockey Night in Canada

> *We hire Molstar under a six-year contract signed in 1988 to produce the games and therefore in that client relationship we dictate certain things. . . . As you saw last year we got rid of the Hockey Night in Canada jackets and put on our CBC jackets [also] ensuring that CBC people host all the broadcasts.*
> —Alan Clark, head of CBC Sports, 1990

> *They get rid of those distinctive Hockey Night in Canada jackets that Foster Hewitt wore and every topflight Hockey Night guy wore from when they were invented, and replace them with CBC jackets that you can see on any bleeping CBC sports show from curling to darts, and they have the nerve to use that slogan, The Tradition Continues.*
> —Ralph Mellanby in an interview, 1989

Those conflicting statements represent, not at all subtly, how much the drive and direction of Hockey Night in

Canada has changed as a direct result of the first "brotherly" partnership between the CBC and the Canadian Sports Network in 1976.

Until then and for nearly 10 years thereafter Hough, as head of CSN, was still the court of last resort. His company was in sole control of the broadcast rights, putting the shows together and in effect hiring the CBC to put the games on the air. Even before the 1976 declaration of brotherhood, CBC as the largest customer usually got most of what it wanted — mainly unquestioned rights to the Saturday night and playoff games. After 1976 that situation still prevailed, with CSN dealing off non-CBC games to other stations or networks wherever a good deal could be made. For the usual reasons — good product and good management — CSN always showed a profit, which as a wholly owned subsidiary wound up in MacLaren Advertising's year-end statements. What happened next was simply that Molson, through its sponsor fees the main contributor to CSN's profitability, decided that it did not wish to continue helping out the MacLaren profit picture year after year. So it looked for a way to cut out the middleman and take over CSN itself.

Asked what they were offering to pay for this acquisition, Molson's said in effect, "Nothing. We'll just take the people off your hands and guarantee them employment."

The vehicle by which this was accomplished bore the name of a successful U.S. company, Ohlmeyer Communications, half-owned by Molson, the other half by the food-based conglomerate, Nabisco. Ohlmeyer had been a successful independent until bought by Nabisco in an earlier diversification program. Under the Ohlmeyer name, in 1986 Molson and Nabisco became the successors to Canadian Sports Network, that name disappearing into sports history.

What ensued was a shakeout of staff in a fairly small way. Some landed on their feet, some didn't. Among core people were Hough, whose retirement was scheduled for 1988, and Frank Selke, for 1989. Bob Gordon's employment, after 33 years was terminated in 1987, with about 18 months of severance. Nancy Carroll, who had been Horler's secretary away back when and had assisted Don Wallace in producing the U.S. hockey network where Don Cherry as a TV personality first saw the light of day, went back to MacLaren.

One thing didn't change much during the brief Ohlmeyer interlude: for 10 years CSN had been a thorn in the CBC's side, and that was not altered much under Ohlmeyer. Molson orchestrated the next change, helped by Nabisco's deciding it did not really belong in the television programming business and allowing Ohlmeyer to buy himself back out. When he did so, Molson bought the Nabisco portion of Ohlmeyer Canada and converted it to Molstar Communications as a wholly owned subsidiary now of Molson's. Soon after, executive producer Don Wallace, feeling uncertain about his future with Molstar, negotiated a deal by which he moved to The Sports Network (TSN) — where he joined, among others, Gordon Craig, the man who, when at the CBC, had relieved Retzlaff of his duties as head of CBC Sports.

These changes left Molstar on the production side and CBC on the network side trying to negotiate a new contract in the spring of 1988, the negotiations being somewhat at a standstill. Molstar (read: Molson Breweries of Canada Limited) was up against certain unacceptable CBC attitudes, and vice versa.

In early June, at exactly the time Ted Hough officially took his retirement, their deadlocked negotiations resulted in a front-page flap: news that CTV network had made an offer to Molstar that, if accepted, would make CTV Molstar's prime broadcasting client and shut out the CBC entirely. One must assume that caught the CBC's attention.

A front-page story by sportswriter Al Strachan in the *Globe and Mail* of May 31 was headed CBC CLOSE TO LOSING SATURDAY HOCKEY. The opening paragraphs said that by the time the next National Hockey League season rolled around in October, Saturday night hockey would almost certainly be shown in Canada exclusively on CTV. Molson Breweries of Canada Limited, parent of Molstar and largest single sponsor of hockey, was finding its association with the CBC "too restrictive." Molson wanted a higher profile on the telecasts, including having the Molson name as part of the show's title. One unnamed Molson executive said the CBC had a condescending and interfering attitude toward sports. Aware that the Dave Hodge firing still rankled with the public, the same unnamed executive, or another, pointed out that it was the CBC, not Molstar, that had led to the dismissal of Dave Hodge and that a similar case of "insisting that the start of its nightly news not be delayed by even three minutes [to finish a game] had led to the firing of HNIC producer John Shannon."

According to the *Globe* story, one thing that could prevent the CTV deal, besides lack of CTV outlets in Quebec, "would be a major policy change at the CBC, and furious last-minute negotiations are taking place to that end."

By coincidence, this story broke about the time of a retirement dinner in Toronto's King Edward Hotel for Ted Hough. Frank Selke, Jr., whose own retirement was only a year away, was master of ceremonies for a gathering of about a hundred of the hockey and broadcasting elite ranging from John Ziegler, the NHL president, and Danny Gallivan, himself retired, to almost everybody who was anybody in broadcasting and hockey — including CBC and CTV executives. During the predinner reception, which in light of the *Globe* story was not being treated by those CBC people present as a happy hour, one senior CBC executive rather sneeringly branded the *Globe* story as part of Molson's power play. But anybody who gets into a power play with Molson soon learns that this is playing with the big boys.

What had happened was that Molson was fed up with the stalled CBC negotiations and had sought and got an offer from CTV that would give Molson all the goodies it was seeking. The CTV offer was described as a strong one by Johnny Esaw, CTV vice president of sports. Despite subsequent pooh-poohing on the "merely a power play" theme by some CBC people, who apparently disregarded the fact that CTV had beaten CBC to a great hockey attraction once before in handling the first Soviet–Canada super series, in 1972, it was the first time ever that the Hockey Night rights had been offered to anyone other than the CBC.

If it was a power play, it worked. With the CTV offer still on the table as a fallback position, Molson and the CBC got together to thresh things out.

At the time there had been changes at or near the top at both Molstar and the CBC. Ron Harrison replaced Don Wallace as Molstar's executive producer on August 8, 1988, and at the same time at the CBC a rising young star named Arthur Smith was named head of CBC Sports. These two and at least one other senior CBC executive, Dave Martin, deputy head of CBC television's English network, met for an intensive two days at a resort north of Barrie, Ontario, and hammered out the main principles of a six-year agreement between Molstar and CBC. "We made some drastic changes," Harrison said later, "but it was a meeting of the minds."

Under that agreement Molson got the commercial concessions it wanted — Molson signs on or near the ice-surface boards and arena entrances within easy camera range, the Molson logo as part of the televised scoreboard, free promotional spots on other CBC programming. The final retreat was calling the show *Molson Hockey Night in Canada on CBC.*

As to what the CBC got, a good guess would be that they got permanent title to Hockey Night in Canada and all its heirs and assigns. Even though Molson still owns the rights and sells them to the CBC, the contract runs until 1994, and by 1990 there was a distinct sense that there wasn't much fighting, if any, going on between the two principals. Molstar is no longer a policy maker. It still contracts and assigns the on-air talent, including more and more CBC employees to work in certain situations, but CBC feels that it has something like a divine right to bounce from its network anybody who doesn't conform à la Dave Hodge, in whose defence Molstar did not lift more than a token finger.

What this means in the long run is that the CBC will run the nuts and bolts of Hockey Night its own way.

The Molson-ization of Hockey Night in Canada 213

When 29-year-old CBC Sports head Arthur Smith early in 1990 accepted a job with Dick Clark Productions in the United States, his successor was Alan Clark, a 41-year-old journalism graduate from Carleton University in Ottawa. Clark quickly made clear what *his* leanings were: a one-way flow of commands. With Clark's observation that Molstar is hired by the CBC and that "in the client relationship we dictate certain things," you can be pretty sure that in future, among other things, there'll be no Ralph Mellanby type defending Don Cherry's right to speak hockey rather than CBC English.

There was even a mildly thought-provoking element when Ron Harrison, who, after all, is a surviving link with Retzlaff, Mellanby and the largely successful past of Canadian Sports Network, said in a 1990 interview that he liked to keep his hand in directing golf, football and other sports. This was because: "Recognizing the fact that everybody has to change direction, there's younger people coming along, you've got to resign yourself to the fact that you're going to go on and do different things." As if he might not be around long.

The CBC has been aggressive in gradually blanketing the show with its own employees and corporate identity — getting rid of Dave Hodge, virtually shutting out Brian McFarlane, changing the HNIC jackets — and it looks like a long-range plan to make it impossible for anyone other than the CBC to run Hockey Night in Canada.

There is also the sense of the show's becoming the entertainment equivalent of homogenized milk. The CBC does not really run to rugged individualists. Ron MacLean is capable, Chris Cuthbert is capable, they are both good broadcasters full of aplomb and quick reactions, but neither has much edge.

In the olden days of CBC radio, Max Ferguson, calling himself Rawhide, had a funny morning show peopled with characters whom he invented and played himself. His stereotypical CBC announcer was called Marvin Mellowbell. Wonder if Marvin's still around and would like to be a Hockey Night host?

Somebody floated a balloon in the media early in 1990, a story printed by the *Globe and Mail* to the effect that the NHL might press the CBC to either muzzle Don Cherry or remove him from the Saturday night games. When a reporter sought his reaction, Cherry said that each week if the CBC hasn't phoned by Thursday, Rose, his wife through thick and thin, will say, "I guess you're still on, on Saturday."

He seems to think that sometime he'll go too far — like sayin' nothin' or 'nothink' twice in the same sentence — and will get the ax, "and that'll be it, but that's the life I chose." One thing sure is that if Hough, Selke or Mellanby were still in charge of Hockey Night talent and the CBC was not in its present commanding role, discussion of Cherry's future would be academic.

There is no doubt that he disturbs the even tenor of a lot of people's ways. When he says that player Kent Nilsson could use a heart transplant, or that the people who pick the player of the week in the NHL are incompetent know-nothings because they've never played the game, the people involved resent it, go to the boss, get him to call the CBC. And don't think that the CBC does not take this seriously. Cherry is news. Alan Clark jokes that when he got the job in midseason of 1989-90, he soon realized he should have asked for a separate contract — the Don Cherry watch.

On the other hand he pointed out that Cherry is careful not to overexpose himself, just does the one show a week and seems likely to have a "good shelf life", which of course is vastly different from being "on the shelf".

Cherry likes his job tremendously, works hard at it, always knows what he is talking about when he refers to some specific incident in a game. He watches dozens a week by home satellite, including every one he comments upon. But he also knows that he has enemies and some of them are in the CBC. As Clark says, "He knows he shouldn't say 'nothin'.' " But Cherry has been torpedoed so often before by experts that he has a pretty good understanding of what he risks. One must note, however, that to the CBC Cherry is a special case on the language front.

A few short days after Clark was talking about Cherry dropping his *g*'s, one Hockey Night show had a player in a penalty box in Hartford shouting a phrase that clearly included the word "fuckin'." Even dropping the *g*! There's *really* dropping *g*'s for you! Is that player under threat of being banned from hockey television?

Also, among the dozens of CBC shows every week, why is there an effete speech discrimination against hockey compared to other programs?

On March 27, 1990, Cherry appeared with Eric Malling on another CBC show called *fifth estate*. Same air time as hockey — eight o'clock Eastern. Not many kids in bed. Near the end they were discussing Cherry's manner of speech, including dangling prepositions (about which, by the way, even *Fowler's Modern English Usage* is ambivalent; or, to put it another way, is ambivalent about). Somehow, in the dangling-preposition line, Cherry worked the issue around to Roger Neilson, at present New York Ranger coach, but earlier the coach in Vancouver.

According to Cherry, once in Vancouver he asked Neilson, "Hey, Roger, where's the men's room at?" and was told that he should not dangle a preposition that way.

"So," Cherry told Malling, "I told him I'd have another go, and said to him, 'Hey, Roger, where's the men's room at, you asshole?'" Cherry would not say that on a hockey show. Immediately, knowing that the show was being taped and could be edited, Cherry grinned and asked Malling, "You gonna use that?"

It was shown unedited. Different show, different rules. One wonders why.

Heading into the 1990s and beyond, what does the future hold for Molson Hockey Night in Canada? When asked that question, Alan Clark responds that the future is pretty well what we see now: that is, mainly crisply produced hockey games following some of George Retzlaff's techniques, some of Gerry Renaud's, some of Ralph Mellanby's, and a few important elements, like new jackets, originated by the CBC. Happily for now, there is no argument here that the broadcasting teams now extant — Cole and Neale, Irvin and Bowman — have to prove their independence or devotion to the game to anyone. With Don Wittman and others, they are the best. What they do so well is roughly comparable to fights in hockey: if somebody wants to fight, they'll fight. But maybe Molson and the CBC will be smart enough not to provoke them.

There is potentially one other element in the equation: the future face of the National Hockey League, in which the seven Canadian teams now are outnumbered by 15 U.S. teams — with more, maybe many more, somewhere just over the horizon. One prime topic for many in the game is how the NHL should handle the pressure of other cities wanting to join the NHL or, if turned down, threatening to form another league in competition. One called the Global League is now in gestation.

Harry Neale, with the advantage of having coached in the NHL and also in the old World Hockey Association, which fought this same fight with the NHL in the 1970s, has a veteran's understanding of the angles. He believes the NHL made a disastrous mistake in stating that expansion was coming but that each new franchise would cost $50 million. He thinks the NHL instead should have figured out a priority list of what cities they want, found out what those cities are willing to pay and negotiate from there.

"These guys who want to get into the action have some great buildings that would be fine for hockey, if they had hockey. Houston, Dallas, Indianapolis, Kansas City, Denver, Atlanta — they could step right in if they had franchises. These rinks need tenants and somebody in each community has more money than he needs, but when you tell them it's going to cost $50 million right off the bat . . . that's when you get guys deciding they'll form another league. If I was the National Hockey League I'd take in three more teams in 1991 wherever they want to do it, and three more in 1995. And name them. Then at least you've tied up six big-time rinks."

The Molson-ization of Hockey Night in Canada 217

Neale thinks a new challenge to the NHL would be more successful than the WHA's attempt. The WHA didn't have as many good rinks to build on. "The new outfit could go after free agents and 17-year-olds, and patch up the holes with older players and Europeans. Doing that, it would take no time to have a second-best league. The NHL should have learned its lesson from the mint it cost to fight the old WHA in court, in talent dilution through loss of stars, in the WHA signing excellent prospects at age 18 before they were eligible for the NHL draft. Years later, the NHL had to take in some of the WHA teams, anyway. Had to — they just wouldn't go away.

"I hear exactly the same comments now about this Global League that I heard when the NHL was trying verbal putdowns on the WHA: 'Ah, they'll never get started.... Ah-h-h-h, they'll never make it, who'd go to that dump?' "

It is obvious that the demand for more hockey is there, that the people wanting it have the money and the buildings to hold ice surfaces, and that when one looks far ahead hockey has a tremendous advantage over any other sport in the possibility of moving into Europe. The two team sports in Europe that matter most are hockey and soccer. It isn't so outlandish to think of a team in Prague, Stockholm or Paris. Calgary and Washington trained in the Soviet Union in 1989, Montreal this year, and although the games that were televised last year didn't draw great viewing audiences in North America, in Europe one estimate was that four million people watched. That's a whole new set of consumers for the sports excitement that Canadians have known for so long — a great deal of it through Hockey Night in Canada.

It seems a long way back to Foster Hewitt's first ringing, "Hello Canada!" and to the old six-team NHL, the old "Hot Stove League", color cameras that weighed three hundred pounds, Conn Smythe and Jack MacLaren shaking hands on a golf course to get things started, a hundred dollars a game for the first TV rights, and the rest. May it all and more, the new stuff, still be there to remember when the first puck is dropped in the year 2000.

INDEX

A

Aird, John 42
Allen, Keith 129
Allen, Ralph 194
Alliance of Canadian Cinema, Television and Radio Artists (ACTRA) 180
American Hockey League 13, 19
Anderson, John 158, 162, 167–8
Anscombe, Mike 130
Apps, Syl 87
Arena Gardens (Toronto) 39, 40, 44
Armitage, Steve 33
Armstrong, Bob 18
Armstrong, George 109
Askin, Mark 6–10, 13–14
Associated Screen News 53

B

Ballard, Harold 10–11, 31, 35, 78, 120, 126, 130, 132–3, 135, 150–2, 155, 163, 166–7, 180–1, 187, 206
Balmy Beach football team 105
Bank of Commerce 42–3
Bassett, John 87, 110, 155, 201
Bathgate, Andy 29
Batten, Jack 199–201
Beaudry, Roland 54
Beddoes, Dick 133
Beliveau, Jean 29
Bell, Joe 70
Bergeron, Julien 6–7
Bester, Allan 14
Black, Joe 99
Blair, Andy 51
Blair, Wren 129
Boivin, Leo 18
Boston Bruins 18, 20, 22, 36, 48–51, 70–1, 107–8, 134, 140, 170, 188, 191, 201
Boston Garden 170
Bouchard, Butch 71
Bouchard, Pierre 134
Boucher, Frank 61
Bower, Johnny 119, 206–7
Bowman, Scotty 13–14, 32–3, 129, 216
Branigan, Andy 70
British American Oil Co. Ltd. 44, 55
British Broadcasting Corporation (BBC) 69
Bruneteau, Modere (Mud) 52
Buchanan, Bruce 33
Buffalo Sabres 20, 130, 174
Buller, Hy 70
Burkholder, Jack 122
Burr, Shawn 43

C

Cain, Herbie 71
Calder, Frank 50

Caldwell, Spence 73
Calgary Flames 33, 188, 192, 217
California Seals 28
Campbell, Clarence 12–13, 134, 152–3, 202–3, 207
Campbell-Ewald Limited 38–9, 44, 54
Canada Building Materials Ltd. 39
Canada Arena Company Limited 71–2, 190
Canadian Broadcasting Corporation (CBC) 5–6, 9–10, 15, 18, 27, 56, 60, 66–7, 71, 73–6, 81–2, 84, 88–9, 96–7, 104, 115, 119–120, 135, 138, 141, 143, 150, 153–5, 178–9, 189; news interruptions on sports broadcasts 22–3, 169–74; gains control of Hockey Night in Canada production 164–7, 184–7, 208–16
Canadian magazine 199
Canadian Radio Broadcasting Commission: *see* Canadian Broadcasting Corporation
Canadian Sports Network (CSN): *see* Hockey Night in Canada
Carleton University 213
Carling O'Keefe Breweries Ltd. 152, 157, 162–4
Carpenter, Doug 10
Carroll, Nancy 210
Carson, Jimmy 8, 14
Castle, Gordon 50–1
Central Professional Hockey League 20
CFCF (Montreal) 31, 57, 120, 128
CFCX (Montreal) 57
CFRB (Toronto) 45, 67, 81, 110, 178, 184

CFTO (Toronto) 100–1, 110, 127, 155, 169, 174, 206
Chad, Johnny 70
Chamberlain, Wilt 108
Charlesworth, Hector 65–7
Charlotte Checkers 25
Chatham Daily News 174
Chayefsky, Paddy 89
CHCH (Hamilton) 138, 166–7, 183, 198
Cherry, Don 13, 15, 16–25, 29–30, 33–4, 60, 62, 88, 134–5, 186, 204–5, 210, 213–15
Cherry, Rose 18–19, 214
Chiasson, Steve 34
Chicago Blackhawks 11, 30, 47–8, 70, 72, 108
Churchill, Winston 200
CITY-TV (Toronto) 166–7
CJRC (Winnipeg) 81
CKAC (Montreal) 54, 57
CKCH (Hull) 88
CKEY (Toronto) 111
CKFH (Toronto) 150–1, 182
CKGW (Toronto) 46
CKLW (Windsor) 66–7
CKNW (Vancouver) 184
CKO (Toronto) 150–2
Clancy, King 58, 61–2, 131, 174
Clapper, Dit 61
Clark, Alan 208, 213–5
Clark, Gordon 196
Clarke, Bob 129
CLCP (Montreal) 57
Club du Hockey Canadien 29
Coach's Corner: *see* Hockey Night in Canada
Cockfield Brown 160
Cole, Bob 13–14, 21, 32–4, 115–16, 184–5, 188, 216
Coleman, Jim 67
Colorado Rockies 20, 135, 180

Conacher, Charlie 61-2
Cook, Bill 61
Cook, Bun 61
Cooke, Jack Kent 99, 103, 110-12
Cornell, Ward 31, 96, 103-19, 130, 136, 148, 173-4, 181, 194
Cotton, Harold (Baldy) 67, 87-8, 201
Cournoyer, Yvan 206
Craig, Gordon 210
CRCM (Montreal) 57
CTV 28, 73, 100, 120, 122-3, 128, 154-5, 169, 206, 210-12
Curran, Brian 35
Cuthbert, Chris 8-9, 13-14, 33, 188-92, 213

D

Dagenais, Gaston 124
Dale, Kay 65-6, 69-70
Dancy, Keith 118, 121, 128
Daniel McIntyre Collegiate, Winnipeg 81
Daniels, Ken 33
Darling, Ted 130
Day, Hap 69, 175
de Courcy, Joe 86
Dennett, Jack 67, 87, 130, 141-2, 178, 194, 200, 203
Detroit Red Wings 9, 15, 30, 32, 34, 36, 48, 51, 70-2, 109
Diefenbaker, John 148-9
Di Stasio, Pat 123
Doraty, Ken 51
Dornhoefer, Gary 29-30
Douglas, Kent 206
Dryden, Dave 106
Dryden, Ken 106
Dufour, Claude 19
Duncan, Art 47
Durnan, Bill 71

E

Eagleson, Alan 138, 153-5
Eastern Provincial Hockey League 19
Edmonton Oilers 33, 35, 188, 192, 228
Ed Sullivan Show 207
Elslinger, Don 101
Esaw, Johnny 105, 155, 211
Esposito, Phil 30

F

Federko, Bernie 34
Ferguson, Elmer 54, 67, 201
Ferguson, Max 213
Feyer, George 86
fifth estate 215
Fisher, Douglas 155
Fisher, Red 131-2
Fitkin, Eddie 29, 99, 111
Flaman, Fern 18
Foley, Tom 93, 104-6
Ford Motor Co. Ltd. (Canada) 122, 159, 161-2
Forman, Dave 20-1
Formby, George 200
Foster, Stuart 95
Frayne, Trent 76
Fred Waring Show 74
Fyfe, Scott 93-5, 99

G

Gallinger, Don 70
Gallivan, Danny 31, 61, 103, 118, 120, 121-2, 128, 130, 170, 178, 194-5, 198, 211
Garrett, John 33
General Electric (U.S.) 74
General Motors Co. of Canada Ltd. 41, 43-5, 48, 53-5, 62
Gibson, John 94-5
Global Television Network 5-6, 10, 28, 130, 167, 187

Goldham, Bob 29–30, 199
Gordon, Barbara 142
Gordon, Bob 99–101, 106–9, 111, 117–8, 140–53, 161, 163, 167, 170–2, 174–5, 177, 179, 180–3, 186, 196–7, 202–3, 206, 209
Gordon, Todd 25–6
Gorman, T.P. 57–8
Grapes (by Don Cherry) 19
Great Western Forum 9, 103, 109, 124, 133
Green, Ted 107–8, 181
Grundman, Irving 132–3
Gzowski, Peter 193

H

Haggert, Bob 114
Haggart, Elsie 114
Hamilton Tiger-Cats 105, 167
Hannan, Dave 34
Harrison, Ron 6, 17, 21, 96, 103–4, 113–15, 170, 172, 183, 204, 212–13, 253
Hartford Whalers 32
Harvey, Doug 12
Harwood, Charlie 51, 54
Hastie, Moe 125
Hay, Charles 154
Hayden, Wilf 101
Henderson, Paul 155
Hershey Bears 18, 19
Hesketh, Bob 110
Hewat, Ron 151
Hewitson, Bobby 67, 200
Hewitt, Barbara 192, 199
Hewitt, Bill 31–2, 103, 119, 128, 130, 141, 150, 175, 192–9
Hewitt, Foster 25, 27, 31, 39–40, 44–48, 53, 59–62, 66, 69–70, 81, 103, 111, 120, 150, 152, 193–6, 196–200, 208, 217; longest game 49–52; TV play-by-play 76–8, 83–4, 89, 125–7; Canada–Soviet series 156
Hockey Hall of Fame 31
Hockey Night in Canada: Conn Smythe and Jack MacLaren strike deal 38–41; the first General Motors Hockey Broadcast 43–7; Imperial Oil enters the picture 55; HNIC goes coast-to-coast 60; HNIC in wartime 66–71; Montreal gets its share of Saturday night 73; television debut 74; first use of goal camera 91; first replay 97–8; color telecasts 206–7; "Hot Stove League" 17, 61, 67–8, 71–2, 87–8, 148, 200–1, 217; "Coach's Corner" 15, 17, 21, 23, 25; first HNIC executive producer 123; Bill Hewitt succeeds Foster 193; Canadian Sports Network 20, 123, 161, 167, 174, 203, 208–9, 213; 25th anniversary broadcast 150; 50th anniversary broadcast 126; HNIC and NABET strike 140–8; Imperial Oil pull out 158; Molson moves in 163; the CBC and Molson Hockey Night in Canada 212
Hodge, Charlie 206
Hodge, Dave 11, 31, 36, 107, 130–2, 141–3, 174–87, 196, 198, 211–12
Hodges, Bob 35
Holden, John 47
Hollett, Flash 71
Horler, Hugh 64–76, 82–4, 86, 90, 94–5, 98–9, 104, 122, 159

Index   223

Horler, Jack 65
Horner, Red 61-2
Hough, H.E. (Ted) 20-1, 27, 33, 79, 96, 98-9, 104, 116, 118-20, 122-4, 127, 129, 133, 138, 140-158, 160-7, 169-70, 172-4, 178, 180, 194, 196, 198, 205-10, 214
Hough, Jim 189-90
Howe, Gordie 29, 61
Howe, Syd 71
Hull, Bobby 11, 61-2, 137
Hull, Cordell 200

I

If You Can't Beat 'Em in the Alley, (Conn Smythe and Scott Young) 43
Imperial Oil Limited 27, 55, 58-60, 62, 66, 69, 71, 74, 76-9, 81, 86, 88, 93-6, 122-3, 126-7, 157, 160-5, 168, 174, 179, 199, 200, 202, 206
Imlach, George (Punch) 11, 104, 109, 180-1, 206
Irvin, Dick (Sr.) 32, 47
Irvin, Dick 31-3, 36, 47, 120, 128-31, 170, 174, 178, 188, 216

J

Jackson, Busher 61
Jennings, Charles 60
Jewison, Norman 81
Jonathon, Stan 134
Jungh, Esse 81

K

Kells, Morley 116, 125-6
Kelly, Dan 120, 128, 129, 194, 198

Kelly, Red 129
Kennedy, Ted 70, 87
Keon, Dave 119
Kielty, Terry 105
King, William Lyon Mackenzie 69, 140
King Edward Hotel, Toronto 211
Kitchener-Waterloo hockey team 19
Kordic, John 8
Korn, Jim 35

L

Labossiere, Gord 129
Lalonde, Phil 54
Lamantia, Joe 10
Lapointe, Karen 6, 9-10
La Presse 30, 54
La Soirée du Hockey 123
Large, Dick 147
LeCavalier, René 118, 178
Le Droit 88
Leeman, Gary 8, 14
Léger, Neil 143-4
Lemberg, Ty 100-1
Lockerbie, Beth 81
Lockwood, John 162
London Lords 105
Los Angeles Kings 6, 9, 24, 33, 99, 103, 111, 143
Louis, Joe 200
Lowe, Kevin 35
Lucas, Rupert 45

M

MacLaren Advertising Co. Ltd. 20, 54-5, 57-8, 60, 62, 64-5, 71, 73-4, 76-8, 84, 90, 93, 96, 98, 104, 120, 122-5, 132, 149-50, 153-5, 158-62, 168-9, 209-10

MacLaren, Jack 38–41, 43, 54–5, 57–9, 62–3, 71, 73, 77, 217
MacLean, Ron 13, 15–17, 21, 23–4, 33, 186, 188, 213
Maclean's Magazine 41, 193
Madison Square Garden 10, 51
Maher, Peter 151–2
Mahovlich, Frank 119, 201
Maida, Maria 116
Malling, Eric 215
Maloney, Dan 31
Maloney, Larkin 38–9, 42
Mallyon, Roger 141–2, 148, 161, 164, 197
Maple Leaf Gardens 5, 7–8, 15, 25, 28, 35, 39, 41–6, 49–50, 55, 59, 61–2, 66, 72, 76–8, 82, 87, 99–100, 109–10, 119, 126–7, 133, 148, 150, 152, 163–7, 184–5, 206–7
Maple Leaf Sports Productions 20
Mariash, Joe 174–5
Marsden, Pat 11
Martin, Dave 212
Maskell, Terry 6
McDonald, Lanny 180–1
McFarlane, Brian 11, 29, 31, 116, 119–20, 126–9, 133, 141, 175, 194–5, 197, 199, 201, 213
McGill University 105
McKechnie, Walt 129
McKee, Ken 188
McKee, Tom 174
McKeigan, Paul 6, 8–9
McKenzie, Don (Shanty) 167
McKnight, Wes 45–7, 67, 71, 87, 201
McMaster, Sam 191
McPhee, George 190
McPherson, Don 172–4
Meeker, Howie 29–30, 62, 88, 131–3, 156, 204

Mellanby, Janet 123–4
Mellanby, Ralph 21, 27–8, 85, 104, 113–4, 116–8, 143, 147–8, 154, 156–7, 159, 163, 171–4, 177–8, 180, 196, 204, 208, 213–4, 216
Memorial Cup 76
Metro-Golden-Mayer (MGM) 206–7
Miles, Jeff 97–8
Miller, Jack 153–4
Minnesota North Stars 141, 143
Mohns, Doug 18
Molson, David 132
Molson, Hartland 159–60
Molson, Herbert 158
Molson, Tom 159
Molson Brewery 122–3, 127, 158–67, 179, 206, 210–12, 216
Molstar Communications 10–11, 28–9, 208–13, 251–2
Momesso, Sergio 34
Moncton hockey team 23
Montreal Alouettes 105
Montreal Canadiens 11–13, 18, 28, 33, 35–6, 47–8, 53, 57, 71–3, 89, 93, 122, 129, 131–2, 134, 140–1, 159, 170, 188–91, 206, 217
Montreal Forum 56–8, 61, 90, 93, 121, 132–3, 158–9
Montreal Maroons 48, 51, 53–4, 57–8
Montreal Royals 159
Montreal Star 131
Moore, Trevor 94
Morenz, Howie 61
Morris, Paul 10
Murray, Rev. Athol 67

N

Nabisco Foods 209–10
Nash, Knowlton 23

Index 225

National Association of Broadcast Employees and Technicians (NABET) 140-8, 153-4, 177
National Hockey League (NHL) 10, 12, 18-20, 23, 28, 57-8, 70, 72, 93, 103, 111, 128, 138-9, 182, 187-8, 195, 198, 202, 204, 210, 214, 216
National Hockey League Players' Association 138, 153-5
National Hockey League-Soviet series, 1972 132, 153-6, 211
Neale, Harry 13, 21-2, 32-7, 60, 116, 188, 216-7
Neely, Cam 22
Neilson, Roger 35, 215
New Jersey Devils 35, 188-90
Newman, Sydney 82-4
New York Americans 48, 70
New York Islanders 135
New York Rangers 30, 33, 35, 48-51, 70, 215
Niagara Falls Thunder 24
Nicholls, Bernie 33
Nienhaus, Kraig 36
Nilsson, Kent 214
Now Back to You, Dick (Dick Irvin) 36, 170
Norris (junior hockey player) 24
Notre Dame College, Wilcox, Sask. 82

O

Oake, Scott 33
O'Connell, Mike 34-5
Ohlmeyer Communications 209-10
Olczyk, Ed 14, 34

Olmstead, Bert 129, 202
Olympic Games 139
O'Neill, Tommy (Windy) 70
Ontario Hockey Association 40
Ontario Hockey League 24
Ontario Rugby Football Union 105
Orr, Bobby 29, 155
Ottawa Senators 48
Ottawa Rough Riders 105

P

Palmateer, Mike 11
Park, Brad 170
Pasmore, C.M. 45-6, 48-50, 55-9, 65-7, 70, 73
Patrick, Lynn 129
Pearson, Lester B. 150
Peterborough Examiner 21
Philadelphia Flyers 30, 135, 170, 221
Phillips, Audrey 170-2
Pittsburgh Penguins 67, 143
Plaza Hotel, New York 207
Pollock, Sam 19
Potts, Lyman 53-4
Pratt, Babe 71, 136, 204-5
Prendergast, Frank 55-6, 58
Prendergast, Walter 55
Preston, Jerry 6
Primeau, Joe 61
Provost, Claude 12

Q

Quackenbush, Bill 18
Quebec Nordique 33
Queen Elizabeth Hotel, Montreal 153
Queen's University 105

R

Radio-Canada 89, 93
Ratelle, Jean 173
Raymond, Donat 159
Reardon, Ken 13, 90–1
Reay, Billy 131
Rechnitzer, Einar 44, 55, 64–5
Renaud, Gerald 80, 88–93, 97–8, 118, 125, 216
Retzlaff, George 16–17, 74–5, 79–86, 88–90, 93, 96–104, 112, 118, 120, 122, 125, 169, 171, 204, 210, 213, 215
Reynolds, Ted 204
Reynolds, Warren 40
Richard, Maurice (Rocket) 36, 61, 70–1, 92
Robert, Philippe 86
Roberts, Leslie 41
Robinson, Larry 9
Robson, Jimmy 204
Rochester hockey team 20
Rochon, Gerry 120–1
Romanelli, Luigi 86
Rosenfeld, Maurice 45, 65
Ross, Art 50
Ross, Victor 55
Ross and MacDonald (architects) 42
Royal Canadian Naval Volunteer Reserve 30
Royal York Hotel, Toronto 42
Russell, Scott 34
Ryan, Tim 100–1, 203
Ryerson Polytechnical Institute 82, 174

S

St. Louis Blues 34, 128–9, 141–2, 152
Salming, Borje 35
Sarnia Imperials 105
Saturday Night 111
Saucier, Roland 90
Saunders, Lloyd 105
Savarin Hotel, Toronto 81
Schriner, Sweeney 68, 71
Scott, Allan 154
Selke, Frank D. 27–8, 109–10, 119–22, 129, 141, 159, 161, 164, 174, 178–81, 203–4, 209, 211, 214
Selke, Frank J. 13, 28, 42–4, 69, 72–3, 91
Sgambati, Fred 143
Shannon, John 211
Shaw, Cecil 43
Shenkerow, Barry 23
Shore, Eddie 19, 51, 61
Sinclair, George 162, 194
Sittler, Darryl 11, 180–1
Slater, Tom 19
Smith, Arthur 212–3
Smith, Floyd 10
Smith, Hooley 61
Smith, Mike 23
Smythe, Conn 13, 38–44, 47–9, 57–9, 62–3, 66, 69, 71–3, 75, 77, 84, 94, 109, 217
Smythe, Stafford 78, 104, 109–10, 131, 206
Spokane hockey team 19
Sportswriters 17
Springfield Indians 19
Stanley Cup 30, 32, 47, 57, 71, 104, 108–9, 129, 134–5, 140, 154, 170, 188, 202–3
Stein, Gil 26
Stellick, Bob 10
Stewart, Nels 61
Storey, Red 11–13, 182
Strachan, Al 210
Suhonen, Alpo 23
Sullivan, Red 129

Sun Life Assurance
  Company   42
Sutter, Brian   34

T

Thatcher, Margaret   171–2
The Globe and Mail   67–8, 71, 99, 201, 210–11, 214
The Sports Network (TSN)   10, 28, 97, 210
Thompson, Jim   96
Three Rivers hockey team   19
Tikkanen, Esa   35
Toronto Argonauts   105, 182, 184–5
Toronto Trades and Labor Council   43
Toronto Maple Leafs (Toronto St. Patricks)   11, 14–15, 24, 30, 33–4, 38–9, 47–51, 60, 67, 69–73, 93, 104, 108, 122, 131–2, 141, 143, 150–1, 159, 162, 170, 173, 180, 185, 187, 199–200, 202, 206
Toronto Maple Leafs baseball team   111
Toronto Marlboros   30, 124
Toronto Star   19, 40, 153, 188
Toronto Symphony   94
Toronto Telegram   67, 110, 201
Travis, Sid   99
Tremblay, Réjean   30
Tulsa hockey team   20
Turner, H.M. (Bud)   74–6, 83, 90–1, 93–5, 99, 104, 122, 149, 158, 160–1, 174
Twaits, Don   127, 161, 174

U

University of Toronto   105

University of Western Ontario   105

V

Vaive, Rick   35
Vancouver Canucks   32, 36–7, 205, 215
Videotape Productions   20

W

Wallace, Don   20–1, 134–5, 174, 185, 205, 210, 212
Washington Capitals   188–91, 217
Washington Redskins   111
Wayne, Johnny   207
Wells, Jack   81, 105
Westbury Hotel, Toronto   110
Western Hockey League   19
Westgate, Murray   86, 88, 94–5, 164, 173
Westinghouse Radio Network   46
White, Art   101
Winnipeg Jets   23
Wittman, Don   32–3, 216
World Hockey Association (WHA)   32, 216–7
World Junior Hockey Championships, 1990   24

Y

Young, Scott   31, 201
Yzerman, Steve   8, 14

Z

Ziegler, John   211
Znaimer, Moses   166–7

M&S

Other favourites from M&S Paperbacks

RIGHT CHURCH, WRONG PEW
A Mystery
by Walter Stewart
"A genuine page-turner." — *Books in Canada*
"Frothy and amusing." — *The Globe and Mail*
0-7710-8301-7 $5.95

ANDY RUSSELL'S ADVENTURES WITH WILD ANIMALS
by Andy Russell
A classic collection of seven tales by one of our best-loved nature writers.
"Andy Russell is a terrific storyteller."
— *Saskatoon Star-Phoenix*
0-7710-7883-8 $5.95 8 illustrations

KISS THE BOYS GOODBYE
How the United States Betrayed Its Own POWs in Vietnam
by Monika Jensen-Stevenson and William Stevenson
"One of the hottest books to come off the presses in a long time." — *The Province* (Vancouver)
"The most complete, current and controversial proof of POWs abandoned in Vietnam." — *The Calgary Herald*
0-7710-8327-0 $7.95 16 pages b&w photos

COURTING MORE DISASTER
by Malcolm Barker with T.C Sobey
"At the top of everyone's 'must read' list...Bookstores [were] scrambling to find copies [of the hardcover original]." — *The Toronto Star*
"The most voyeuristic account yet written by a former member of the Royal Household."
— *The Daily Telegraph* (England)
0-7710-8227-4 $6.95 16 pages b&w photos

Hot titles from M&S Paperbacks

CHANGING HEAVEN
by Jane Urquhart
"Throbs with the storm and wind of passion and the bitter cold of its withdrawal...a brilliant success."
— *Saturday Night*
0-7710-8658-X $6.95

THE ONLY TICKET OFF THE ISLAND
Baseball in the Dominican Republic
by Gare Joyce
"A beautifully written book...with a terrific range of anecdotes, observations and inside stuff."
— Jack Batten, *The Globe and Mail*
0-7710-4435-6 $6.95   8 pages b&w photos

HUNGRY GHOSTS
An Investigation into Channelling and the Spirit World
by Joe Fisher
"Undoubtedly one of the most important and interesting books about spiritualism ever written...Un-putdownable."
— Colin Wilson, author of *The Outsider*
0-7710-3146-7 $6.95   8 pages b&w photos

SAFE AT HOME
A Kate Henry Mystery
by Alison Gordon
"As fast and furious as its predecessor [*The Dead Pull Hitter*]...Gordon weaves a nice plot."
— *The Globe and Mail*   0-7710-3417-2 $5.95

AUTHENTIC PASSION
Loving Without Losing Your Self
by Bonnie Kreps
"A witty, wise and powerful analysis of the grand delusion [of romantic love]...a survival kit for men and women who regularly drown in their own fantasies." — June Callwood   0-7710-4554-9 $6.95